EXPOSURE

AN INFOGRAPHIC GUIDE TO PHOTOGRAPHY

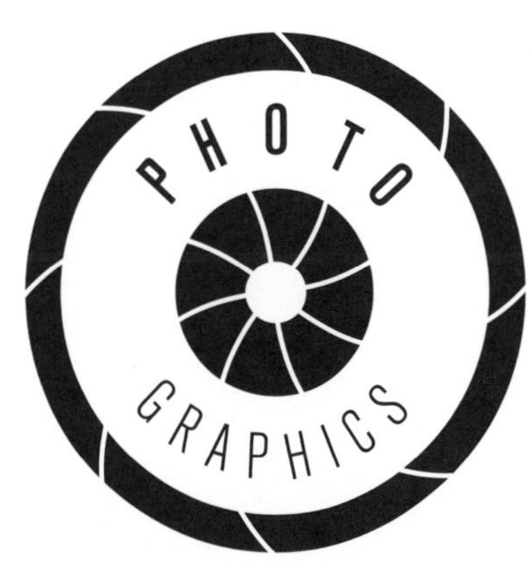

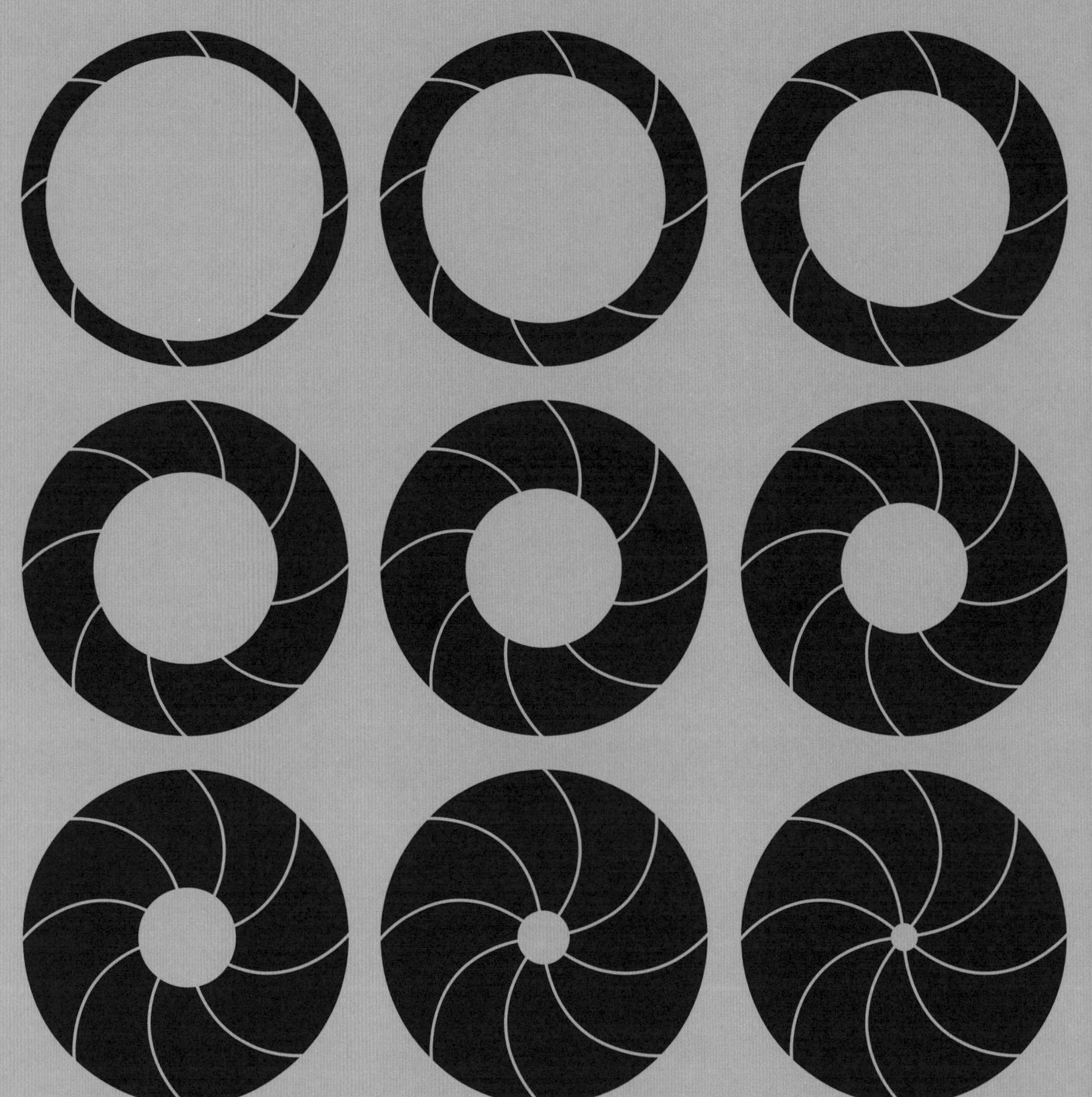

EXPOSURE

AN INFOGRAPHIC GUIDE TO PHOTOGRAPHY

DAVID TAYLOR

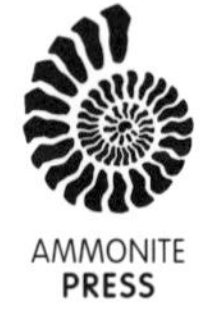

AMMONITE
PRESS

First published 2016 by
Ammonite Press
an imprint of Guild of Master Craftsman Publications Ltd
Castle Place, 166 High Street, Lewes,
East Sussex, BN7 1XU, United Kingdom

ISBN 978 1 78145 270 7

Publisher: Jason Hook
Design: Robin Shields
Illustration: Rob Brandt
Project Editor: Chris Gatcum
Editor: Jamie Pumfrey

Color reproduction by GMC Reprographics
Printed and bound in China

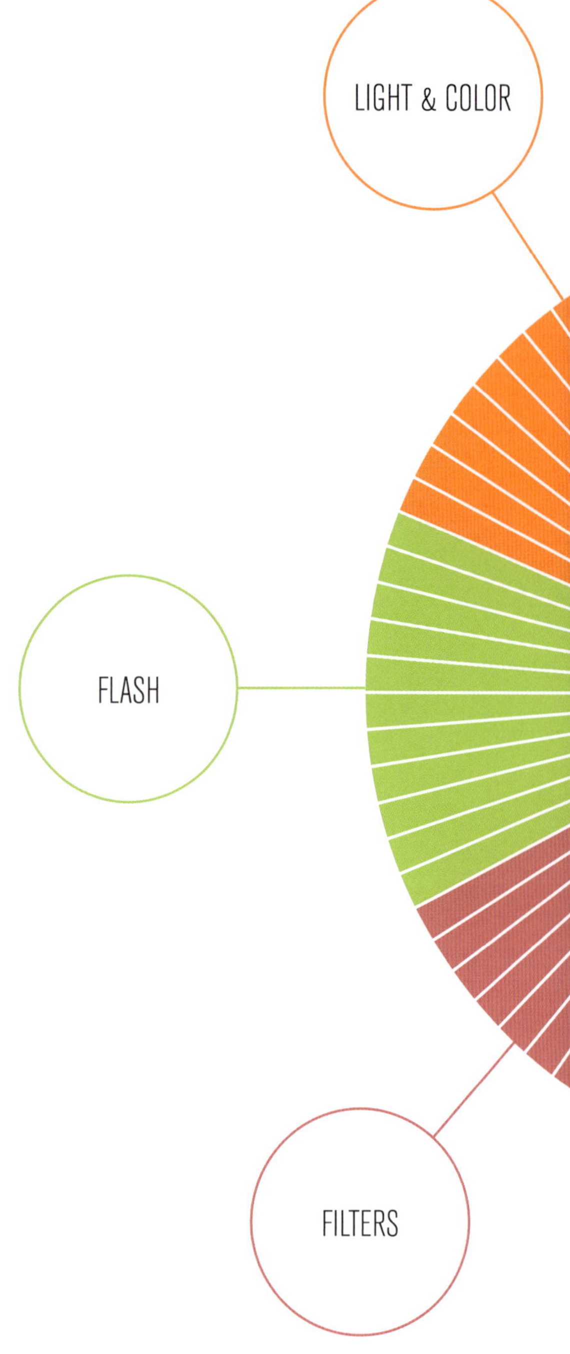

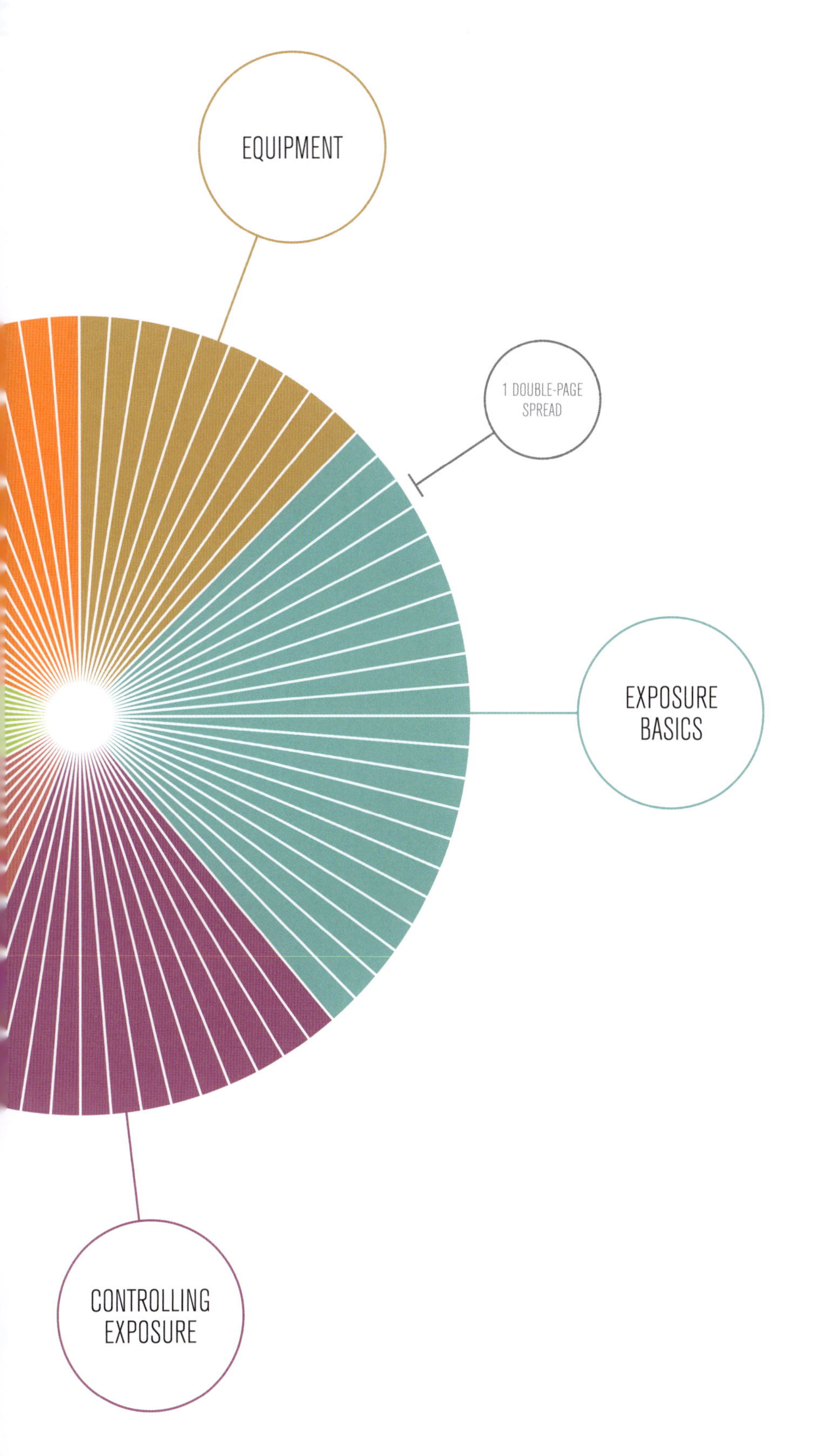

EQUIPMENT
1 DOUBLE-PAGE SPREAD
EXPOSURE BASICS
CONTROLLING EXPOSURE

Contents

INTRODUCTION 8

1 LIGHT & COLOR 10

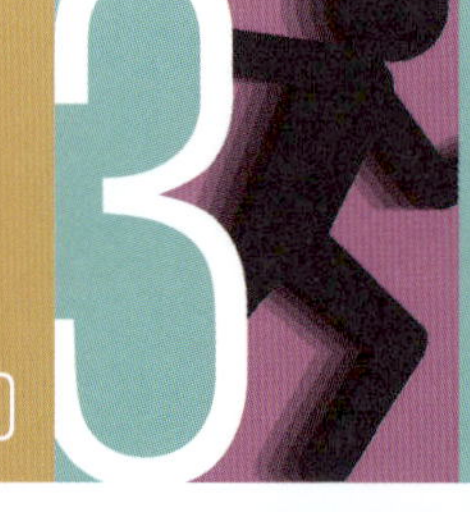

Introduction	12
Wavelengths Of Light	14
Splitting Light	16
Color	17
Color Wheel	18
Color Perception	20
Color Temperature	22
White Balance	24
Light Direction	26
Backlighting & Contrast	28
The Sun	30
Sunrise & Sunset	32
The Sun's Path	34
Qualities Of Light	36
Softness	38

2 EQUIPMENT 40

Introduction	42
Cameras	44
Lenses	46
Wide-Angle Lenses	48
Angle Of View	50
Crop Factor	52
The Shutter	54
The Lens Aperture	56
Keeping Your Camera Steady	58

3 EXPOSURE BASICS 60

Introduction	62
Sensors	64
First Principles	66
Stops	68
The Exposure Triangle	70
Shutter Speed	72
Freezing Movement	74
Blurring Movement	76
Panning	78
Aperture	80
Depth Of Field	82
Differential Focusing	84
ISO	86
Noise	88
Dynamic Range	90
Long-Exposure Noise	92
The "Sunny 16" Rule	94
Exposure Values	96
Histograms	98
File Formats	100

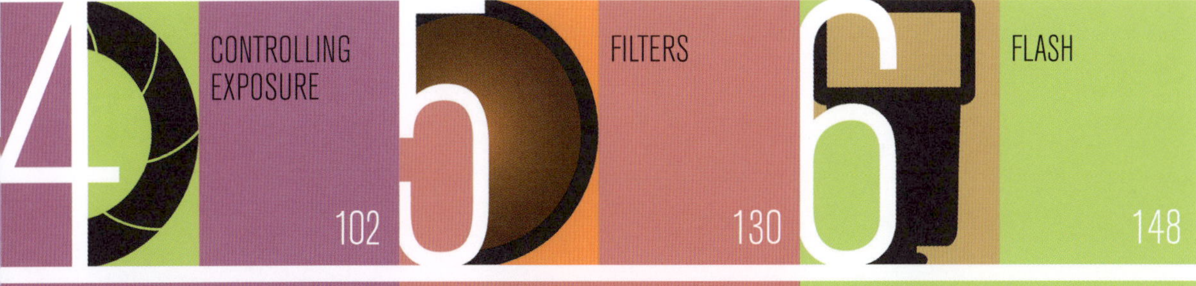

Introduction	104
Midtones, Shadows & Highlights	106
Exposure Meters	108
Metering Modes	110
Spot Metering	114
Picture Parameters	116
Exposure Modes	118
Exposure Compensation	120
Bracketing	122
Sequences	124
Video	126
HDR	128

Introduction	132
Filter Thread Sizes	134
Filter Holder Sizes	136
Filter Types	138
Filter Factors	140
Neutral Density Filters	142
Polarizing Filters	144
Black & White	146

Introduction	150
The Inverse Square Law	152
Guide Numbers	154
Flash Sync Speed	158
Slow Sync Speed	160
Flash Curtain Sync	162
High-Speed Sync	164
Bounce Flash	166
Lighting Ratios	168

Glossary	170
Useful Web Sites	172
Index	173
Acknowledgments	176

INTRODUCTION

Photography has never been so popular. Each and every day, millions of exposures are made around the world. Yet despite photography's ubiquity, it's unusual to find someone who fully understands what his or her camera is capable of. Unfortunately, automated modes hide the underlying processes, and this is done so well that you could be forgiven for thinking that photography involves nothing more than "pointing" and "shooting." This is a great pity, because automation wastes the potential of both you and your camera; automatic modes can only get you so far before you hit their limits.

Taking control of a camera and turning off automatic is a major step in learning how to intentionally craft images you are proud to call your own. However, it is also a daunting process, with a potentially steep learning curve. Exposure is one aspect of photography that's especially complex. For a start, it involves a lot of numbers, or more specifically, a lot of fractions and percentages. Fortunately, there's a logic to the numbers; they weren't arbitrarily invented to torture would-be photographers—even if it feels that way at times!

This book is a visual guide to exploring exposure, with a view to understanding how to take control of these numbers. By the time you reach the end you'll be ready to turn off automation and embrace a more creative way of shooting.

"How do you get to Carnegie Hall? Practice!" It's an old joke, but one that contains a valuable truth. No one mastered any subject without first honing their skills of that subject through practice. Photography—and achieving an understanding of exposure—is no exception. Fortunately, digital photography has made this task less onerous than it once was. Digital cameras let you shoot and shoot and shoot without incurring any further cost. They also give you instant feedback, and as an added bonus, the camera settings selected at the time of shooting are embedded in every image file saved to the memory card. All of this means that it's possible to practice very intensively and quickly grasp how to make full use of your camera.

It's all too easy to become discouraged at any task when mistakes are made. However, mistakes are useful. Mistakes help to expand knowledge—even if it's only to reinforce what not to do in a particular situation. Mistakes can also lead to fruitful new ways of working; making mistakes is as valuable to your on-going creative development as success. Indeed, in many ways *not* making mistakes is worse: it means that you're not trying out new techniques and are sticking rigidly to your own personal comfort zone. No one ever reached Carnegie Hall that way!

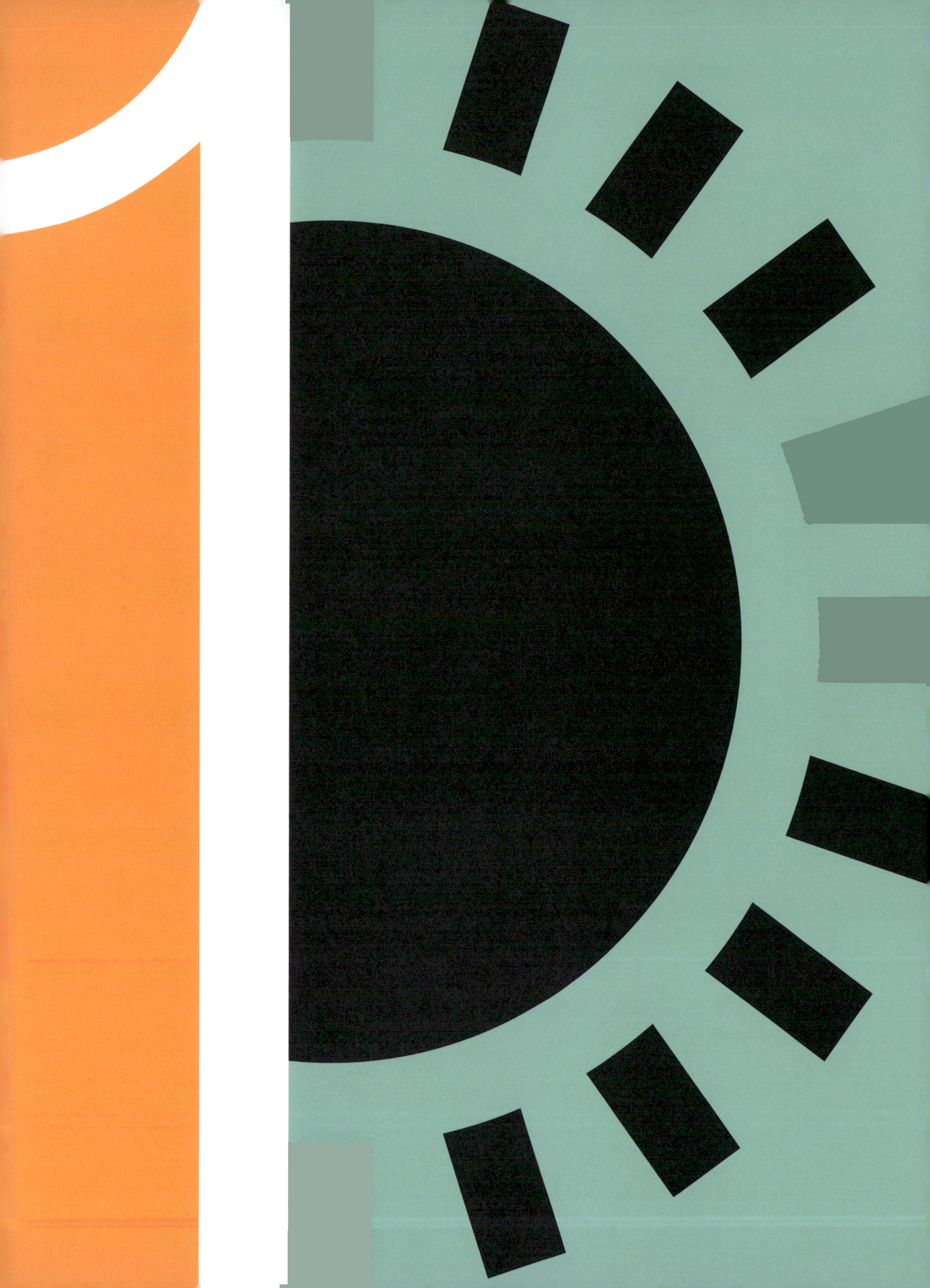

LIGHT & COLOR

PAINTERS USE OILS OR WATERCOLORS TO CREATE THEIR ART; SCULPTORS USE STONE OR METAL; PHOTOGRAPHERS CAPTURE LIGHT.

Without light you cannot make an exposure. In fact, light is so fundamental to photography that the word itself literally means "drawing with light," from a combination of the Greek words for light and drawing. To progress as a photographer it's essential to develop an understanding of light and how it affects a photograph visually; shooting under light that doesn't suit the subject can mar an otherwise good photo.

Determining the best light for your subject is a decision that needs to be made at the time of shooting. There's a photographer's mantra that states "there's no such thing as bad light, only bad photography." This essentially means that you should modify what and how you shoot depending on the light that you have. In a studio it's relatively easy to control the quality and position of the light that falls onto your subject, which includes its intensity, color, and hardness (or softness). Shoot outdoors, though, and you lose that luxury. This means that the time of day and the weather both need to be taken into account before you set off to shoot. If the light changes due to a change in the weather, a good photographer will switch to shooting different subjects more suited to these changes.

Photographers don't have to rely entirely on nature to provide them with light—there are various tools that photographers can use to help them achieve a particular result. Whether it is natural or artificial, you can modify light by diffusing it or reflecting it. This creates a "softer" light that is ideal when photographing close-up details or organic subjects.

Diffusers are sheets of cloth or paper that are placed between a light source and the subject to soften the light; in doing this, they also help to reduce contrast. Commercial "softbox" diffusers are commonly fitted over flashes to improve the light, although taping tissue paper over the flash head can create a similar effect; sunlight is naturally diffused when the sky is overcast or hazy.

Reflectors are panels of material that can be used to bounce light falling on one part of a scene toward another, typically an area of a scene that's in shadow. As with diffusers, reflectors are used to reduce contrast, so a camera can capture the full tonal range of a scene. Commercial reflectors come in a variety of colors and materials, the simplest of which has a neutral white surface. However, reflectors with a colored surface—such as gold—can be used to add a color tint (gold reflectors are often used in portraiture to add warmth to an image). Bouncing the light from a flash is another way that a reflective surface can be used to modify a light source.

Wavelengths Of Light

Visible light is one small part of the full range of frequencies known as the "electromagnetic spectrum." The various frequencies of the electromagnetic spectrum are referred to by their wavelength, with the wavelengths of visible light (in which the full spectrum of colors is found) measured in nanometers and ranging from red at 700nm to violet-blue at 400nm. When the full spectrum is present, the result is neutral or "white" light.

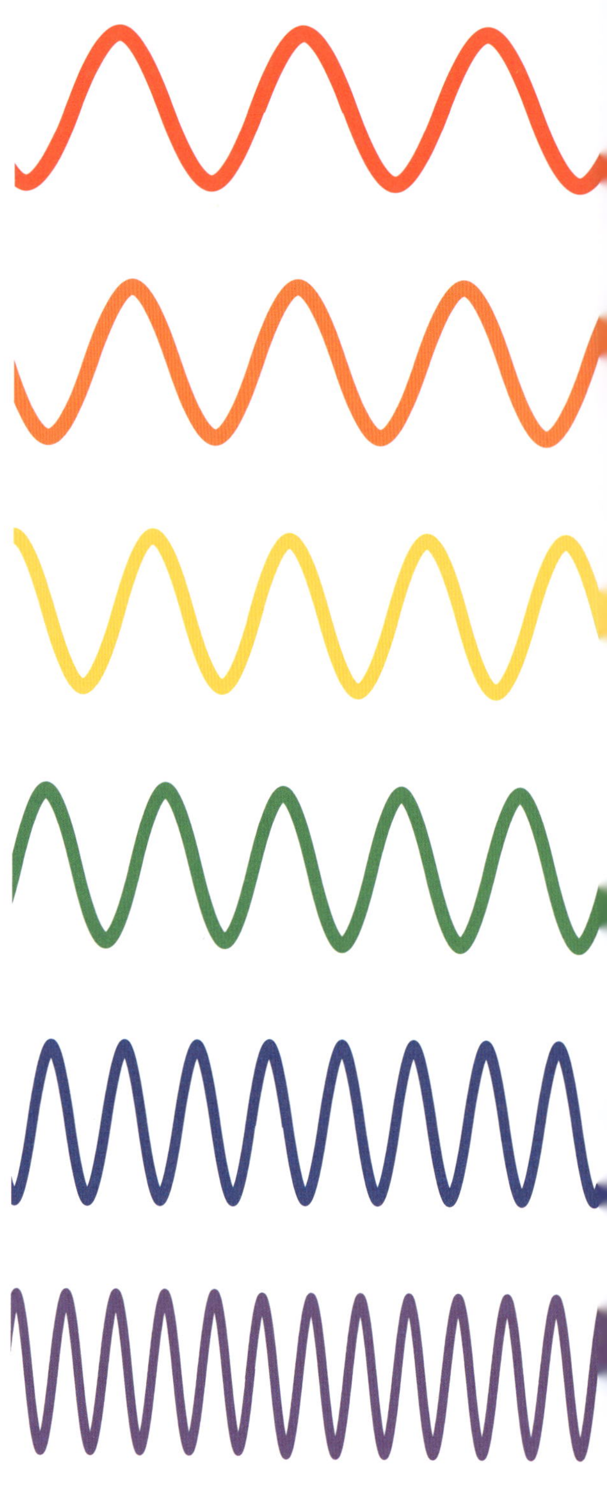

Visible light is made up of wavelengths of light that are visible to the human eye. The size of the wavelength is measured as the distance from the crest of one wave to the crest of the next. Each color has a different wavelength, with red (700nm) having the longest wavelength and violet (400nm) the shortest.

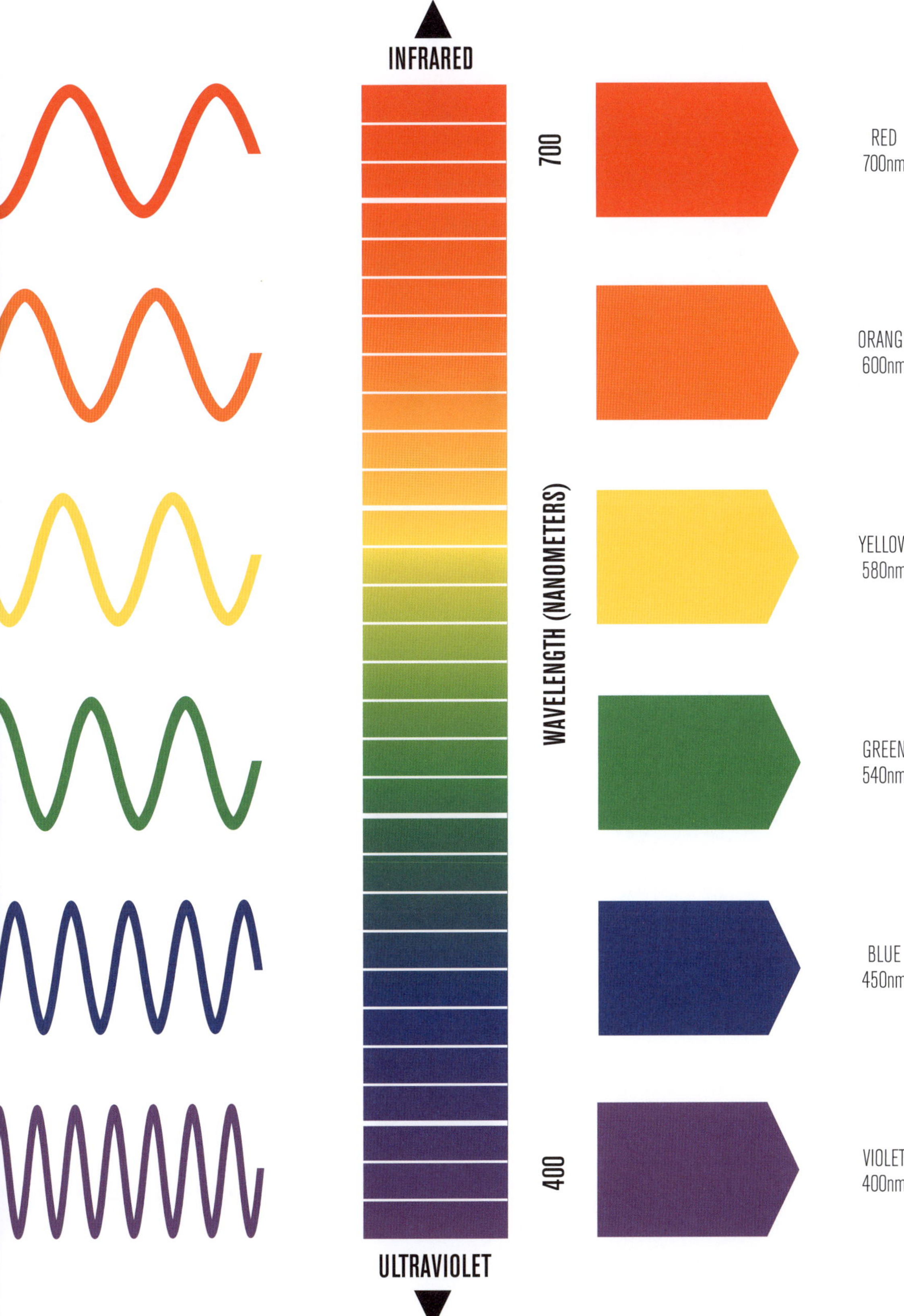

INFRARED
WAVELENGTH (NANOMETERS)
700
400
ULTRAVIOLET
RED
700nm
ORANGE
600nm
YELLOW
580nm
GREEN
540nm
BLUE
450nm
VIOLET
400nm

Splitting Light

The full spectrum of wavelengths of light can be seen by shining a beam of white light through a prism. The various wavelengths are refracted (or change direction) as they enter and exit the glass of the prism. The longer red wavelengths are refracted less than the shorter violet–blue wavelengths, resulting in a spread of colors. A similar effect is seen when white light passes through drops of rain to produce a rainbow.

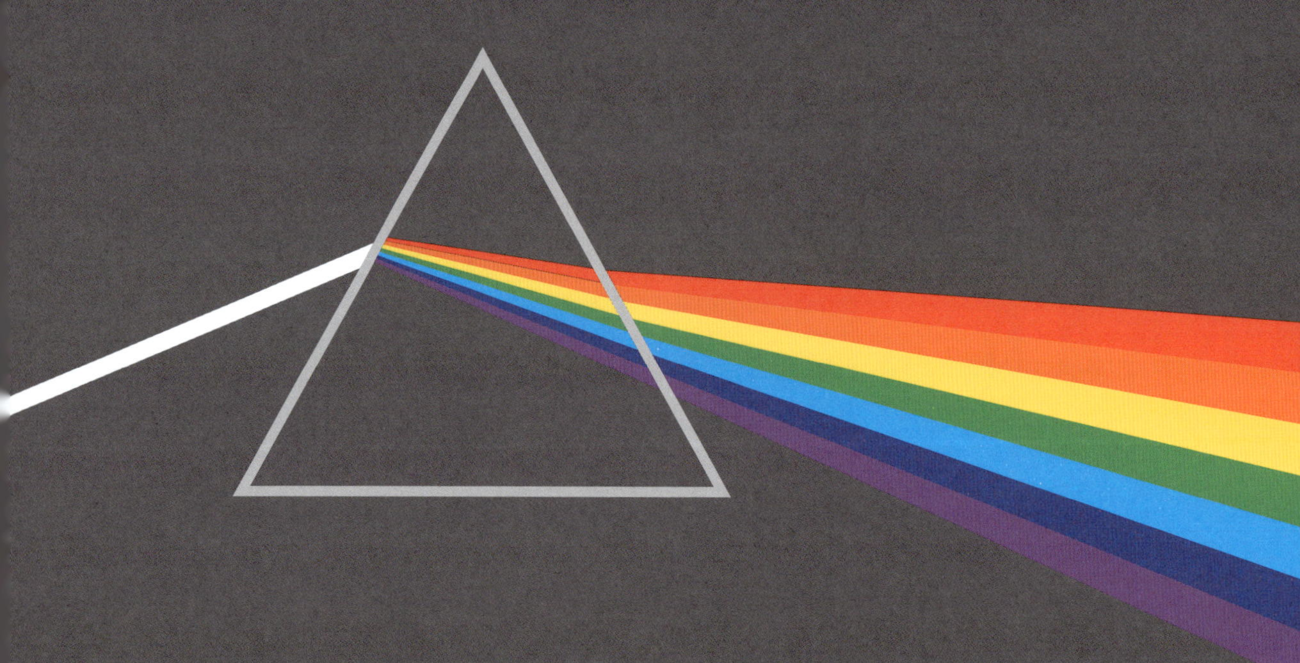

Color

There are two principal ways in which color is created and experienced by the human eye. The first is when a light source (such as fireworks and neon signage) emits some of the wavelengths that make up visible light. The second is when light hits a colored object's surface. Then, some wavelengths of light are absorbed by the object and others are reflected. The apparent color of the object is that of the reflected wavelengths.

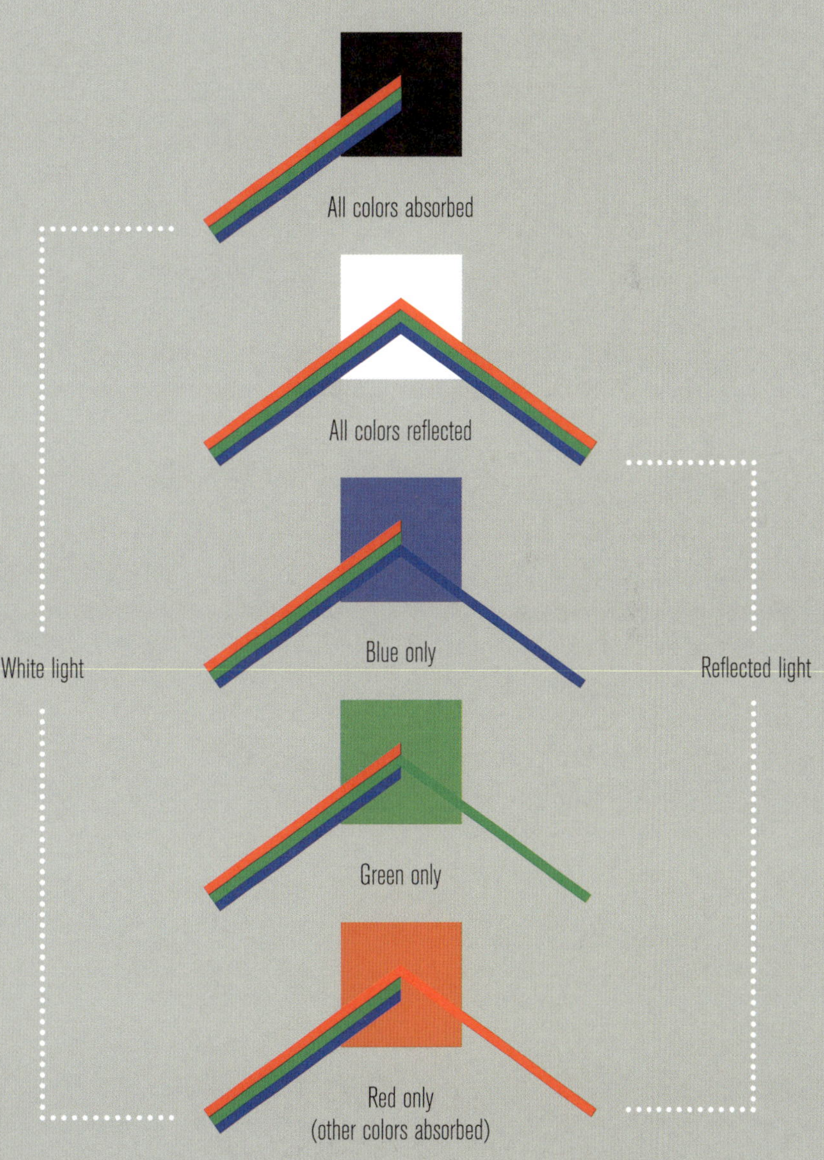

Color Wheel

A color wheel is a useful tool that can help you visualize the relationships of the full spectrum of colors. The three most important colors are the primary colors, which are colors that can't be created by combining other colors. If you combine two primary colors together you produce a secondary color; combine two secondary colors and you get a tertiary color.

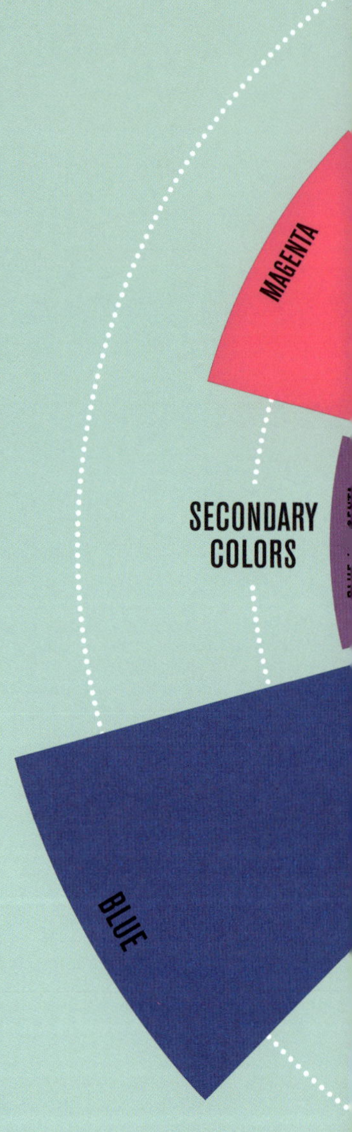

The three primary colors of light and digital imagery created by a camera or displayed on a monitor are red, green, and blue (or RGB). This is an "additive" color system in which the primaries are added together to produce further colors. An absence of all three primaries results in black; a combination of all three at maximum strength produces white.

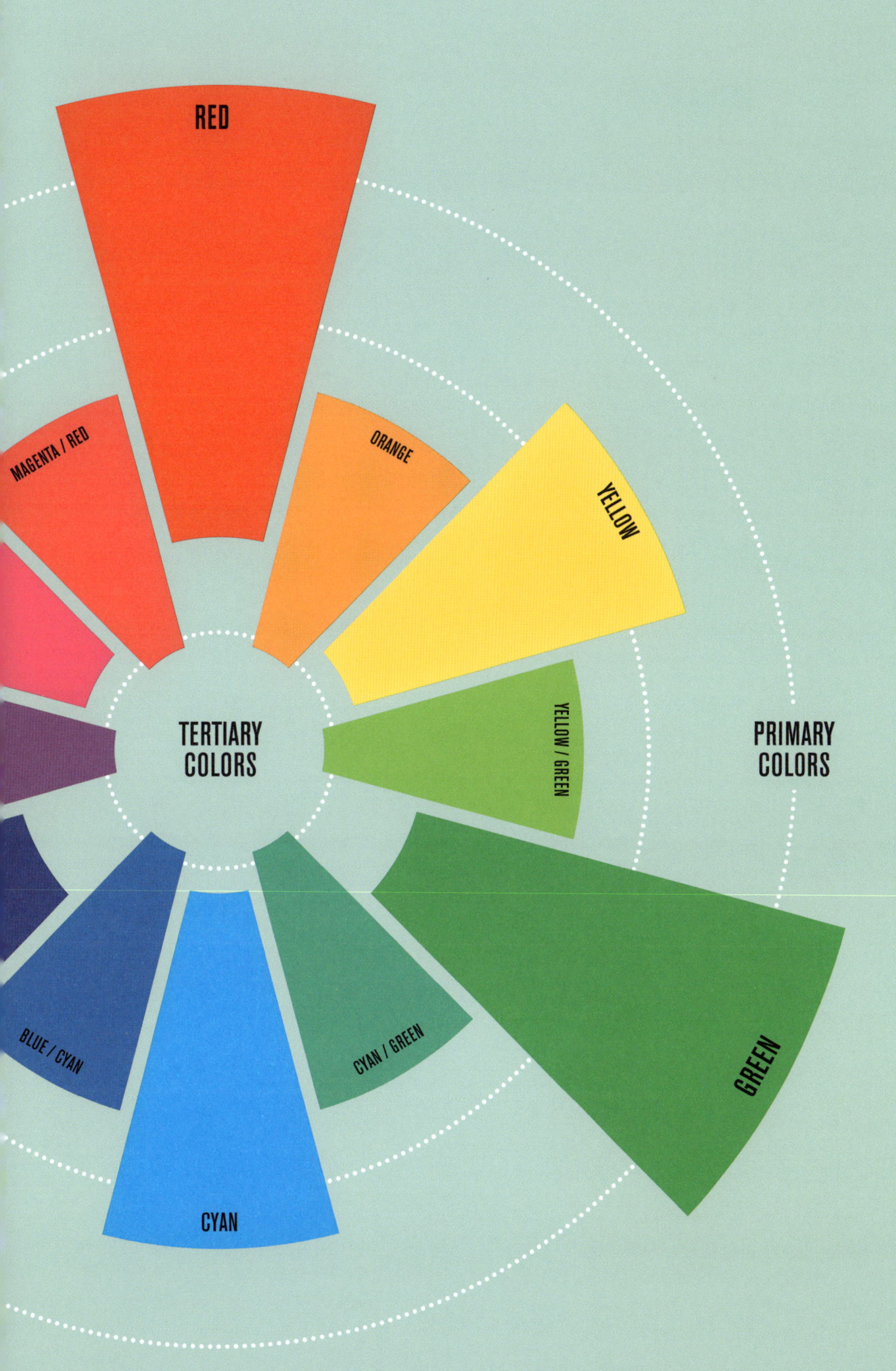

RED
MAGENTA / RED
ORANGE
YELLOW
YELLOW / GREEN
TERTIARY COLORS
PRIMARY COLORS
BLUE / CYAN
CYAN
CYAN / GREEN
GREEN

Color Perception

POSITIVE

Colors have an emotional impact that can be both positive and negative. Therefore, the colors that dominate a photograph can (and will) affect, in combination with the subject matter, how that photograph is perceived and interpreted by the viewer.

warmth, energy, stimulation, love, passion, strength, excitement

warmth, passion, fun, sensuality, security, happiness

optimism, emotional strength, friendliness, creativeness, confidence

harmony, refreshment, nature, health, balance, calm, peace

intelligence, serenity, logic, cool, calm, reflection, trust, efficiency

sophistication, spirituality, luxury, authenticity, truthfulness

reliablity, stability, seriousness, friendliness, nature, strength

purity, cleanliness, efficiency, innocence

solidity, practicality, timelessness

sophistication, security, substantiality, authority

NEGATIVE

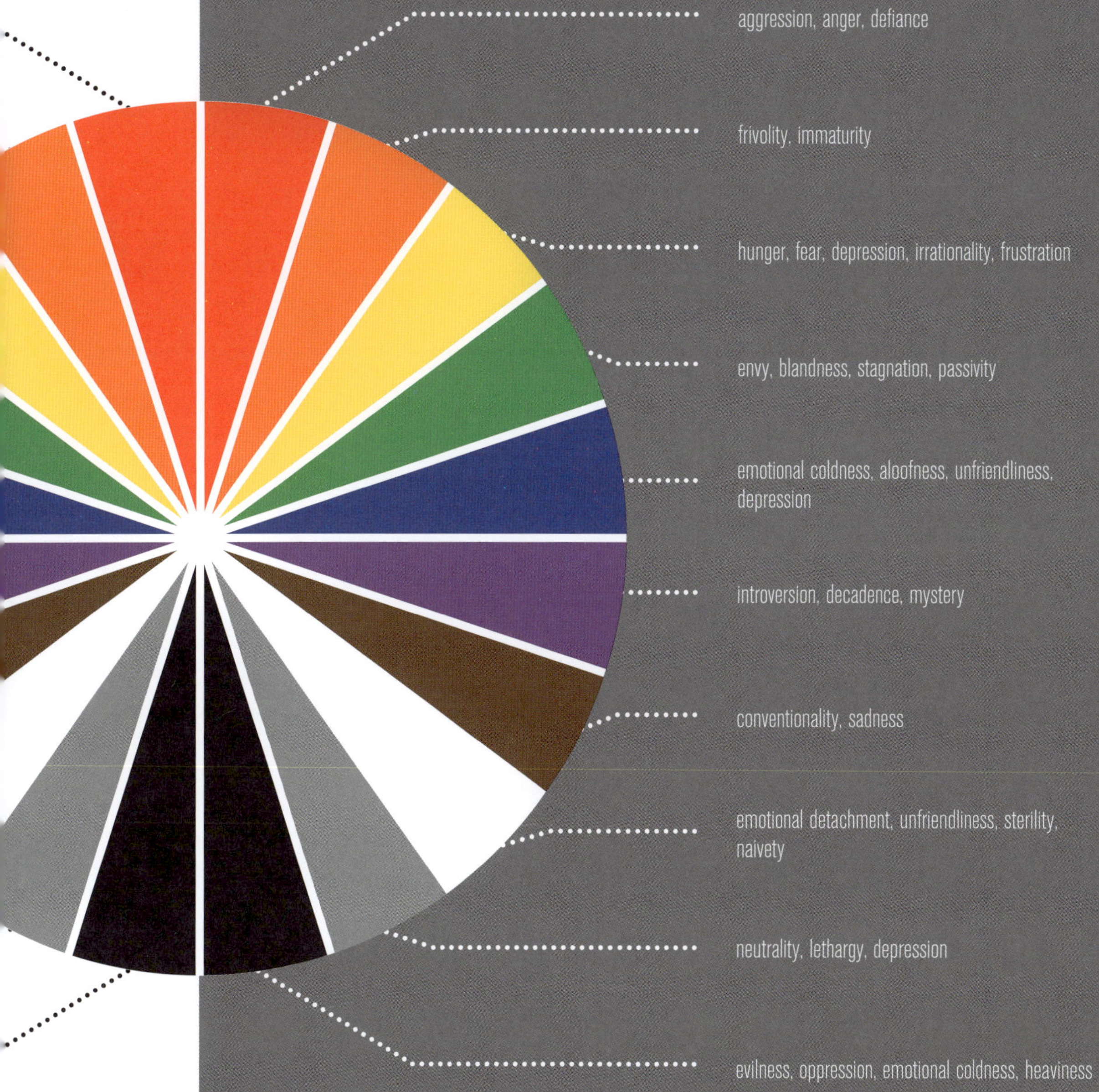

aggression, anger, defiance

frivolity, immaturity

hunger, fear, depression, irrationality, frustration

envy, blandness, stagnation, passivity

emotional coldness, aloofness, unfriendliness, depression

introversion, decadence, mystery

conventionality, sadness

emotional detachment, unfriendliness, sterility, naivety

neutrality, lethargy, depression

evilness, oppression, emotional coldness, heaviness

Color Temperature

Light often has a color bias toward red or blue (or green in the case of fluorescent lighting), which is determined by the color temperature of the light, as measured in Kelvin (K). The lower the Kelvin value of a light source, the more red it is; the higher the color temperature, the more blue the light source is. Because we associate red with warmth and blue with the cold, we consider a higher temperature to have less of a warm feeling.

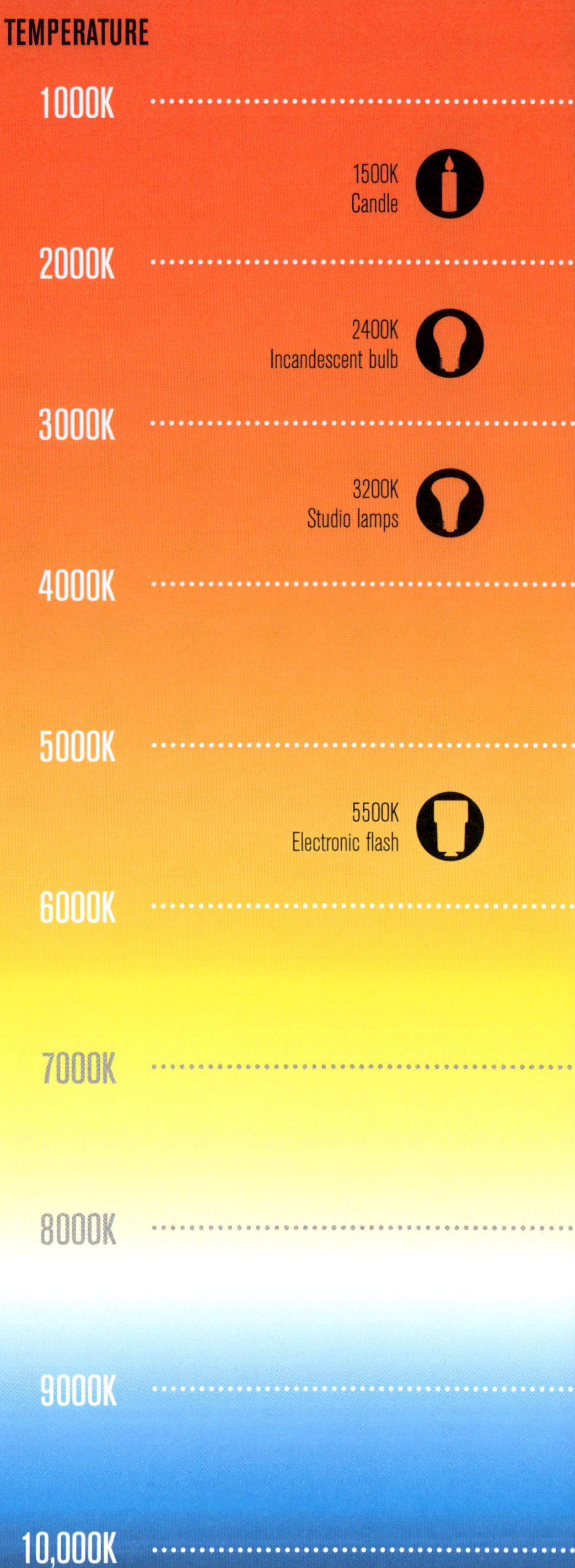

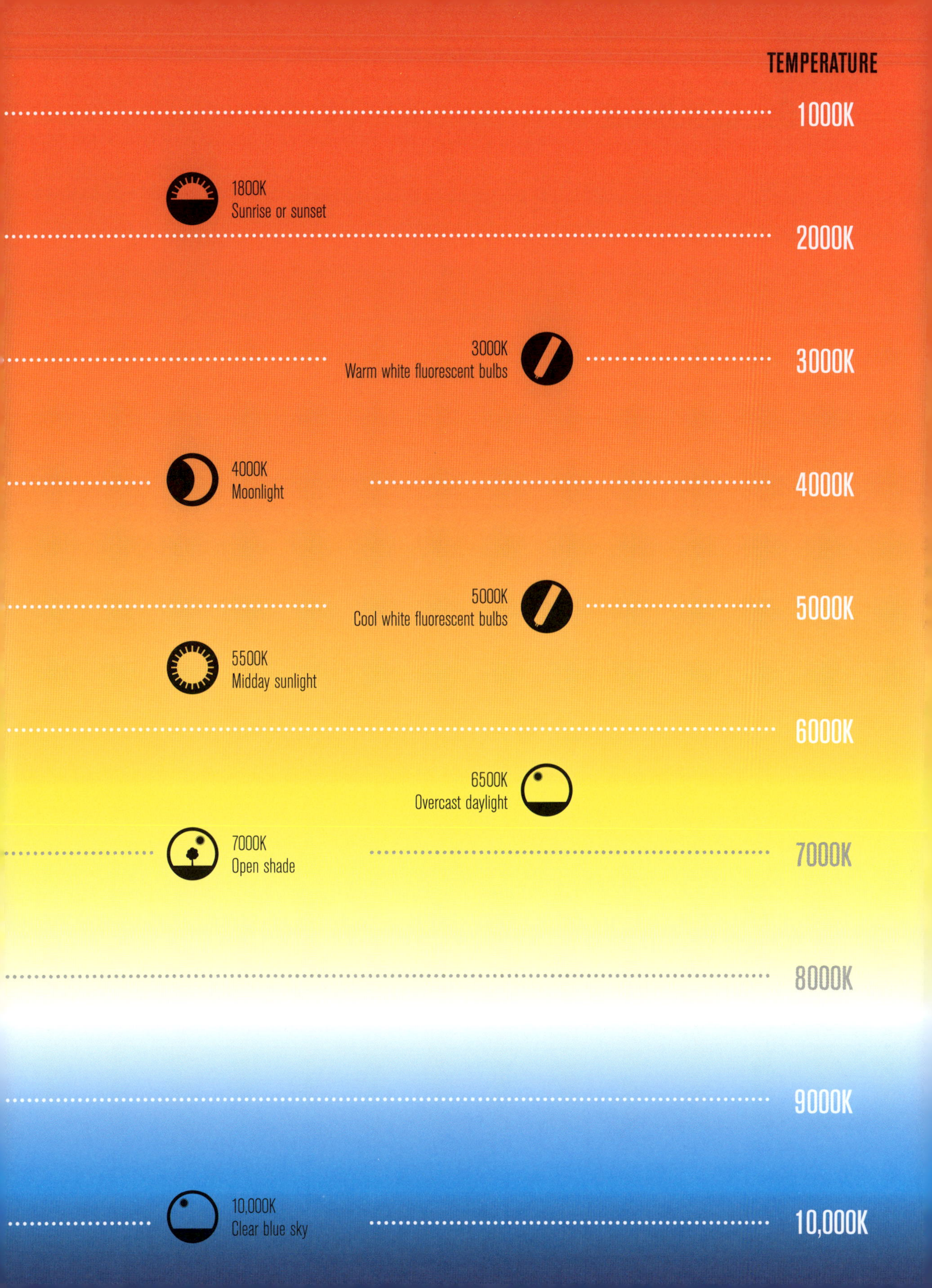

TEMPERATURE

1000K

1800K
Sunrise or sunset

2000K

3000K
Warm white fluorescent bulbs

3000K

4000K
Moonlight

4000K

5000K
Cool white fluorescent bulbs

5000K

5500K
Midday sunlight

6000K

6500K
Overcast daylight

7000K
Open shade

7000K

8000K

9000K

10,000K
Clear blue sky

10,000K

White Balance

White balance (WB) is a camera function that lets you adjust for the color bias of light. This can be done automatically, by selecting a WB preset that matches the light source illuminating the scene; by choosing a specific Kelvin value; or by creating a custom white balance. White balance works by adding the complementary color of the light's color bias to an image, so red is added to neutralize a "cool" color temperature, for example.

AWB

The camera "reads" the scene and automatically sets what it believes is the best white balance.

Incandescent

Corrects the warm bias of incandescent (tungsten/halogen) lighting by adding blue.

Fluorescent

Corrects for the color bias of fluorescent lighting. Cameras often offer several fluorescent WB options including Warm white and Cool white.

Daylight

Corrects for direct sunlight at midday.

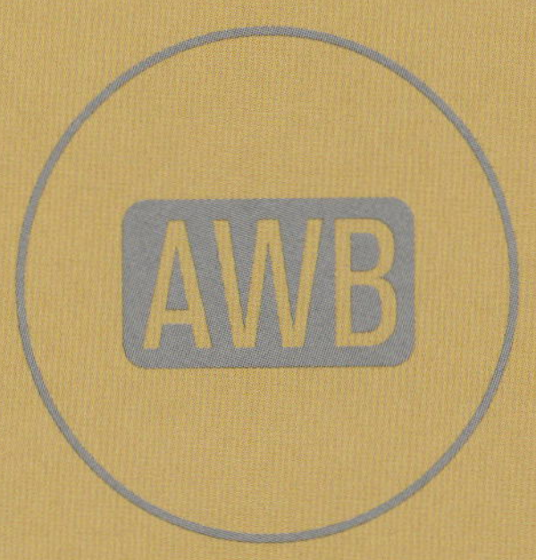

Flash

Select when using flash. Flash is a very neutral light source so very little color correction is applied.

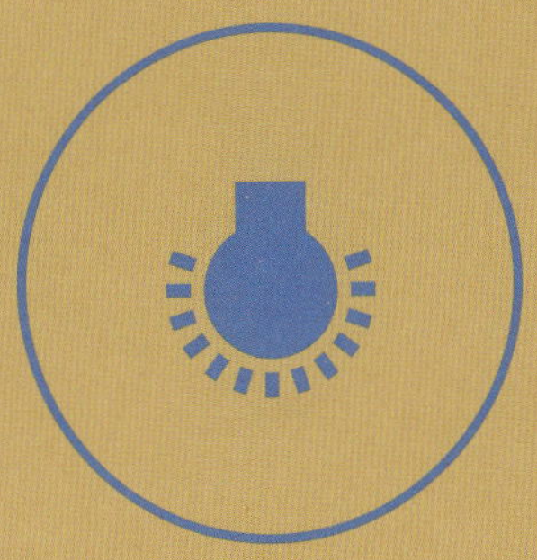

Cloudy

Corrects the cool blue bias of light on an overcast day by "warming" the shot.

Shade

Increases warmth to correct the very cool blue bias of ambient light in open shade.

Custom WB

Lets you set a specific white balance for a particular light source, often by photographing a white or gray reference target.

Light Direction

Lighting direction is measured relative to the camera position. The direction of light determines where shadows are cast from your subject and therefore how three-dimensional your subject will appear in the final photograph.

1 **Frontal lighting** is the simplest lighting direction. This is light that falls from behind the camera onto the scene in front of the camera. Frontal lighting tends to flatten a photograph, as any shadows cast by objects in the scene fall behind those objects, out of sight of the camera.

2 **Three-quarter lighting** is commonly used in portraiture. The light falls so that either three-quarters of the subject is lit and one quarter is in shadow, or one quarter is lit and three-quarters are in shadow.

3 **Backlighting** is light directed toward the camera. Contrast is high, as shadows are cast toward the camera. The high contrast of backlighting makes it an ideal light source when shooting silhouettes.

4 **Side lighting** is light that is cast from either side of the camera's position. Side lighting helps to add a sense of depth to a photograph as shadows fall across the scene.

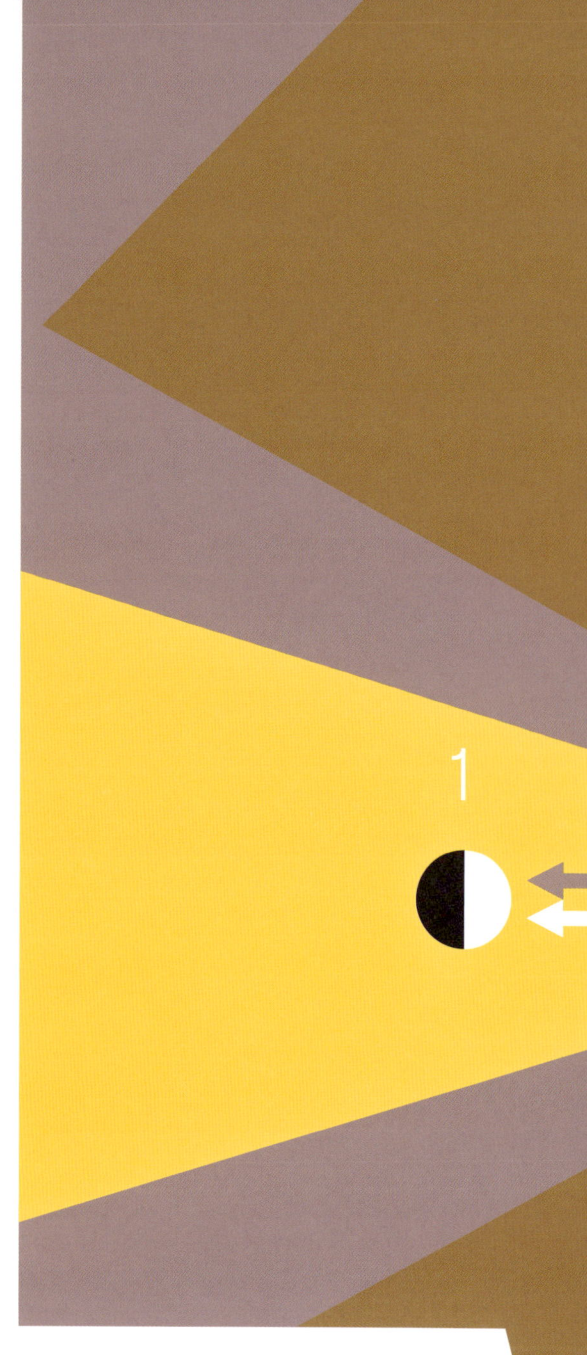

Before you shoot an image it is important to identify where the main light source is in relation to your camera position, as this will have a profound effect on how your subject is lit.

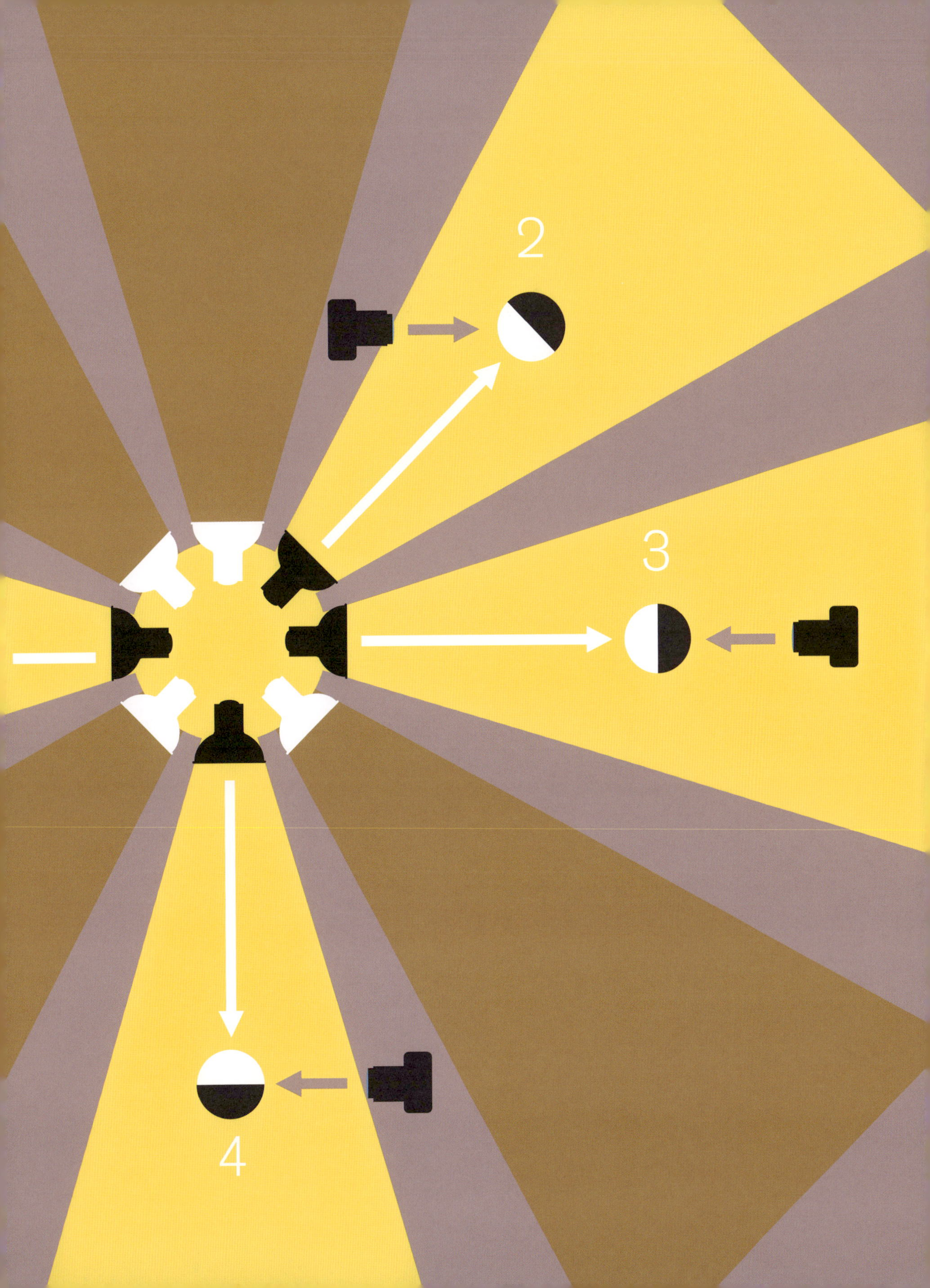

2
3
4

Backlighting & Contrast

Contrast is high when a scene is backlit, particularly when the light source is within the picture space too. In this shot, the setting sun is backlighting a rain-soaked window. I had to underexpose the shot slightly to avoid the sun burning out. In postproduction I had to lighten the darker areas of the shot to reveal some of the hidden detail.

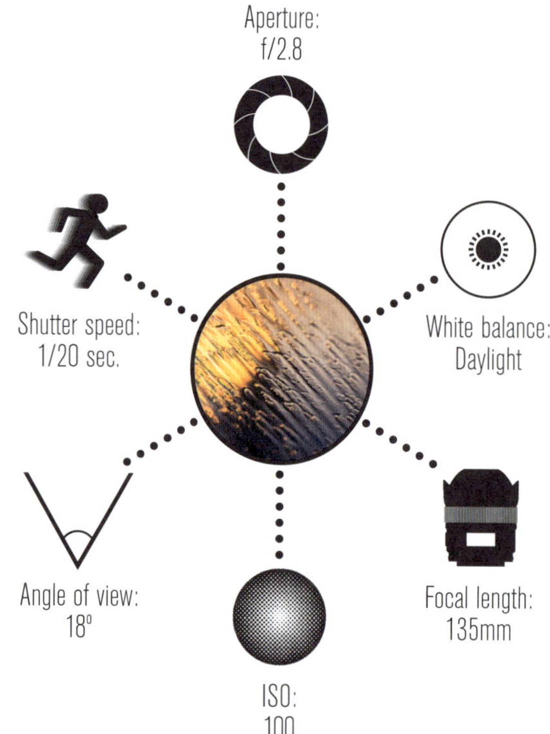

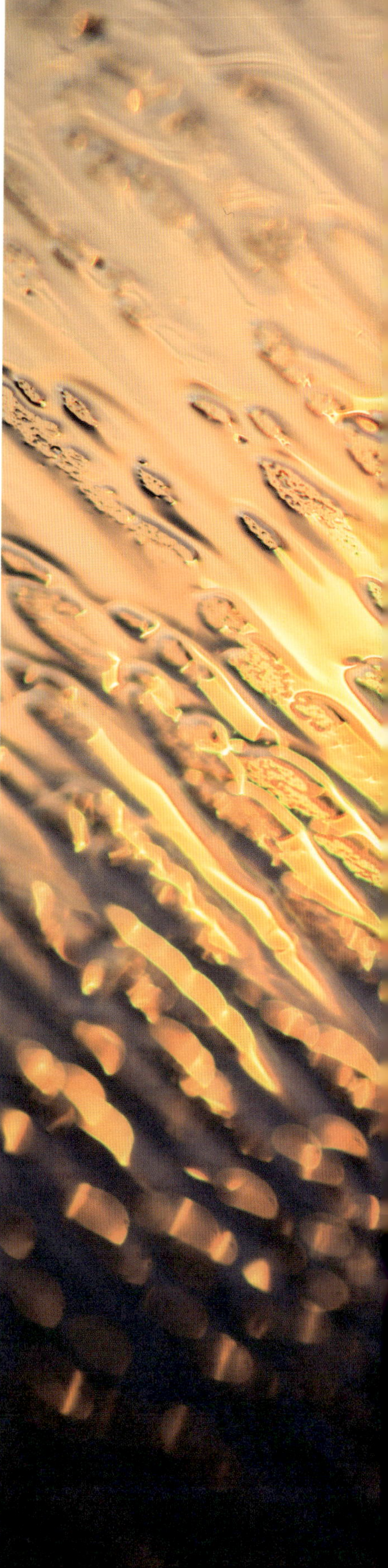

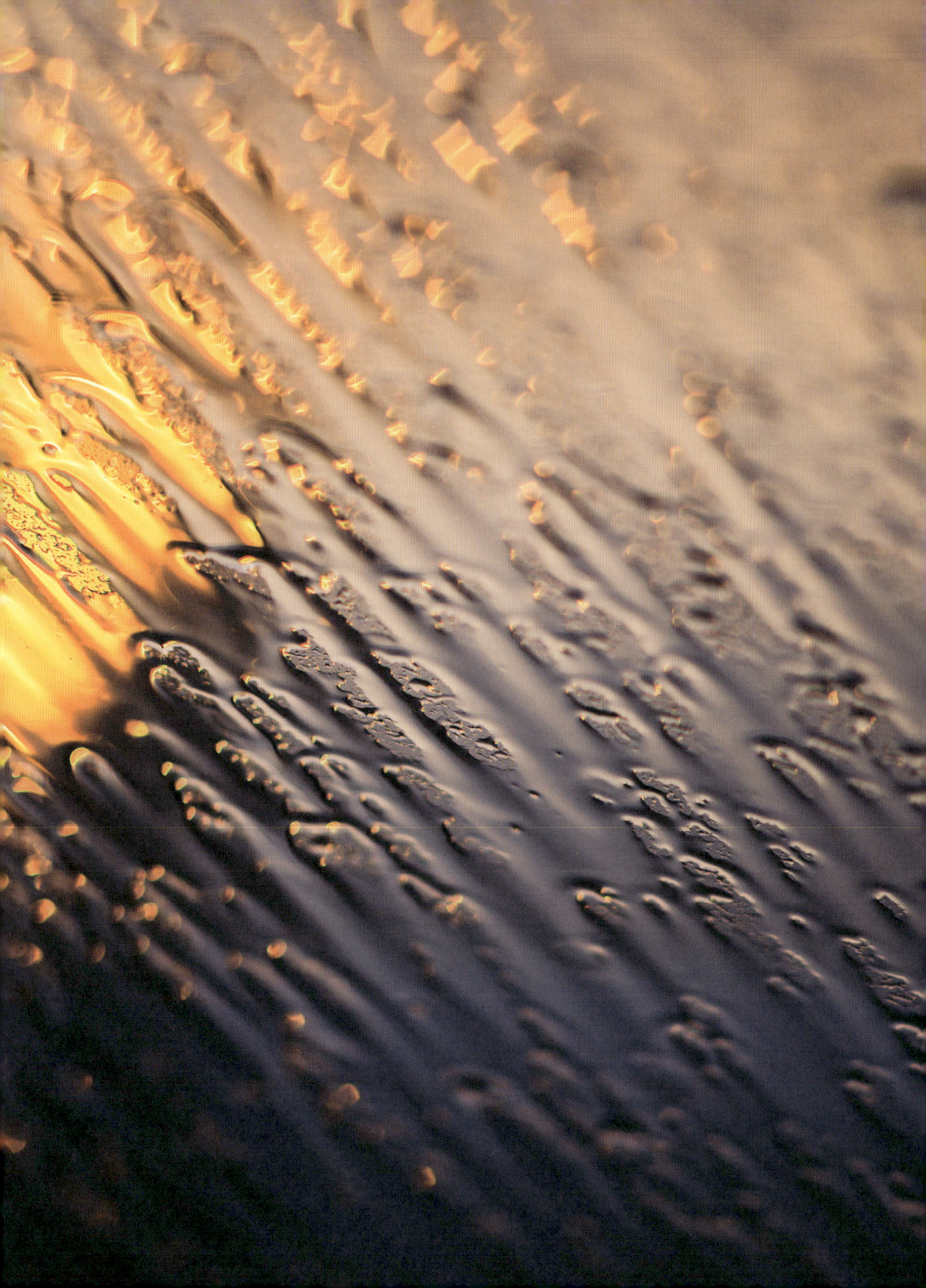

The Sun

Shooting outdoors generally means using the sun as your main light source. The length of the day and the direction of the rising/setting sun will depend on the time of year and the latitude of your location.

It is important to know where and when the sun rises or sets when shooting outdoors. This will let you arrive at your location in good time and allow your intended subject to be lit pleasingly.

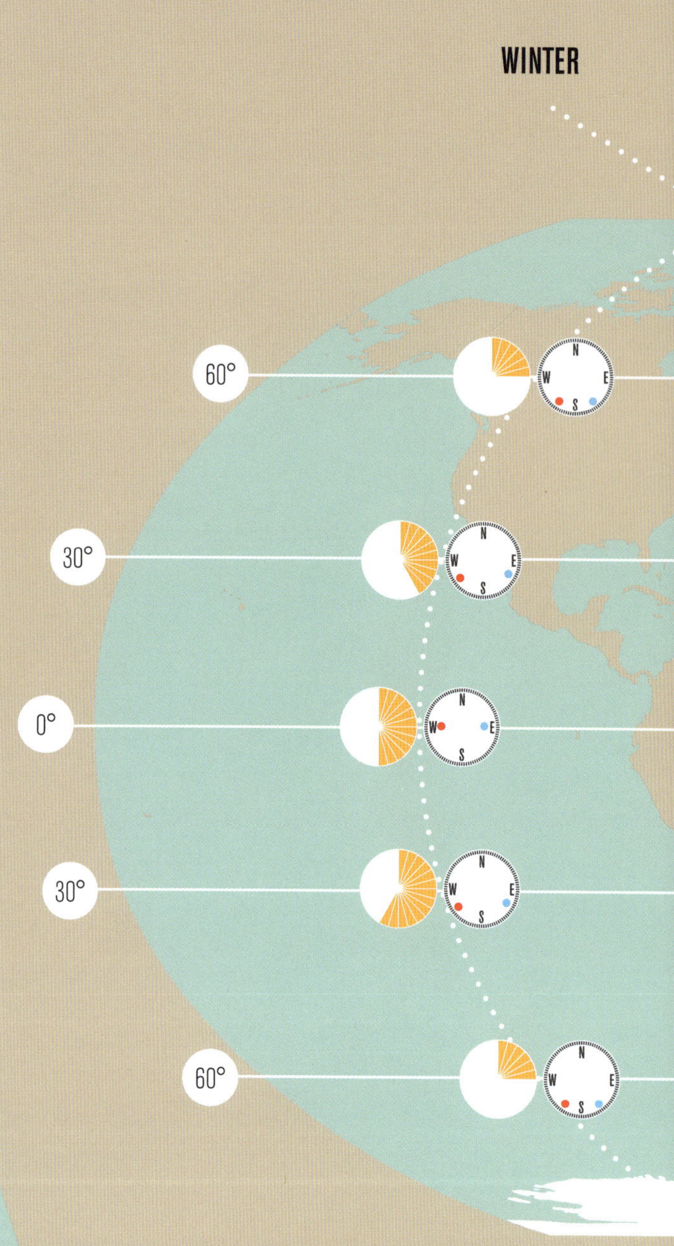

The variation in daylight hours and the direction of sunrise and sunset become more extreme the further north or south you travel from the equator.

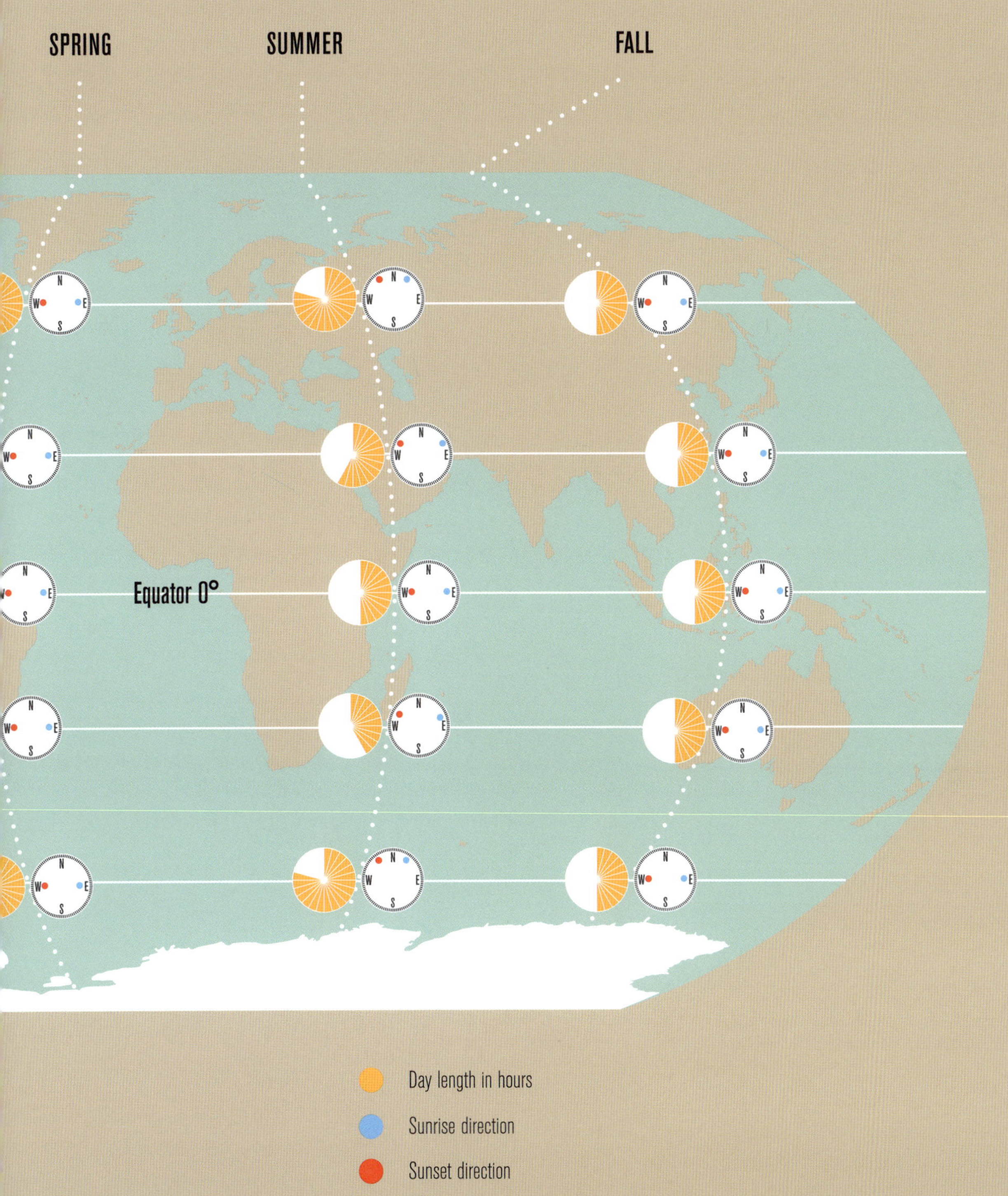

SPRING
SUMMER
FALL
Equator 0°
N
S
E
W
Day length in hours
Sunrise direction
Sunset direction

Sunrise & Sunset

The color temperature of sunlight changes over the course of the day. At sunrise and sunset the light from the sun passes through a thick slice of the earth's atmosphere. This causes the blue wavelengths of the sun's light to be scattered and for sunlight to be heavily biased toward red. When the sun is at solar noon sunlight is more neutral in color as fewer blue wavelengths are scattered.

Warm early morning or late evening light is more esthetically pleasing than the neutral light of midday. The sixty minutes after sunrise and before sunset is known as the "Golden Hour" because of the warmth of the light during this time.

The diagram shows the position of the sun at sunrise and sunset (orange) and solar noon (yellow) and the thickness of the atmosphere the sunlight has to penetrate to reach the earth.

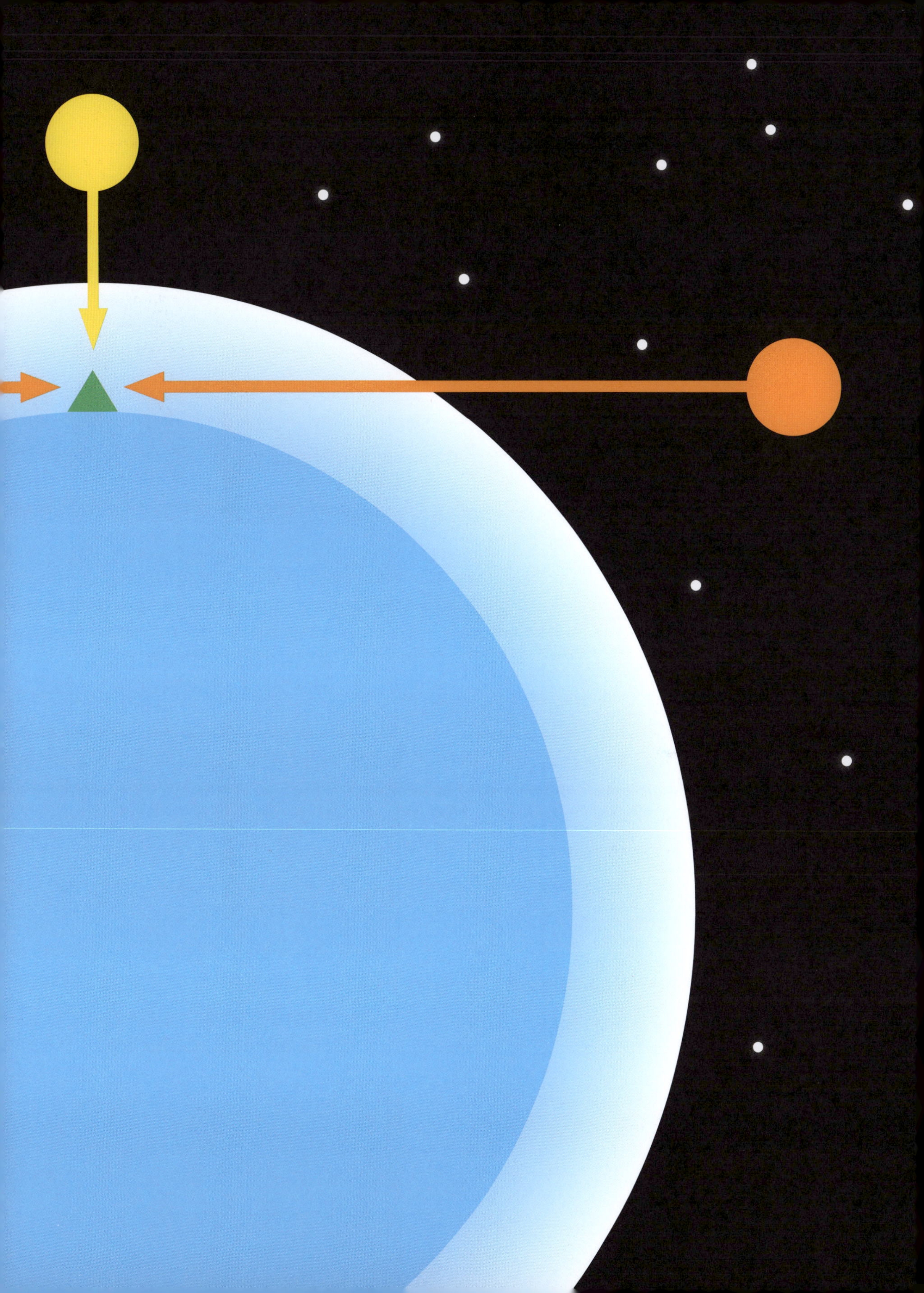

The Sun's Path

The path and position of the sun are critical to outdoor photography. The season and your position on the planet affect not only sunrise and sunset times, but also the height that the sun reaches in the sky. This has an impact on the angle of light striking a subject and the length of shadows.

Taking a position at 40° latitude in the northern hemisphere as an example, we can see how the path and position of the sun change throughout the year. The summer sun rises in the north-east, peaks slightly south of overhead, and sets in the northwest. The winter sun rises in the south-east, peaks at a low angle in the south, and sets in the south-west. On the equinoxes, the sun rises due east and sets due west.

In the northern hemisphere on the equinoxes, the sun reaches its highest point about halfway up from the horizon in the southern half of the sky. There is a marked difference in the sunrise and sunset positions, and in the arc and height of the sun, between the summer solstice (the longest day) and the winter solstice (the shortest day).

Summer Solstice, 40° latitude
June 21/22, longest day

Spring Equinox / Fall Equinox, 40° latitude
March 21/22 / September 22/23,
day and night approximately equal in length

Winter Solstice, 40° latitude
December 21/22, shortest day

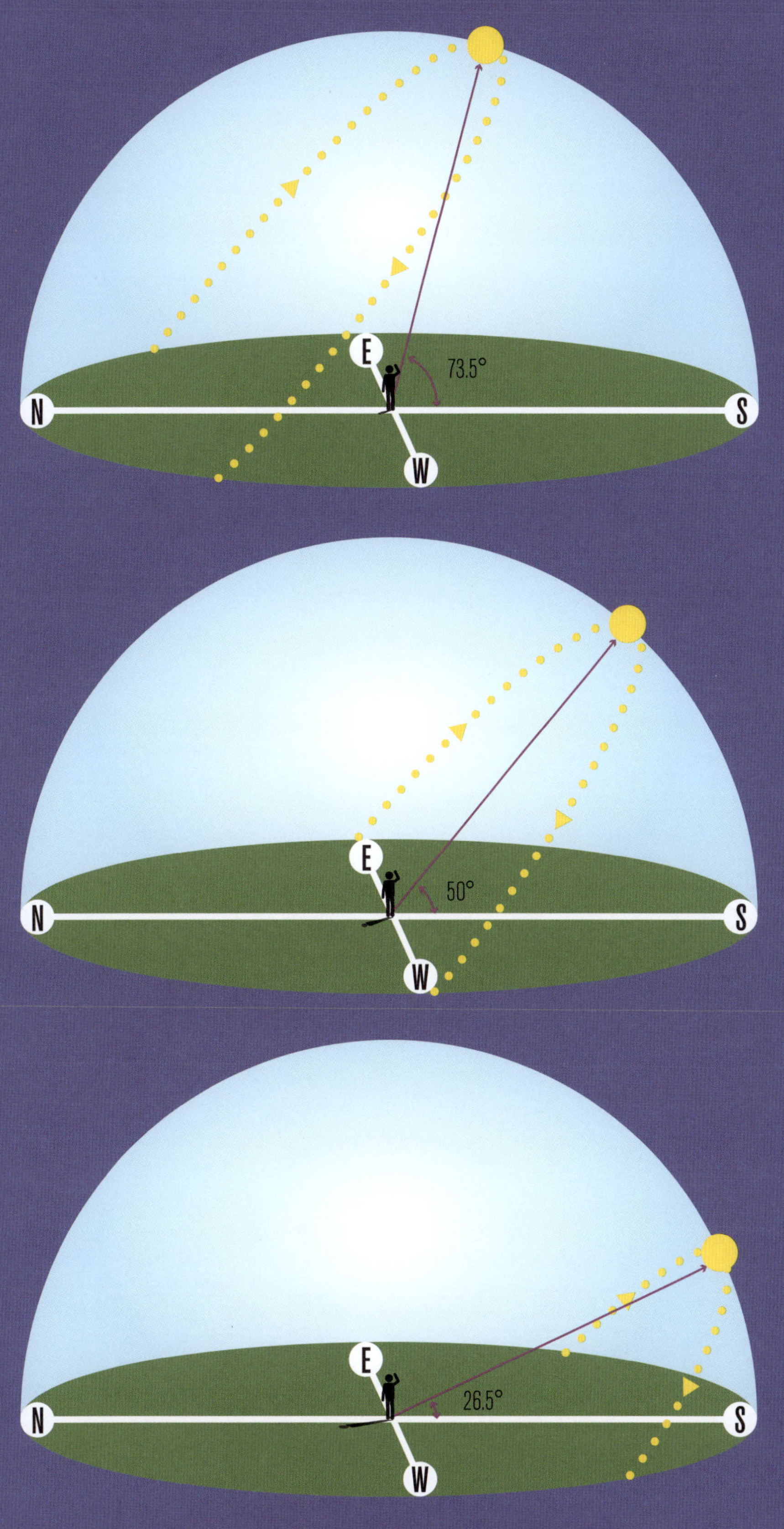

N
E
S
W
73.5°
N
E
S
W
50°
N
E
S
W
26.5°

Qualities Of Light

Hard light is caused when a light source—known as a "point light source"—is small relative to the object being illuminated. The characteristics of hard lighting are dense, sharply defined shadows and bright highlights, which often means that contrast levels are high. Hard lighting is caused by midday sun on a cloudless day and artificial light sources such as direct flash and spotlights.

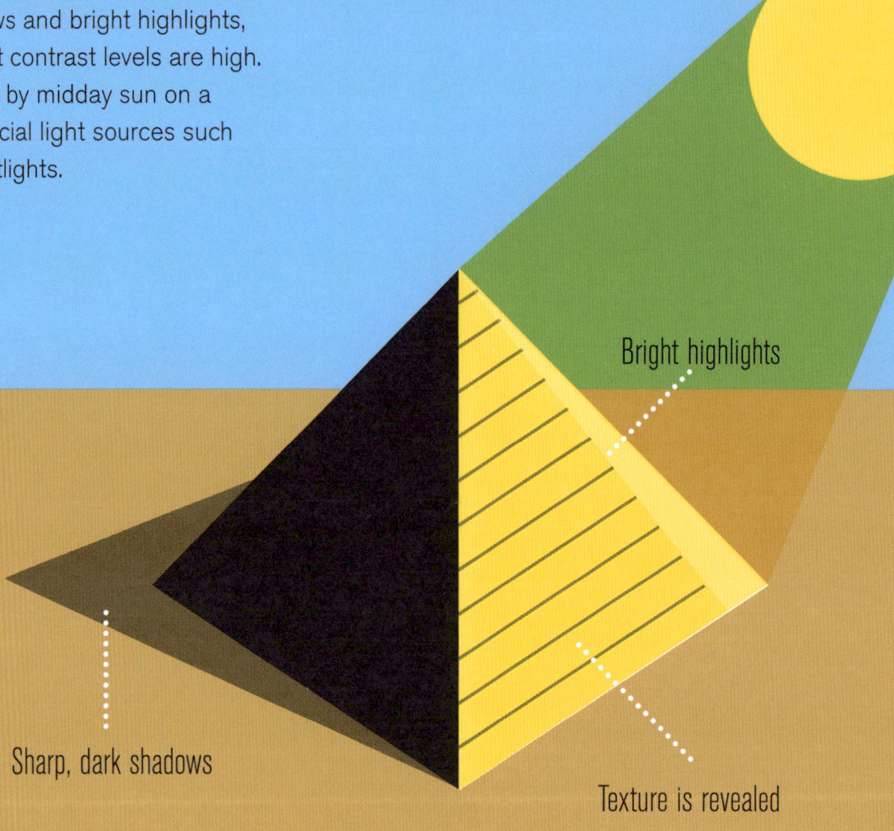

Soft light is cast by a diffused light source or one that is larger than the object being illuminated. The characteristics of soft lighting are low contrast and pale, soft-edged shadows and highlights. Soft lighting is seen on overcast days and when a light source such as direct flash has been bounced or diffused.

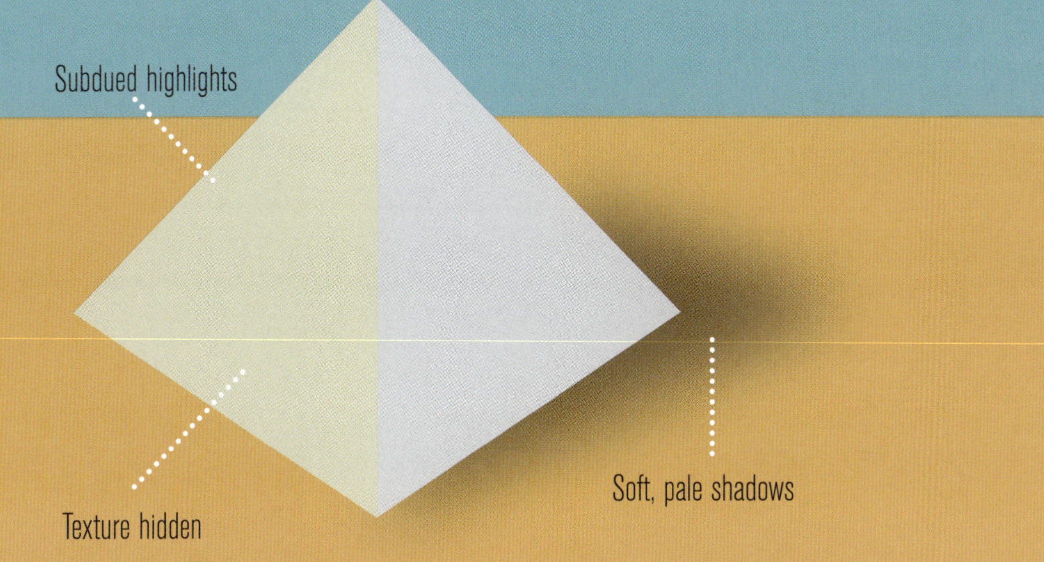

Softness

Whether you use hard or soft lighting will depend largely on your subject—soft lighting is ideal for organic subjects, such as flowers. It's easy to create soft lighting to order in a studio, but more difficult outside. One solution is to wait for suitable weather conditions—the sun passing behind cloud, for example—although for small subjects it's often possible to soften the light by casting a shadow over the subject using your hand or a sheet of card.

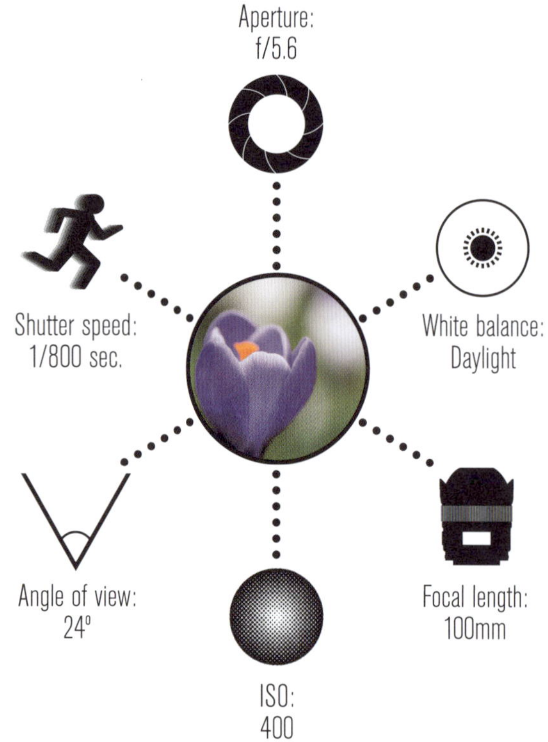

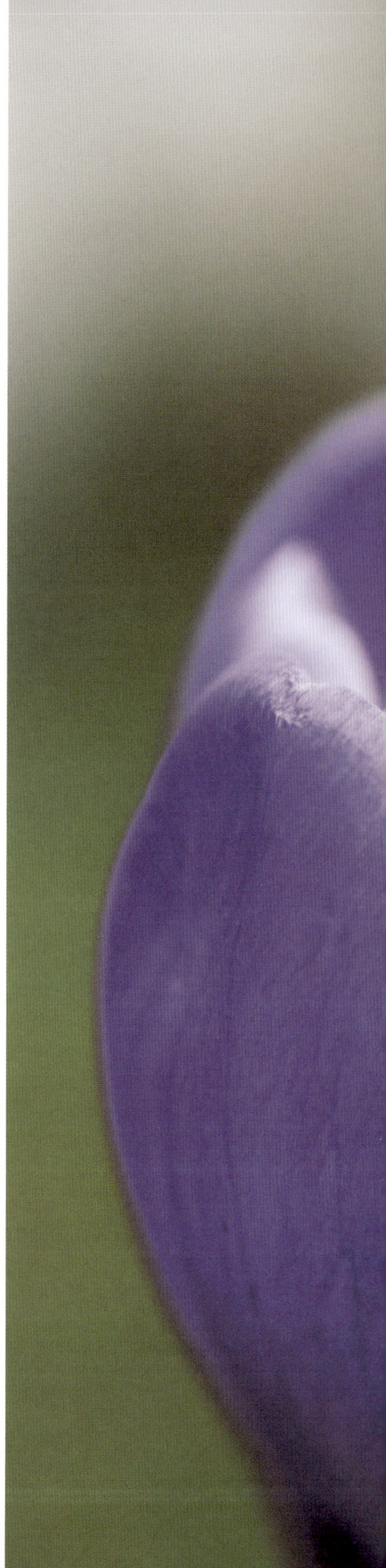

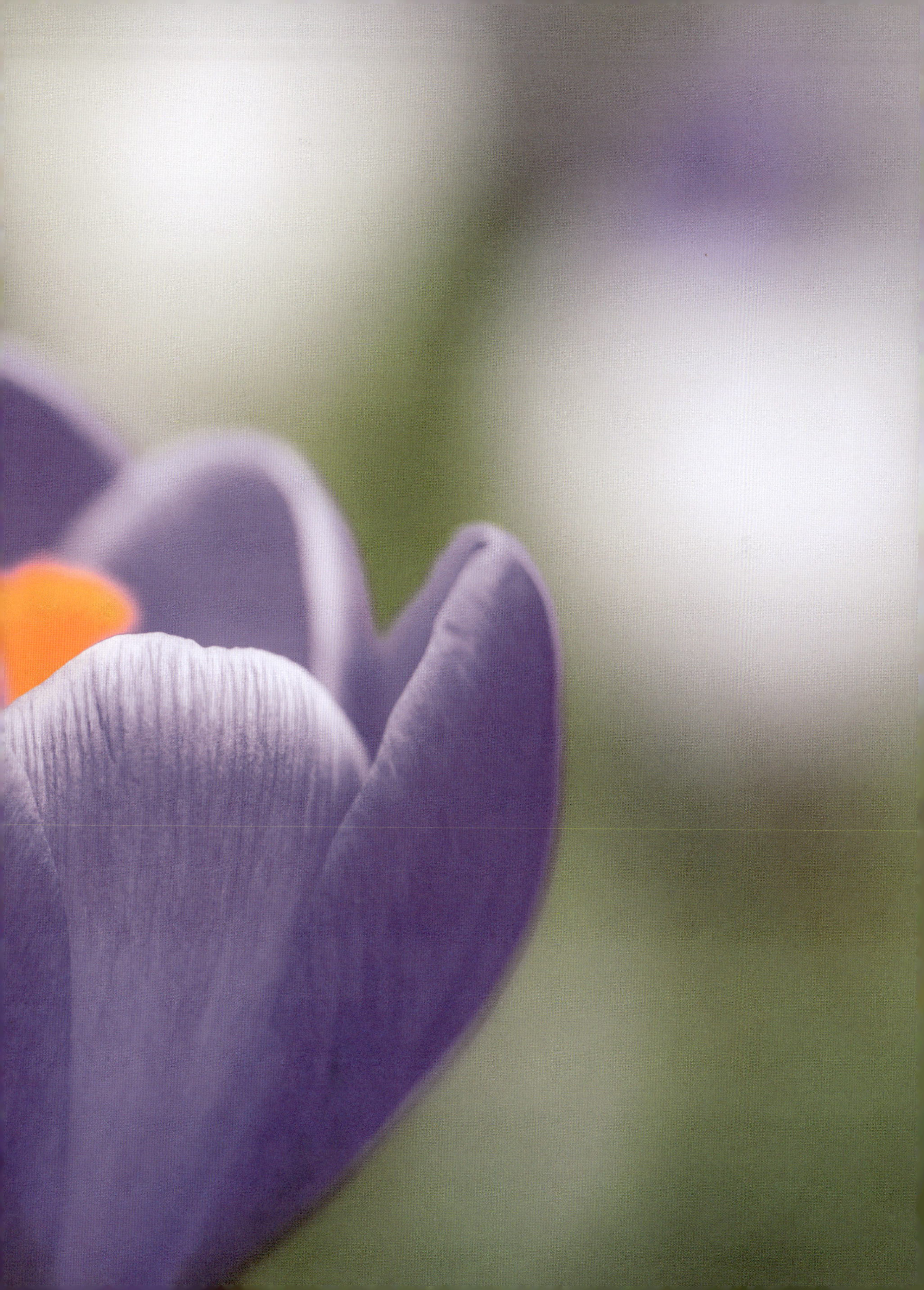

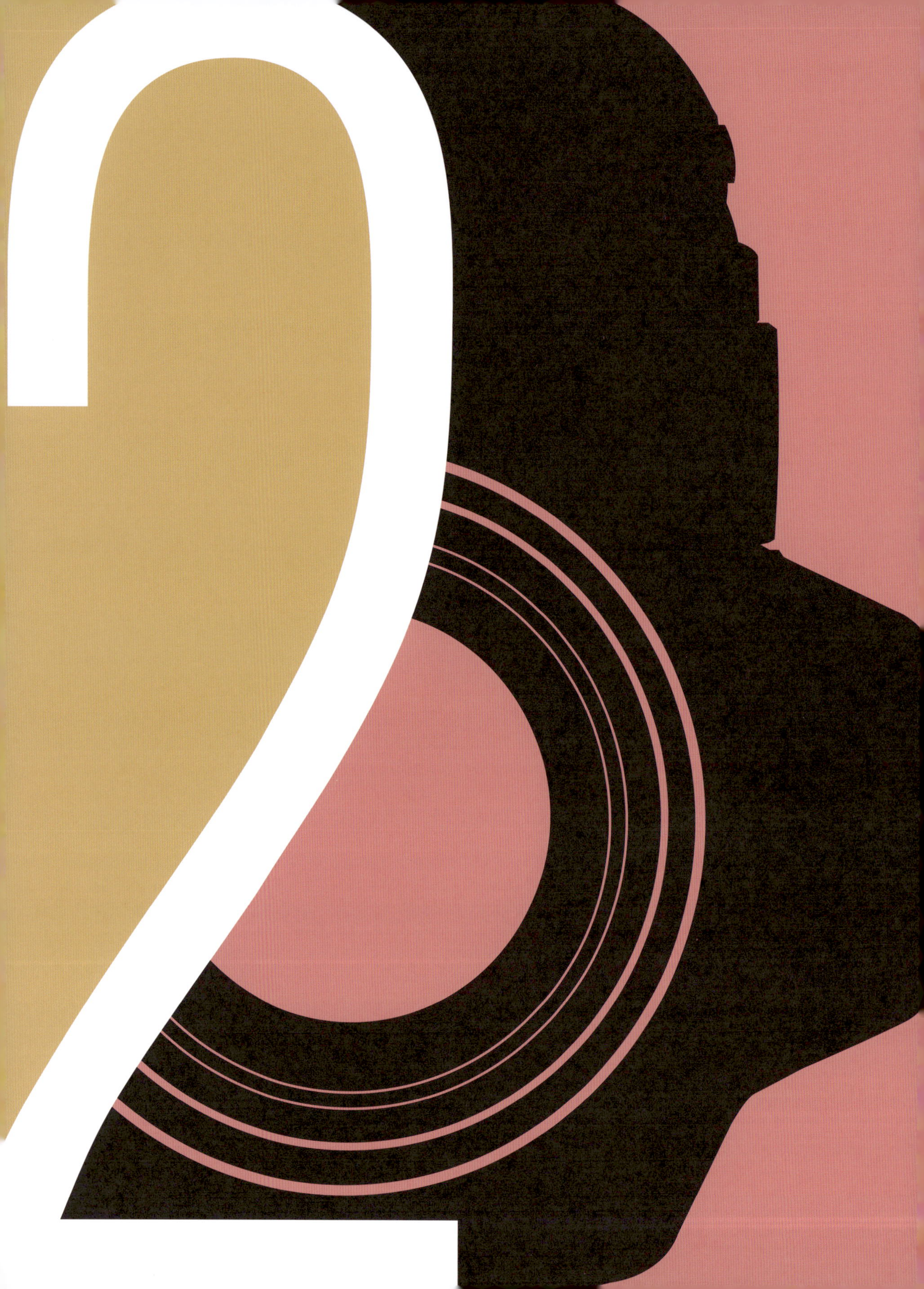

EQUIPMENT

THERE ARE ESSENTIALLY TWO TYPES OF CAMERA: SYSTEM AND NON-SYSTEM.

A system camera (also referred to as an interchangeable lens camera). allows you to change the lens to suit your shooting needs. It can also be expanded by adding accessories such as a flash or battery grip.

A non-system camera is more self-contained, and cannot be added to as easily: lenses are usually fixed in place, and although most non-system cameras come with a built-in flash, they rarely allow you to add an external flash. Non-system cameras include cameras built into cellphones and compact cameras.

Another big difference between system and non-system cameras is the level of exposure control. System cameras typically offer full control, so you can set functions such as shutter speed, aperture, and ISO. When non-system cameras offer exposure controls (and not all of them do), these are often buried in menu systems and so aren't immediately accessible. Non-system cameras therefore make you rely more on automated shooting functions, taking exposure decisions away from you. While automation can sometimes prove useful, exposure is as much a creative element of photography as composition. Losing control over exposure will therefore reduce your level of input when it comes to determining how an image looks.

System cameras come in two main forms: Digital Single Lens Reflex (DSLR) cameras and mirrorless cameras. DSLRs feature an optical viewfinder (OVF). Light is directed straight through the lens via a reflex mirror and pentaprism to the OVF. When the shutter-release button is pressed down, the reflex mirror swings up out of the way to reveal the shutter, the shutter opens, and light hits the sensor to make an exposure. At the end of the exposure the shutter closes and the mirror returns to its "down" position. Because light is directed straight from the lens to the OVF, you see what the sensor will ultimately "see," which makes composing a shot accurate and straightforward. You can also see where the camera is focused. The disadvantage to this system is that the OVF is temporarily blacked out during the exposure.

As the name suggests, mirrorless cameras lack a reflex mirror. In mirrorless cameras the shutter is held open and the sensor constantly receives light through the lens. The image projected by the lens is then fed to an LCD on the back of the camera and/or to an electronic viewfinder (EVF). When the shutter-release button is pressed, the shutter closes, temporarily pausing this feed. The shutter then opens to begin the exposure, before closing again at the end of the exposure. Finally, the shutter re-opens to resume the image feed back to the LCD or EVF. Just like a DSLR you see what the sensor "sees," but you can also see how contrast, white balance, and the current picture parameters will affect the final image.

Cameras

There is no such thing as the perfect camera. All cameras have certain advantages and disadvantages, so choosing the right model for your needs will often involve seeing where the balance lies.

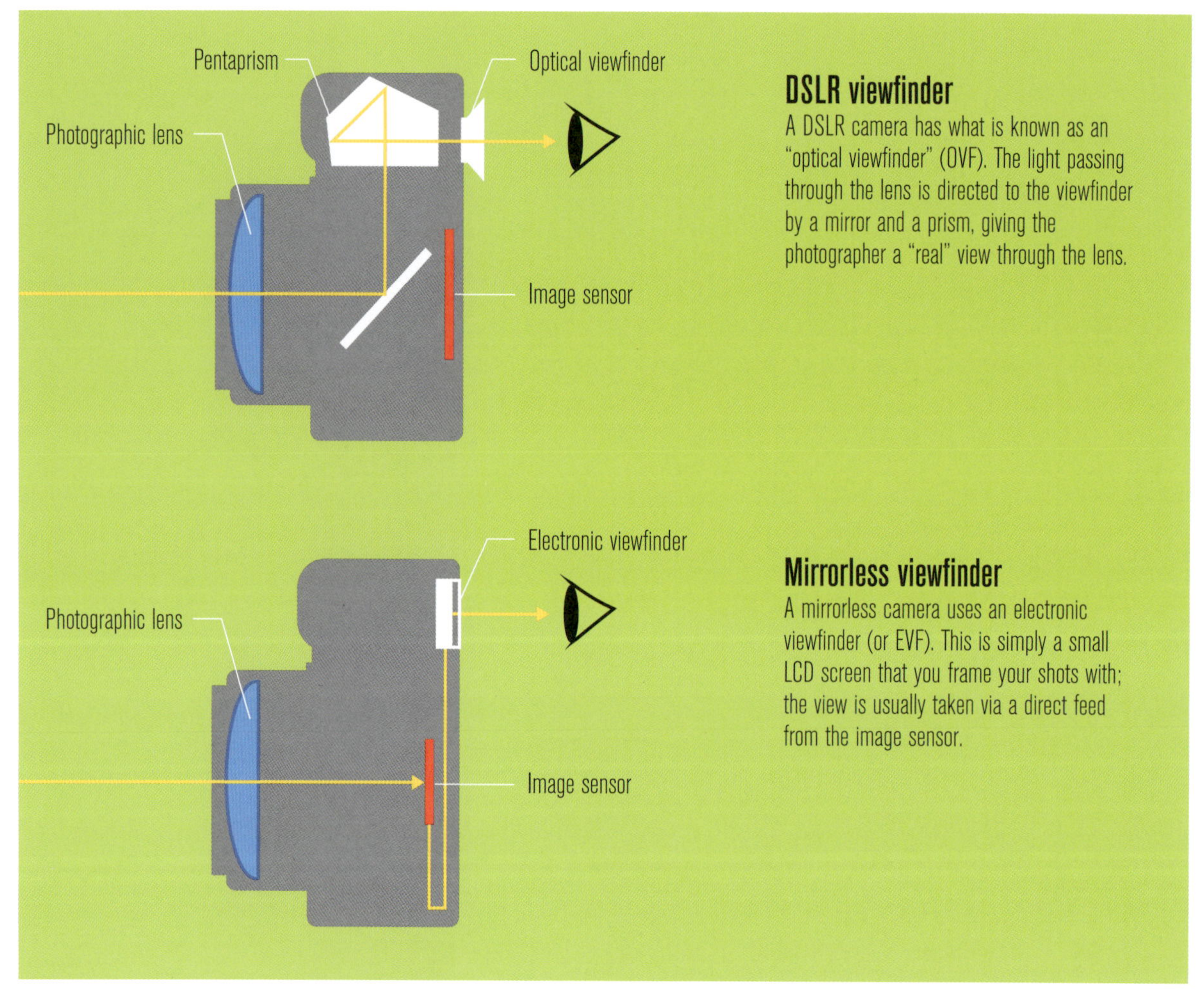

DSLR viewfinder

A DSLR camera has what is known as an "optical viewfinder" (OVF). The light passing through the lens is directed to the viewfinder by a mirror and a prism, giving the photographer a "real" view through the lens.

Mirrorless viewfinder

A mirrorless camera uses an electronic viewfinder (or EVF). This is simply a small LCD screen that you frame your shots with; the view is usually taken via a direct feed from the image sensor.

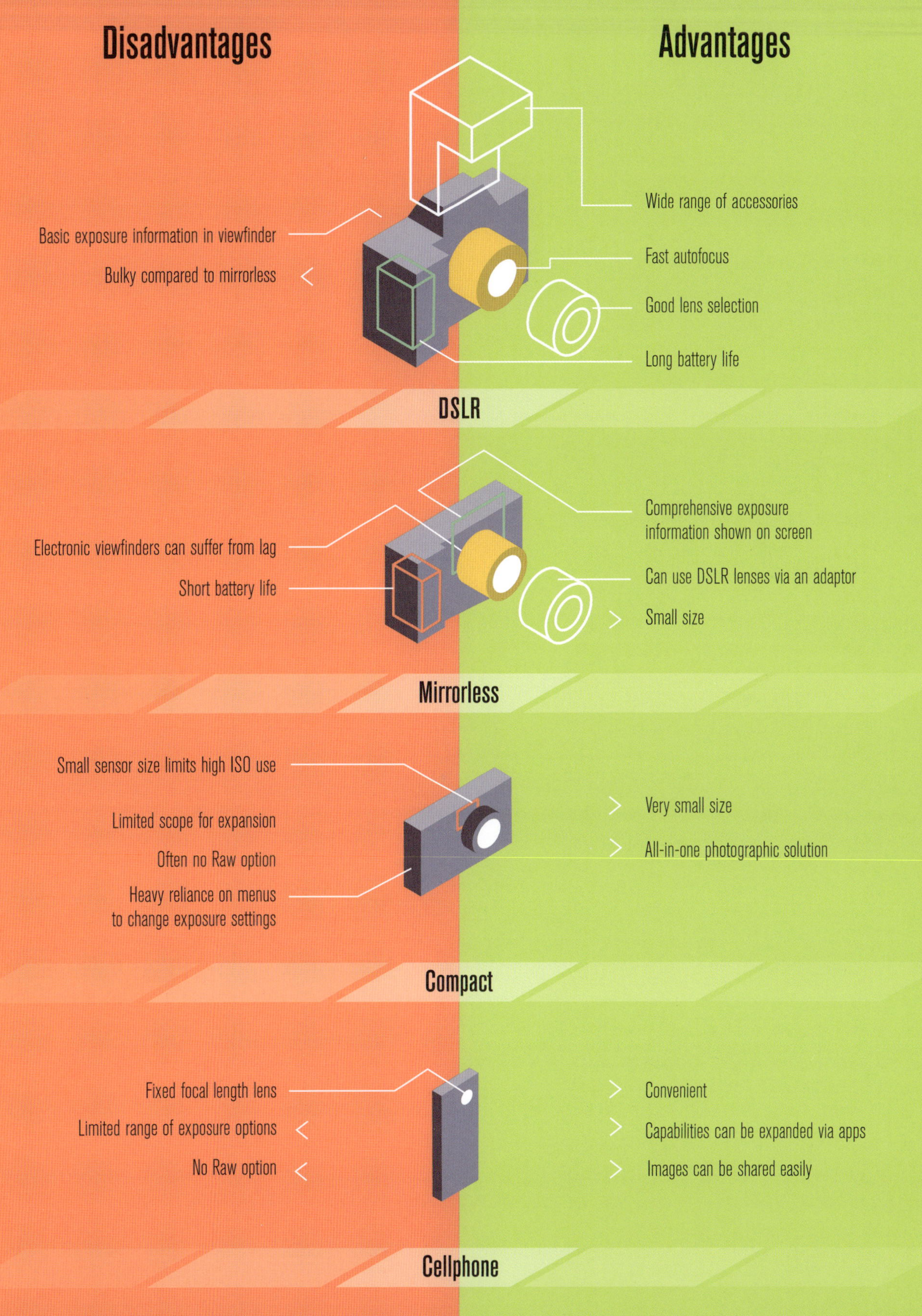

Disadvantages
Advantages

Basic exposure information in viewfinder
Bulky compared to mirrorless
Wide range of accessories
Fast autofocus
Good lens selection
Long battery life
DSLR

Electronic viewfinders can suffer from lag
Short battery life
Comprehensive exposure information shown on screen
Can use DSLR lenses via an adaptor
Small size
Mirrorless

Small sensor size limits high ISO use
Limited scope for expansion
Often no Raw option
Heavy reliance on menus to change exposure settings
Very small size
All-in-one photographic solution
Compact

Fixed focal length lens
Limited range of exposure options
No Raw option
Convenient
Capabilities can be expanded via apps
Images can be shared easily
Cellphone

Lenses

The lens you use will have a profound effect on your images. Lenses fall into three broad categories: wide-angle, normal (or "standard"), and telephoto. The category that a lens falls into depends on its focal length (which is the distance—in mm—from the sensor to the optical center of a lens) and the size of the sensor inside the camera.

The focal length of a lens affects how much of the scene in front of a camera will be recorded. This means that you can vary how an image is composed by varying the focal length of the lens.

Wide-Angle

Subject small in frame
Large angle of view
Perspective distortion
Increased depth of field

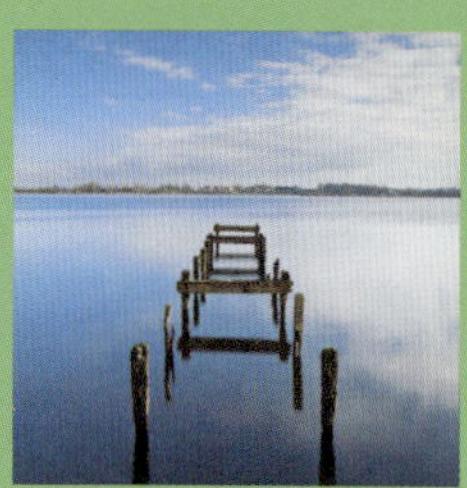

Good for: landscapes
architecture

Normal

Moderate magnification of subject
Moderate angle of view
Natural perspective
Moderate depth of field

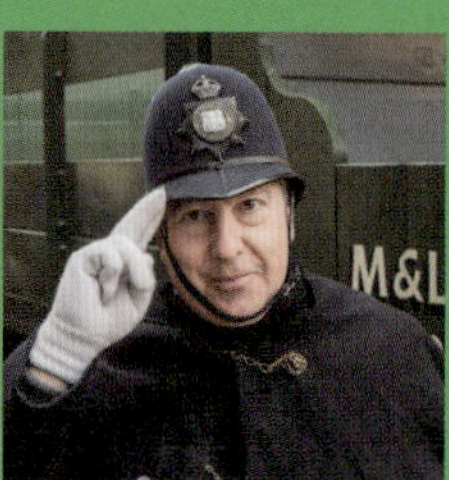

Good for: portraiture
documentary

Telephoto

High magnification of subject
Small angle of view
Appears to compress space
Limited depth of field

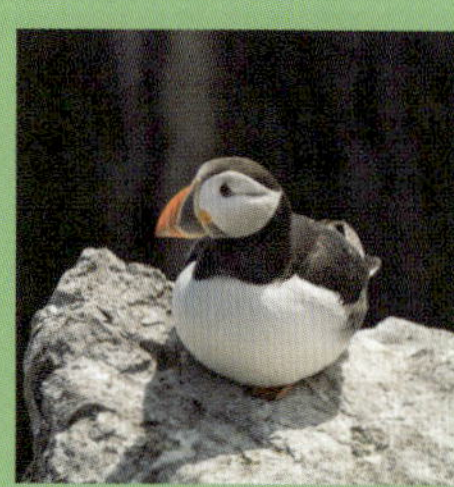

Good for: portraiture
nature

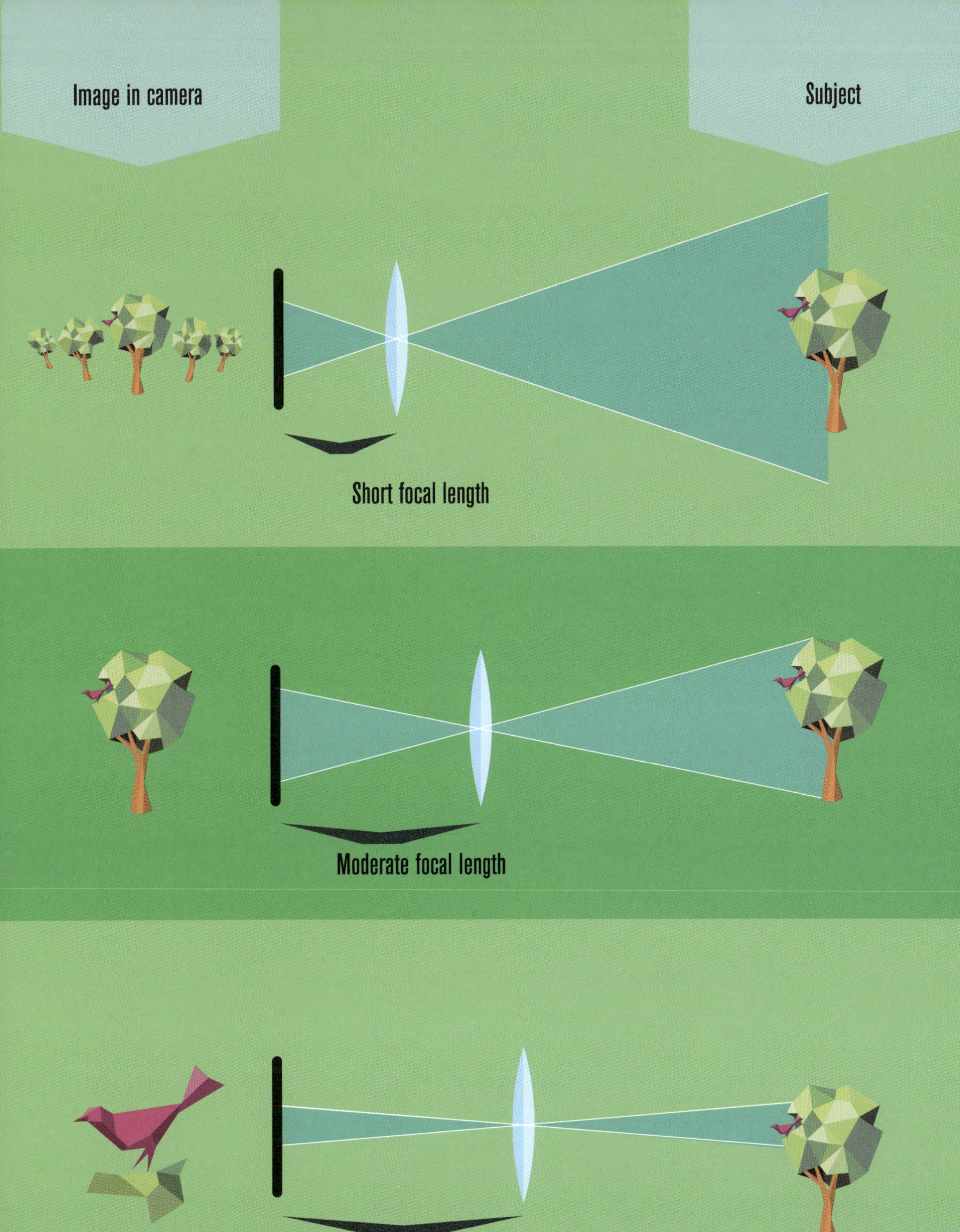

Image in camera
Subject
Short focal length
Moderate focal length
Long focal length

Wide-Angle Lenses

Landscape and architectural photographers frequently use wide-angle lenses to convey a sense of space. The chief characteristic of a wide-angle lens is that spatial relationships are distorted: the relative sizes of objects in a scene change. Those closest to the camera will appear far larger relative to those some distance away. The key to using wide-angle lenses well is to think carefully about the relationships of the various elements in a scene: the distant view in this shot was not as far away as it actually appears, and the foreground rock only looms large because it was so close to the camera.

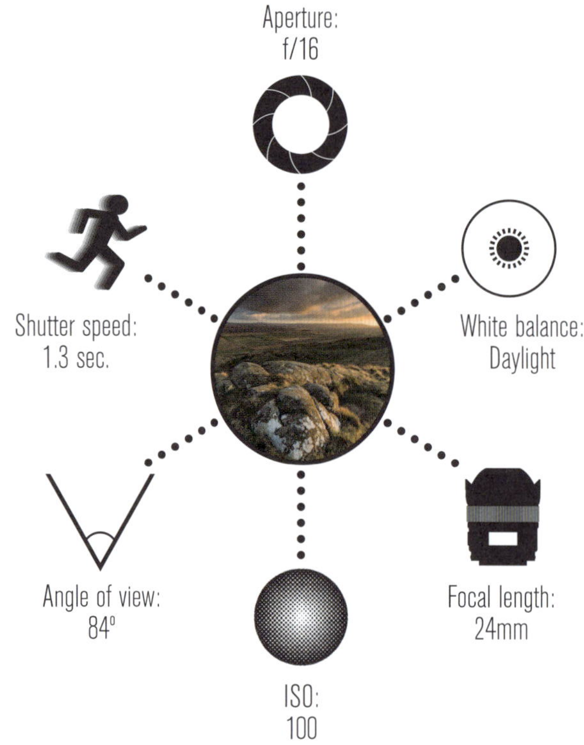

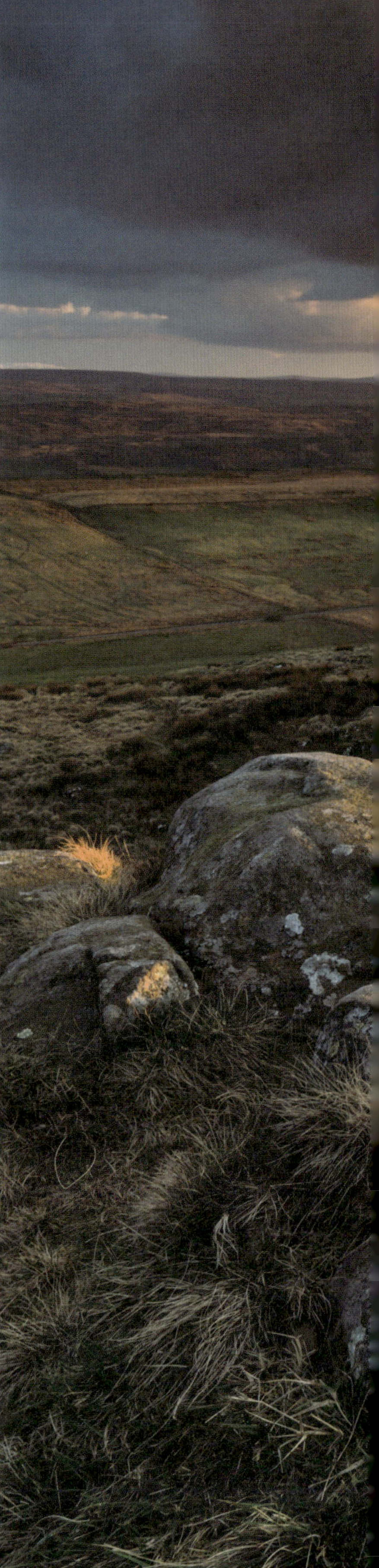

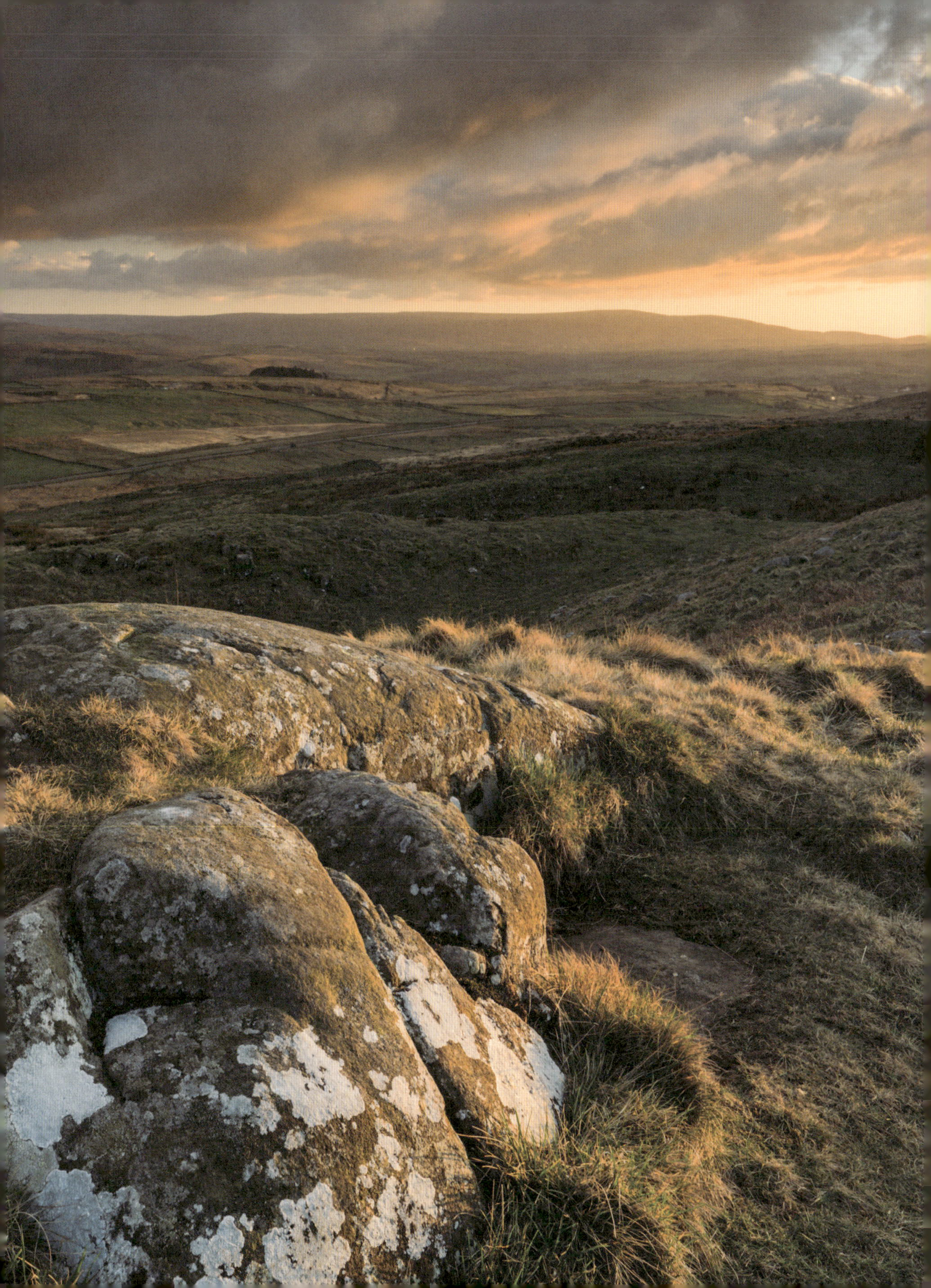

Angle Of View

The angle of view of a lens (measured in degrees) determines the amount of a scene projected by the lens onto the digital sensor inside a camera. The focal length of the lens is one factor that determines the angle of view, but another factor is the size of the camera's digital sensor. Wide-angle lenses have a large angle of view. The angle of view of a telephoto lens is narrow but the image is magnified, making distant objects appear larger within the frame.

The angle of view of a lens can be measured three ways. Horizontally, vertically, or diagonally across the frame. If you only see one figure it's generally safe to assume that this is the diagonal angle of view, which is what has been used throughout this book.

This diagram shows how much of a scene would be recorded, in degrees, when using a lens with a specific focal length (mm) on a camera with a particular sensor type.

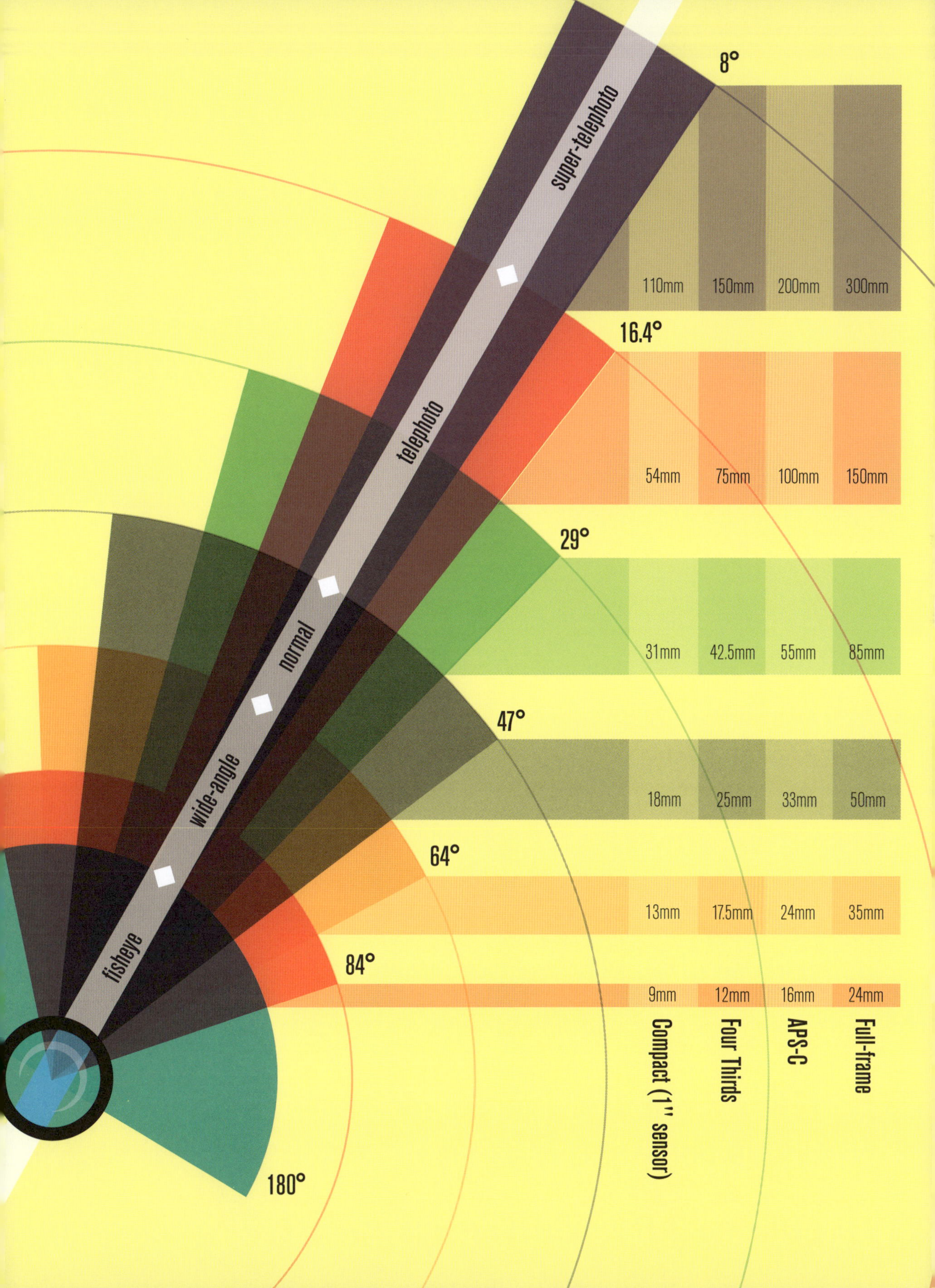

super-telephoto
telephoto
normal
wide-angle
fisheye
8°
16.4°
29°
47°
64°
84°
180°
110mm 150mm 200mm 300mm
54mm 75mm 100mm 150mm
31mm 42.5mm 55mm 85mm
18mm 25mm 33mm 50mm
13mm 17.5mm 24mm 35mm
9mm 12mm 16mm 24mm
Compact (1" sensor)
Four Thirds
APS-C
Full-frame

Crop Factor

The angle of view of a lens largely depends on the physical size of the sensor inside the camera. The difference in the angle of view of a lens when fitted to a 35mm/full-frame camera and a camera with a smaller sensor is known as the crop factor: the smaller the sensor, the greater the crop factor.

Sensor size	Size in mm (w x h)
1/2.5"	5.76 x 4.29
1/2.3"	6.17 x 4.55
1/1.8"	7.18 x 5.32
2/3"	8.8 x 6.6
1"	13.2 x 8.8
Four Thirds/Micro Four Thirds	17.3 x 13
Canon APS-C	22.3 x 14.9
Other APS-C	23.6 x 15.6
APS-H	27.9 x 18.6
35mm/full-frame	36 x 24
Medium format	56 x 36

In this illustration the white outline shows the actual size of a full-frame sensor, while the solid white area shows the actual size of smaller format sensors. This smaller area is effectively a "crop" of the full-frame area, which is why the angle of view of the lens changes.

Sensor Sizes

FULL FRAME
36 x 24mm/864mm^2

APS-H
27.9 x 18.6mm/548mm^2

APS-C
23.6 x 15.6mm/370mm^2

MICRO FOUR THIRDS
17.3 x 13mm/225mm^2

1/2.5"
5.76 x 4.29mm/25mm^2

Common Sensor Sizes

There is a wide variety of sensor sizes in use, ranging from medium format, right the way down to 1.25". This graphic shows the relative size difference between them (note it is not to scale).

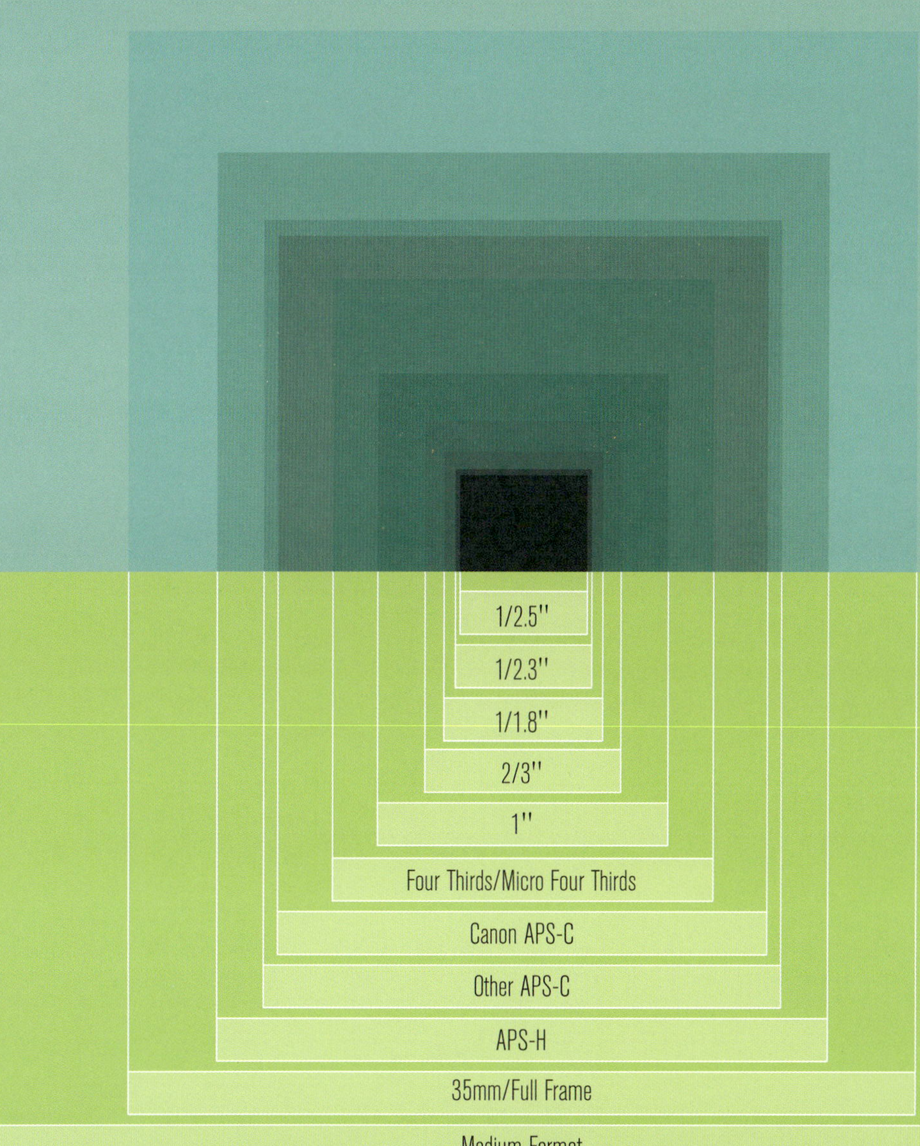

The Shutter

There are two types of camera shutter commonly used in cameras: leaf shutters and focal plane shutters. Leaf shutters are generally found in compact cameras and lenses for medium- and large-format cameras, while focal plane shutters are used in mirrorless and DSLR cameras.

Some digital cameras now use an electronic shutter. This removes the need for a mechanical shutter mechanism as the sensor is simply turned on and off again to make the exposure.

Leaf shutter

A leaf shutter is made up of a series of identical overlapping blades that form a light-tight seal when closed. When the shutter-release button is pressed, these blades pivot outward to create an opening that lets light reach the sensor. At the end of the exposure the blades close once more.

Advantages
- Flash can be used at any shutter speed
- Simplicity

Disadvantages
- Limited range of shutter speeds

Focal plane shutter

A focal plane shutter uses two light-tight curtains. When the shutter-release button is pressed down the first curtain moves to begin exposing the sensor to light. The second curtain follows on, creating a slit. Once the second curtain has completed its travel the exposure ends. The time between the first curtain moving and the second is the time selected by you or the camera as the required shutter speed.

Advantages
- Wide range of shutter speeds

Disadvantages
- Low flash synchronization speed
- Complexity

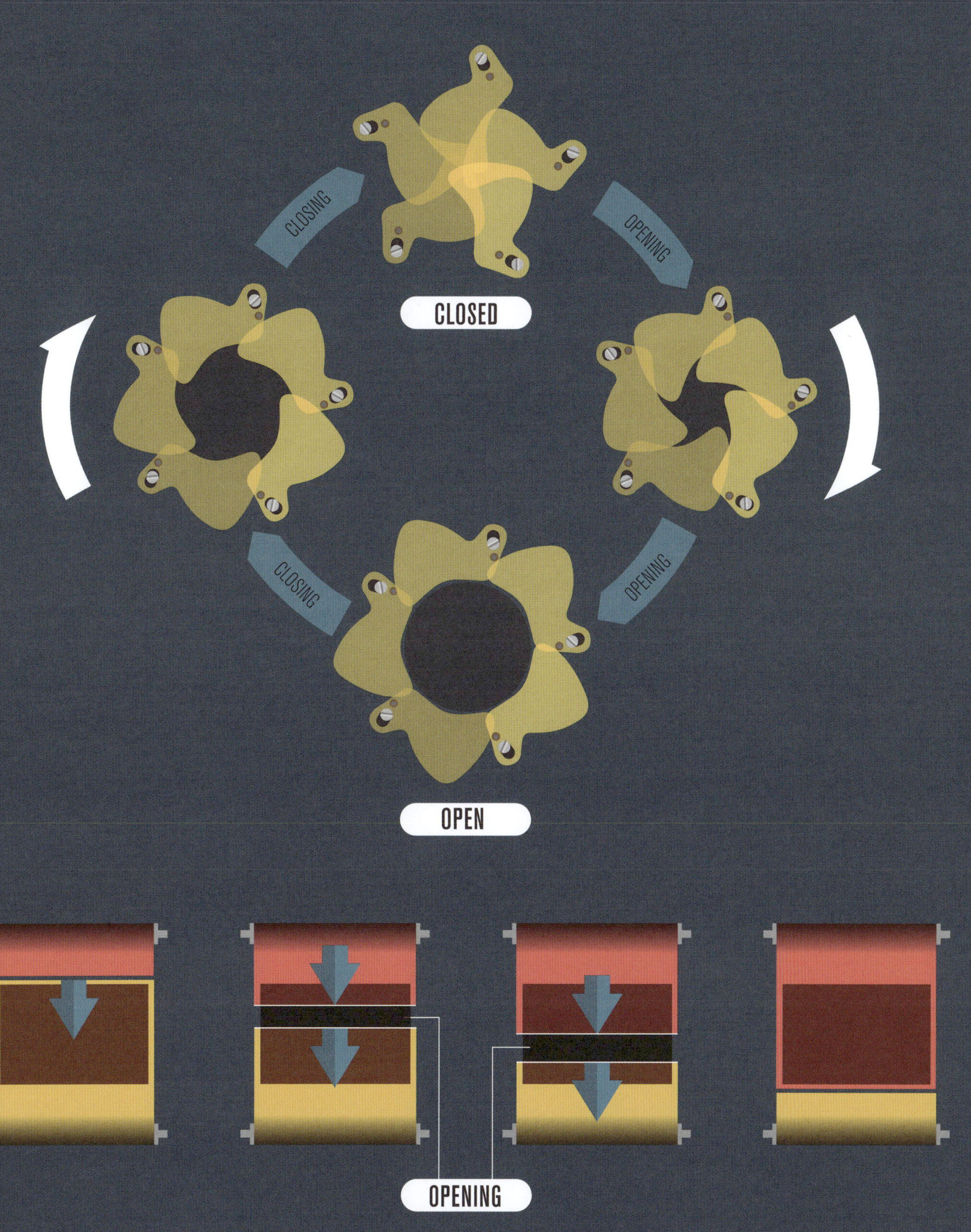

CLOSING
OPENING
CLOSED
CLOSING
OPENING
OPEN
OPENING

The Lens Aperture

The aperture in a lens is a variable iris that can be made larger or smaller to control the amount of light reaching the sensor. An aperture is made up of a number of identical blades (like a leaf shutter, although the aperture cannot be closed completely). One significant way that lenses differ is in the range of aperture settings available. Prime lenses—lenses that have a fixed focal length—typically have a wider range of aperture settings than zoom lenses.

Lenses vary in the number of aperture blades used. The greater the number of aperture blades, the more round the aperture will be as it is closed down. This affects a lens' bokeh, which is the esthetic quality of out-of-focus highlights.

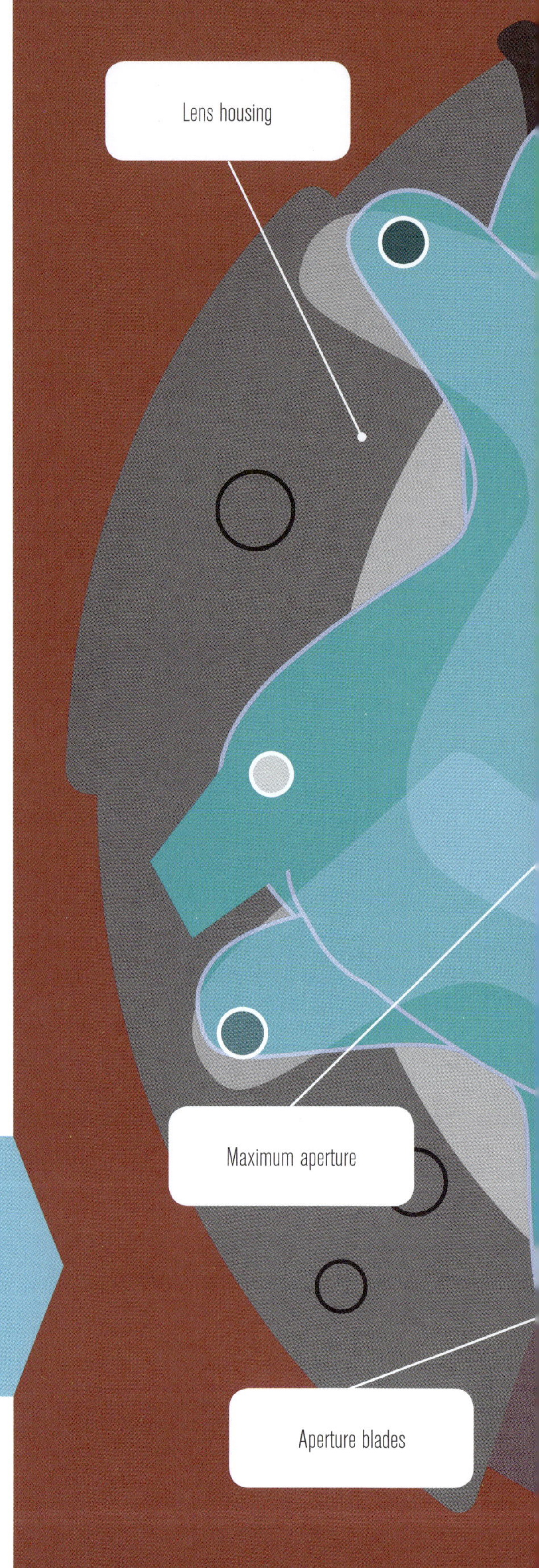

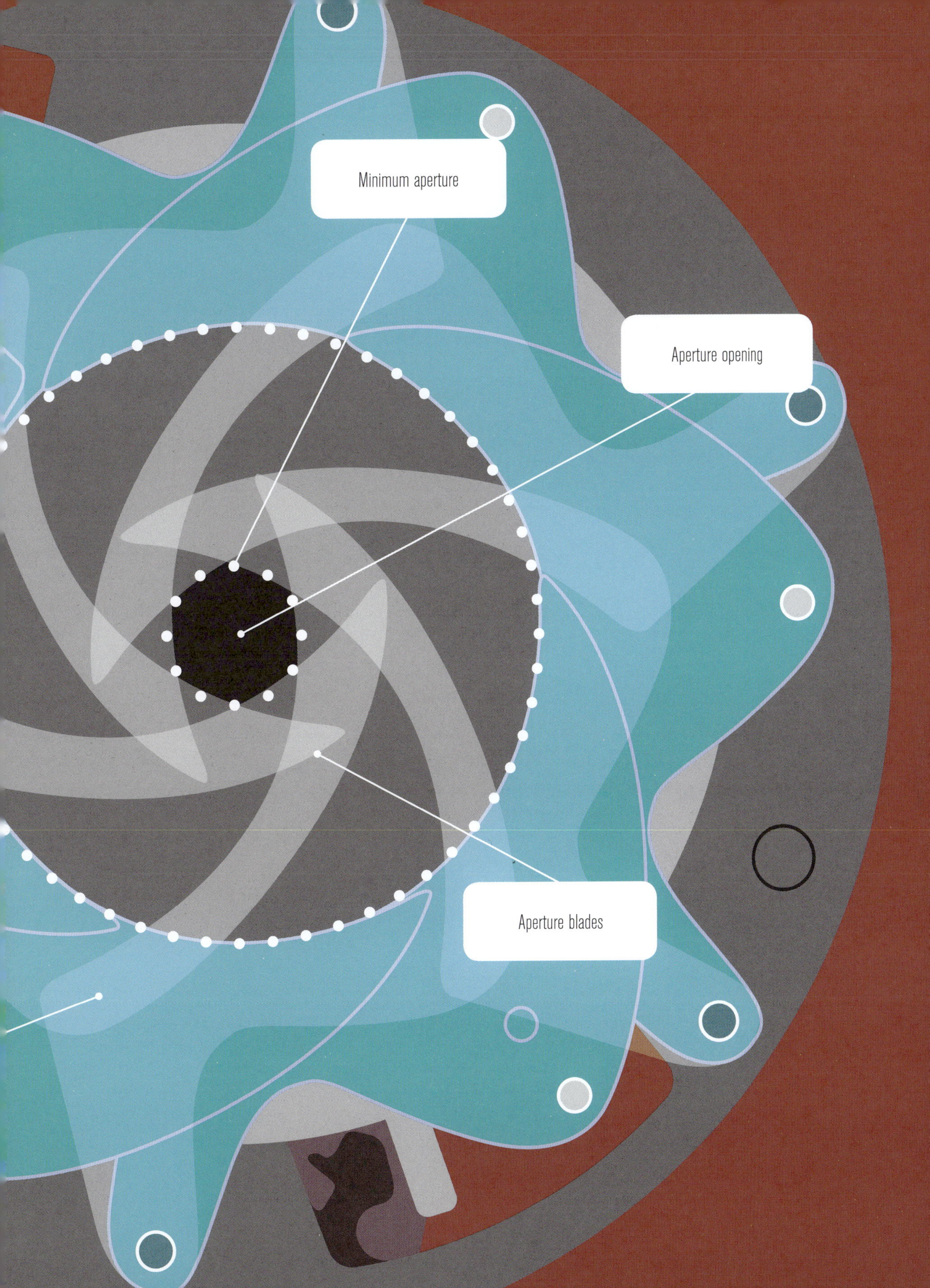

Minimum aperture
Aperture opening
Aperture blades

Keeping Your Camera Steady

A tripod provides a stable support for a camera. This is particularly useful when shooting in low light, as slow shutter speeds are often necessary. However, tripods need to be set up carefully to maximize their stability.

Handholding a camera in low light often results in "camera shake," which is image softness caused by camera movement during an exposure. Image stabilization systems—either lens-based or built into the camera—can help reduce the risk of camera shake, but may not prevent it entirely.

Wrong

- Do not lean over
- Do not hold your camera at arm's length
- Do not have your camera bag dangling from one shoulder
- Do not keep your feet tightly together

Right

- Support the lens
- Tuck your arms against your body
- Stand upright
- Keep your feet apart with one foot slightly farther forward
- Use a fast shutter speed
- Squeeze the shutter button gently
- Find something to lean against if possible

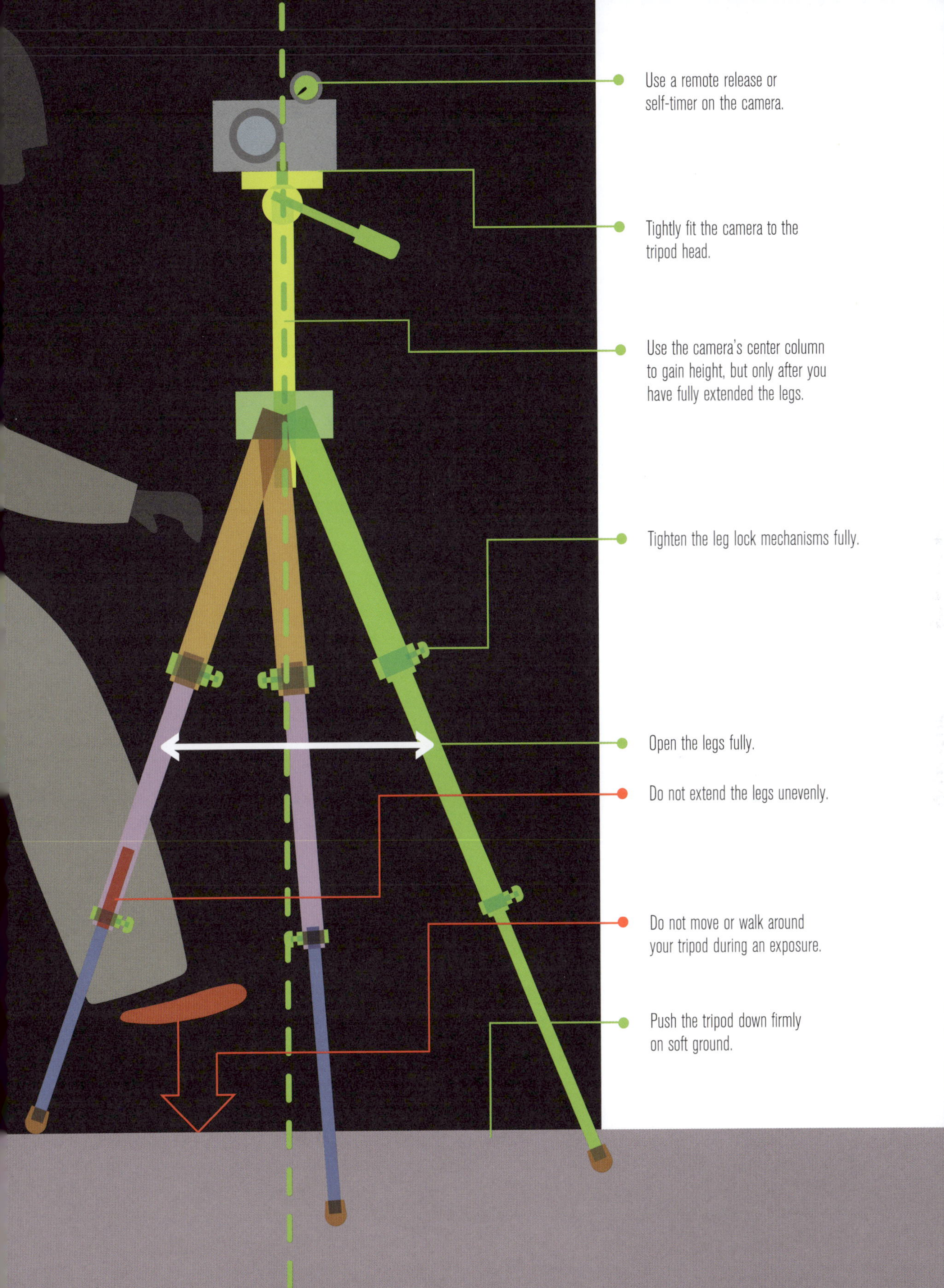

Use a remote release or self-timer on the camera.
Tightly fit the camera to the tripod head.
Use the camera's center column to gain height, but only after you have fully extended the legs.
Tighten the leg lock mechanisms fully.
Open the legs fully.
Do not extend the legs unevenly.
Do not move or walk around your tripod during an exposure.
Push the tripod down firmly on soft ground.

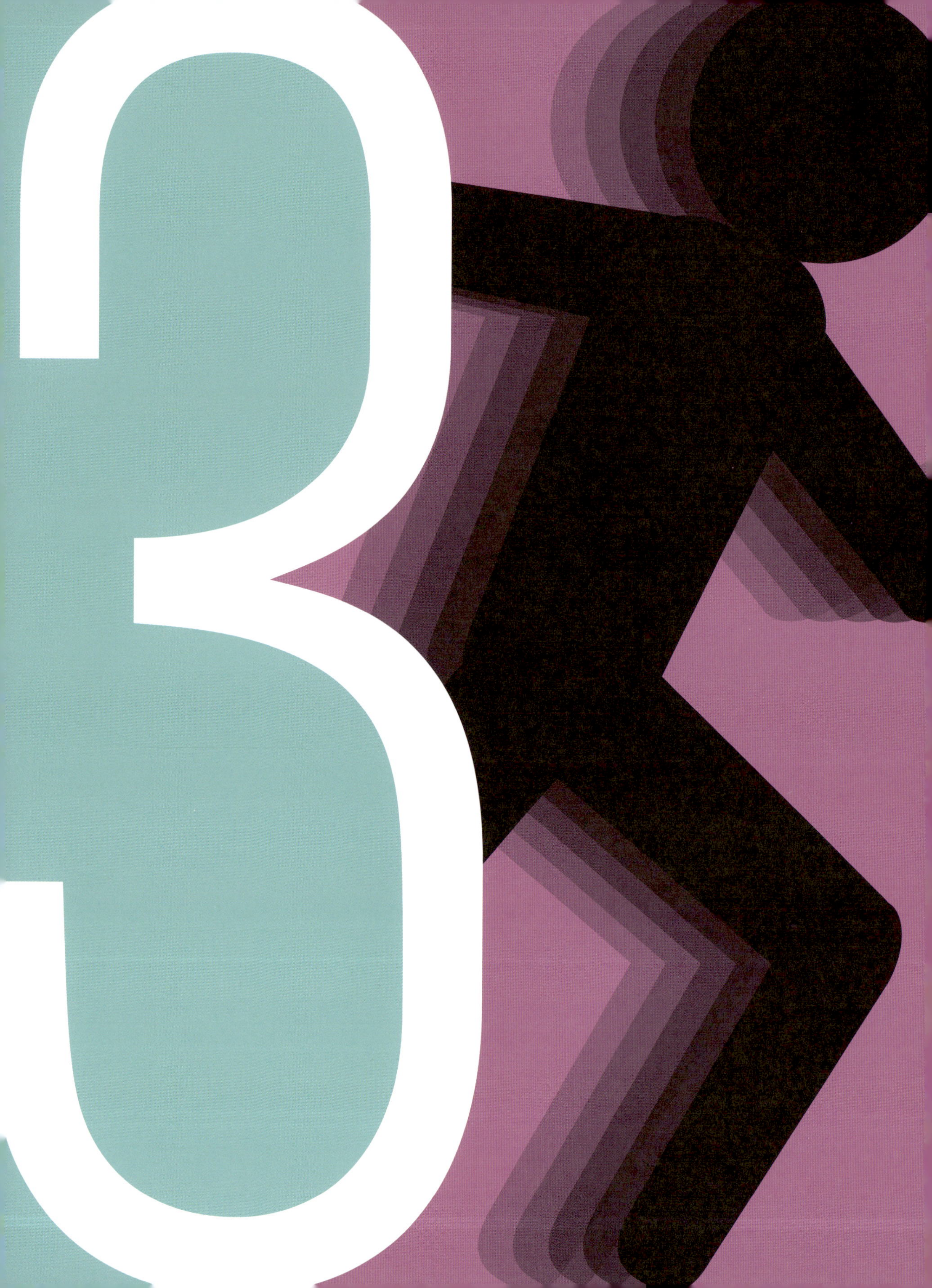

EXPOSURE BASICS

THE BASIC PRINCIPLES OF EXPOSURE APPLY TO BOTH FILM AND DIGITAL CAMERAS. Both require light to hit a light-sensitive surface inside the camera—to "make an exposure" in other words. The light-sensitive surface—whether that's a sheet of film or an electronic sensor—needs just the right amount of light to make a successful image, the basic principles of which are the subject of this chapter.

Although composition is commonly seen as the most important element in the esthetic success (or otherwise) of a photograph, this is slightly unfair, as exposure offers just as much scope for artistic expression. There is generally a technically correct level of exposure for a particular scene, but that doesn't mean it will be the most artistically pleasing level: there's no reason that an image can't be intentionally over- or underexposed for creative effect. Ultimately it's up to you how you interpret a scene and how your shots are exposed to reflect that interpretation.

Deliberately underexposing an image will produce an effect similar to a lighting technique known as "low key." Low-key imagery is dominated by dark tones, with few, if any, bright highlights. Consequently, low-key photographs tend to have a heavy, moody, and often somber feel—not something you would use if you wanted your pictures to make people feel warm inside when they looked at them.

Overexposure produces a look that is similar to high-key imagery. High key is the exact opposite of low key, and results in images that are dominated by bright tones, with few—if any—dark tones. This produces a lighter and more airy effect than low key, which helps to convey a sense of romance, of innocence, and of youth; a high-key approach is popular with wedding photographers for this reason.

There are other aspects of exposure that help you create particular effects as well. These include whether movement is frozen or blurred and the degree of sharpness through the image. In this way, exposure is like a language, and once you've learned the basic vocabulary you can start to craft images that convey a particular message, feeling, or mood.

Sensors

The digital sensor inside a camera gathers the light that passes through the lens. The light first passes through an array of microlenses and colored filters, before reaching light-sensitive photodiodes that "collect" the light. The light is then turned into an electronic signal, which goes on to form a digital photograph.

Microlenses

Microlenses focus light onto the photodiodes below them.

Colored filter

To create color, light passes through either a red, green, or blue filter before it reaches the photodiode behind it. This lets the sensor calculate the mix of colors in the scene it is recording.

Photodiodes

The strength and quality of the electronic signal is determined by the amount of light that falls onto the photodiodes. Too much light and the photodiodes are flooded, causing overexposure. Too little light and the signal is not strong enough to create an image, causing underexposure.

Circuitry

The light received by the photodiodes is read, processed, and converted from an analog signal into a digital one, before the data is saved onto the memory card.

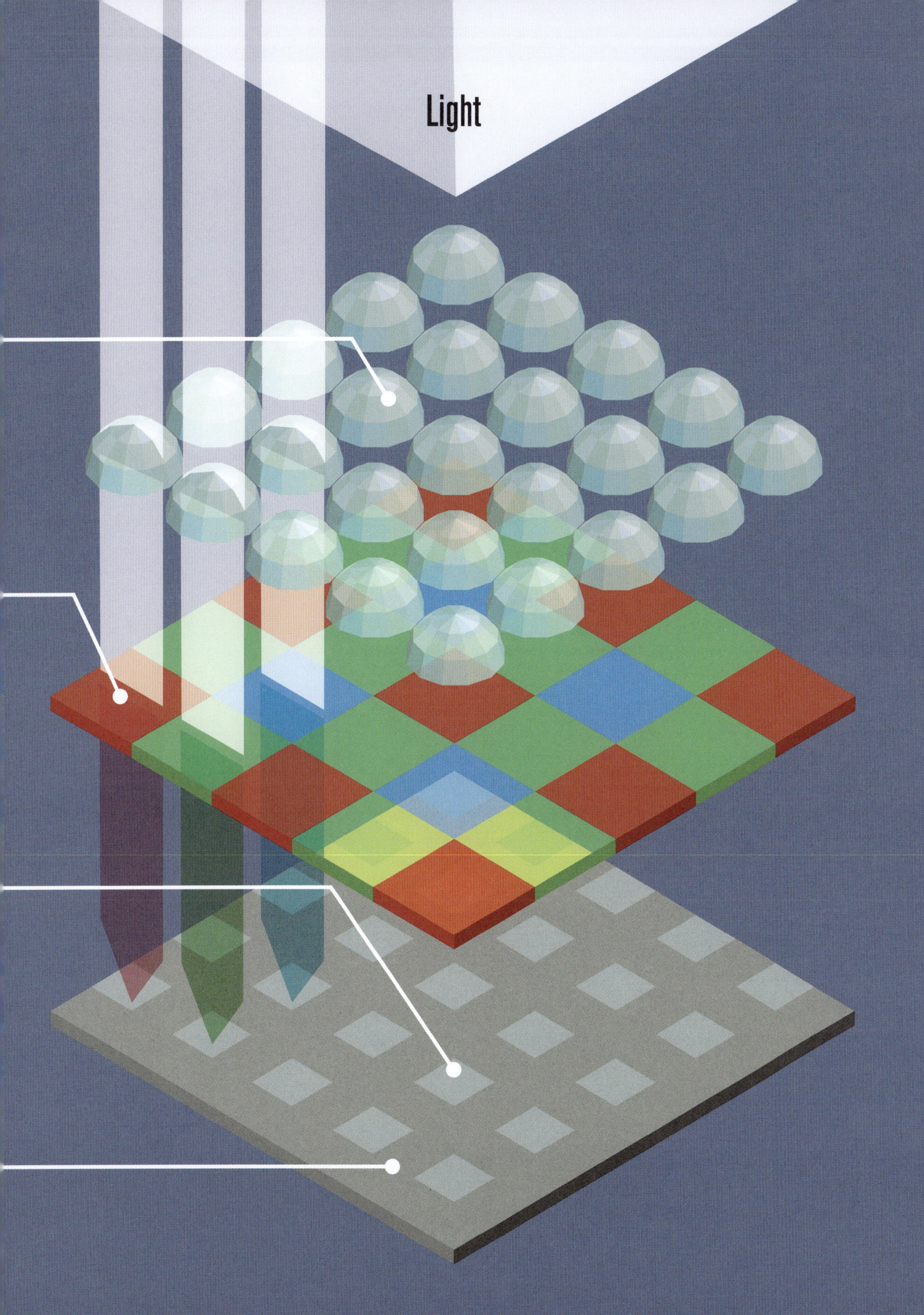

Light

First Principles

Creating an image means letting light reach the sensor—not too much, nor too little. It's a lot like filling a bucket with water from a tap. If you fill the bucket too much it will overflow—similar to overexposing an image. However, running too little water into the bucket is equally unwelcome—this is the equivalent of underexposing a photograph.

Fitting a light-sapping filter such as a polarizer is the equivalent to a partial blockage in the tap that also restricts the flow of water. This means the water has to flow for longer just as you also need to increase the exposure.

Light level

The pressure of the water coming out of the tap is similar to the level of light in a scene. Low light is like low water pressure, meaning less water coming through the tap. Bright conditions are like high water pressure—water gushes out of the tap more quickly.

Shutter speed

Shutter speed is equivalent to the length of time you run the tap to fill the bucket. The longer your run the tap for, the more the bucket fills.

Aperture

The diameter of the tap nozzle is similar to the aperture in a lens. A wide nozzle lets more water through than a narrower nozzle.

ISO

ISO determines the size of the bucket. A low ISO is equivalent to a large bucket, requiring lots of water to fill it. A higher ISO value shrinks the size of the bucket so that less water is needed to fill it.

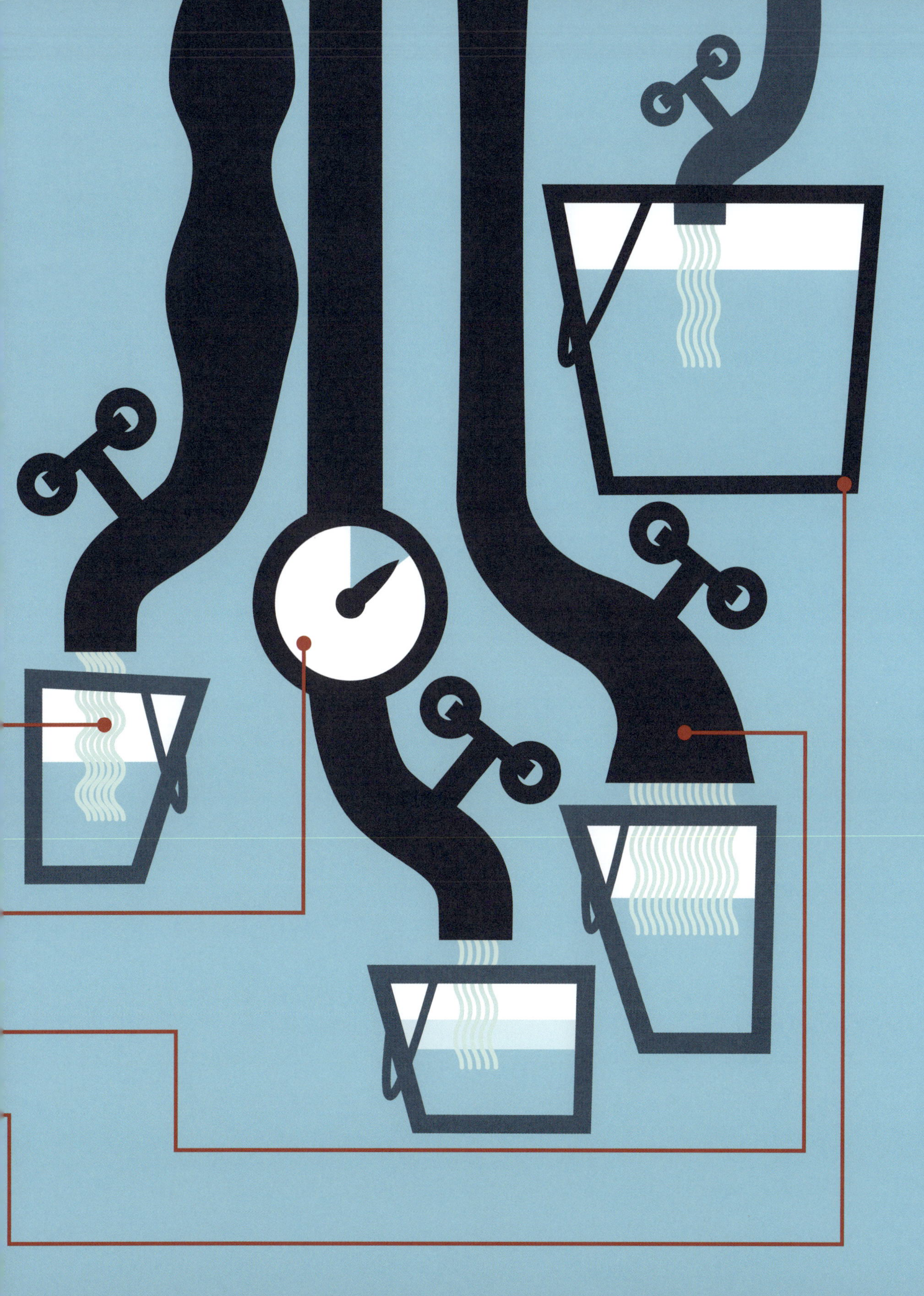

Stops

When photographers refer to a "stop" they mean one simple thing: that the amount of light reaching the sensor is being either halved or doubled. This is achieved in one of two ways: by adjusting the size of the aperture or altering the shutter speed. The ISO setting can also be adjusted in stops, but this affects how much light is actually needed by the sensor to make a successful exposure.

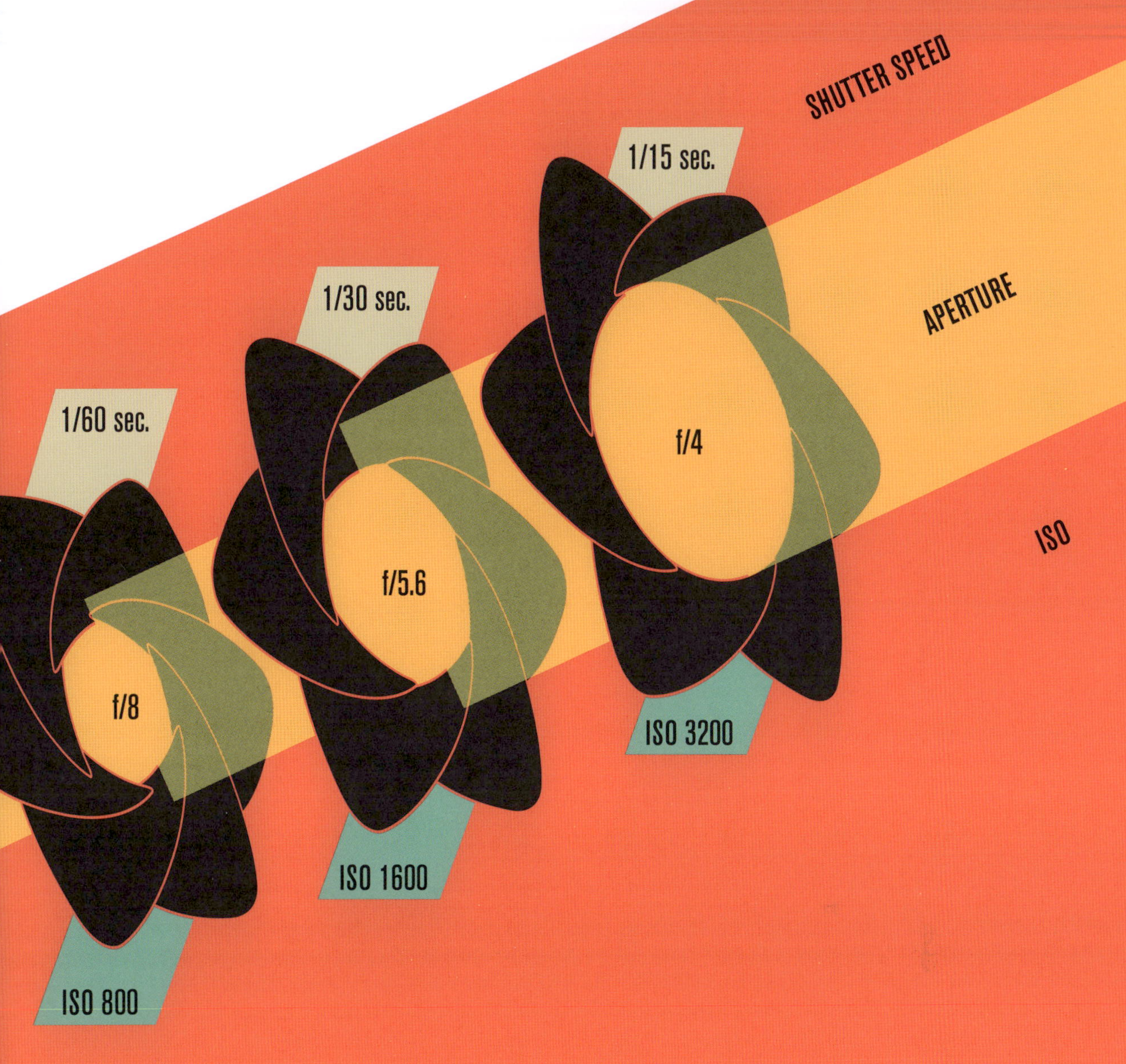

Follow the graphic from right to left and the shutter speed decreases in length by one stop, the aperture decreases in size by one stop, and the ISO decreases in sensitivity by one stop.

The Exposure Triangle

If you adjust one of the exposure controls—aperture, shutter speed, or ISO—you need to make a corresponding adjustment to one or both of the other two to maintain the same level of exposure overall. The exposure triangle is a useful way to visualize how these three controls are related.

Each exposure control has an effect on the esthetic qualities of an image, so you need to decide what is more important to you: the degree of movement blur, the depth of field, or the amount of noise. Then, look at the relevant corner of the triangle to see how you may need to compromise one of the other two qualities.

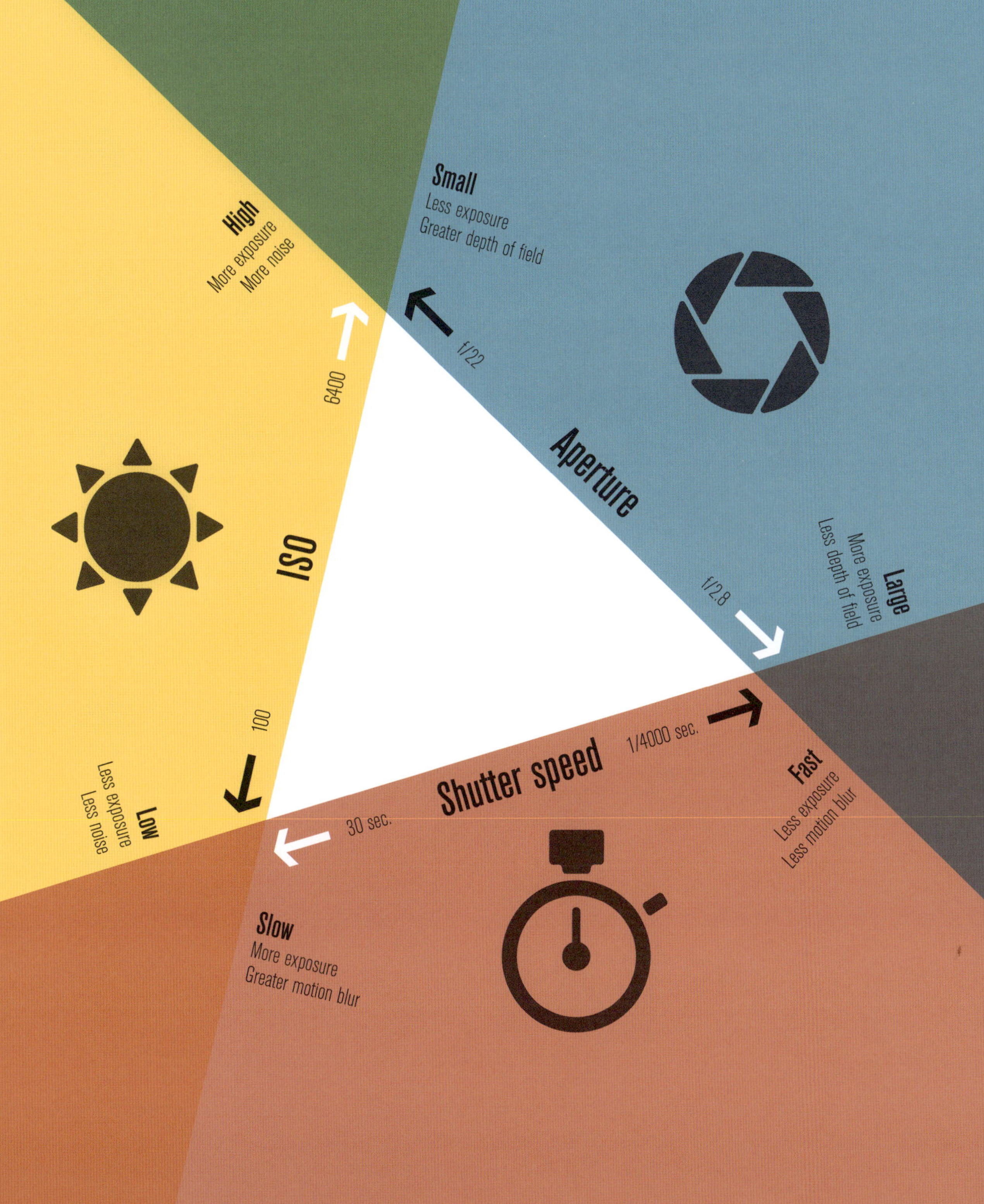
ISO
High
More exposure
More noise
6400
100
Low
Less exposure
Less noise
Aperture
Small
Less exposure
Greater depth of field
f/22
Large
More exposure
Less depth of field
f/2.8
Shutter speed
Slow
More exposure
Greater motion blur
30 sec.
1/4000 sec.
Fast
Less exposure
Less motion blur

Shutter Speed

When you take a photograph, the length of time the shutter is open for is known as the shutter speed. If your subject is static, the shutter speed selected is relatively unimportant, but it will have a far more noticeable effect with moving subjects. The range of available shutter speed varies from camera model to camera model, but is typically in the region of 30–1/4000 sec.

Shutter speed is less important when shooting a static subject such as a still life. You could use any shutter from the full range without it making a difference (other than depth of field due to the necessary aperture changes or image noise if you vary the ISO).

A moving subject such as a person running will look more blurred the longer the shutter speed you set on your camera. Blurring softens fine detail and will make your subject look less solid.

1/500 sec.

1/250 sec.

1/125 sec.

1/60 sec.

1/30 sec.

1/15 sec.

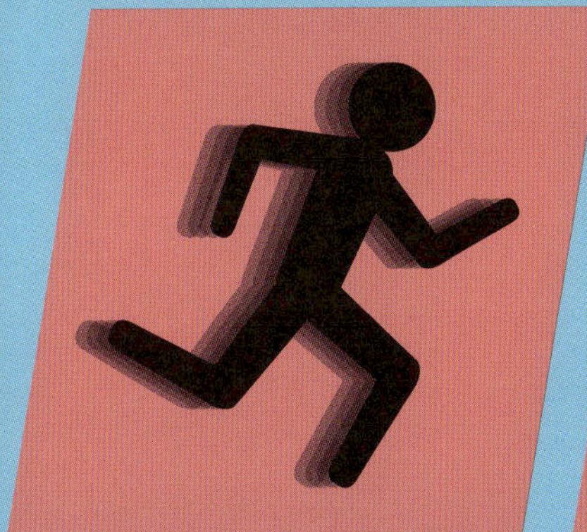

1/8 sec.

1/4 sec.

1/2 sec.

Freezing Movement

Freezing a subject that's moving across the frame requires the use of a fast shutter speed. The faster the subject is moving (and the larger it is in the frame), the faster the shutter speed needs to be.

Using the faster shutter speeds on your camera means either using a high ISO or a large aperture. Use a large aperture and your focusing will need to be more precise due to the restriction of depth of field, particularly when using longer focal length lenses.

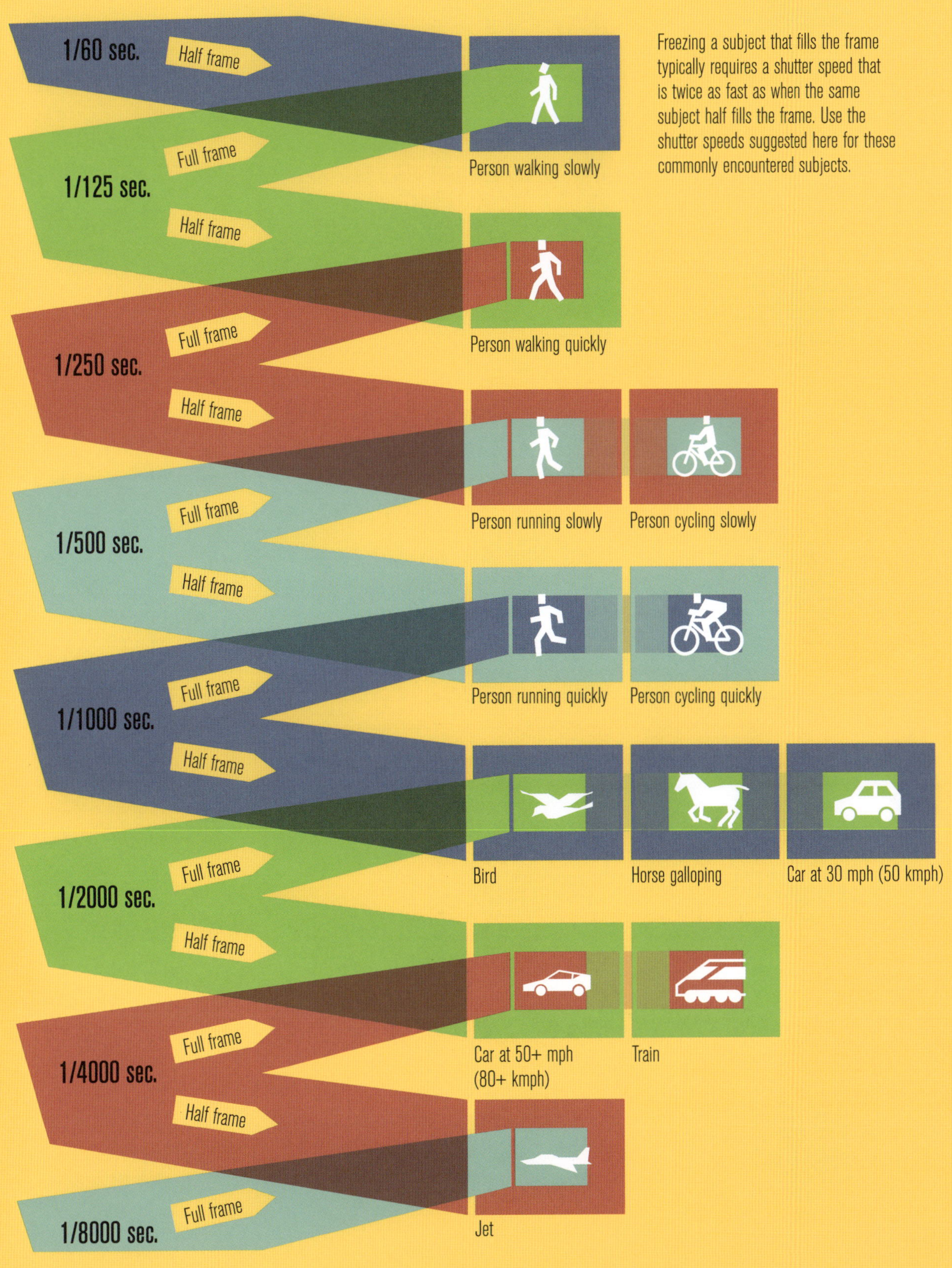

Freezing a subject that fills the frame typically requires a shutter speed that is twice as fast as when the same subject half fills the frame. Use the shutter speeds suggested here for these commonly encountered subjects.

Blurring Movement

Movement does not need to be frozen. In fact, "frozen" movement can sometimes look oddly static, whereas using a long shutter speed to add blur to a moving subject can help to convey motion. The slower the subject moves (or the smaller it is in the frame), the slower the shutter speed will need to be.

There's no right or wrong answer to how much blur is acceptable. It's very much your own personal choice as to how an image should be shot. However, use too long a shutter speed and your moving subject may disappear from the image completely!

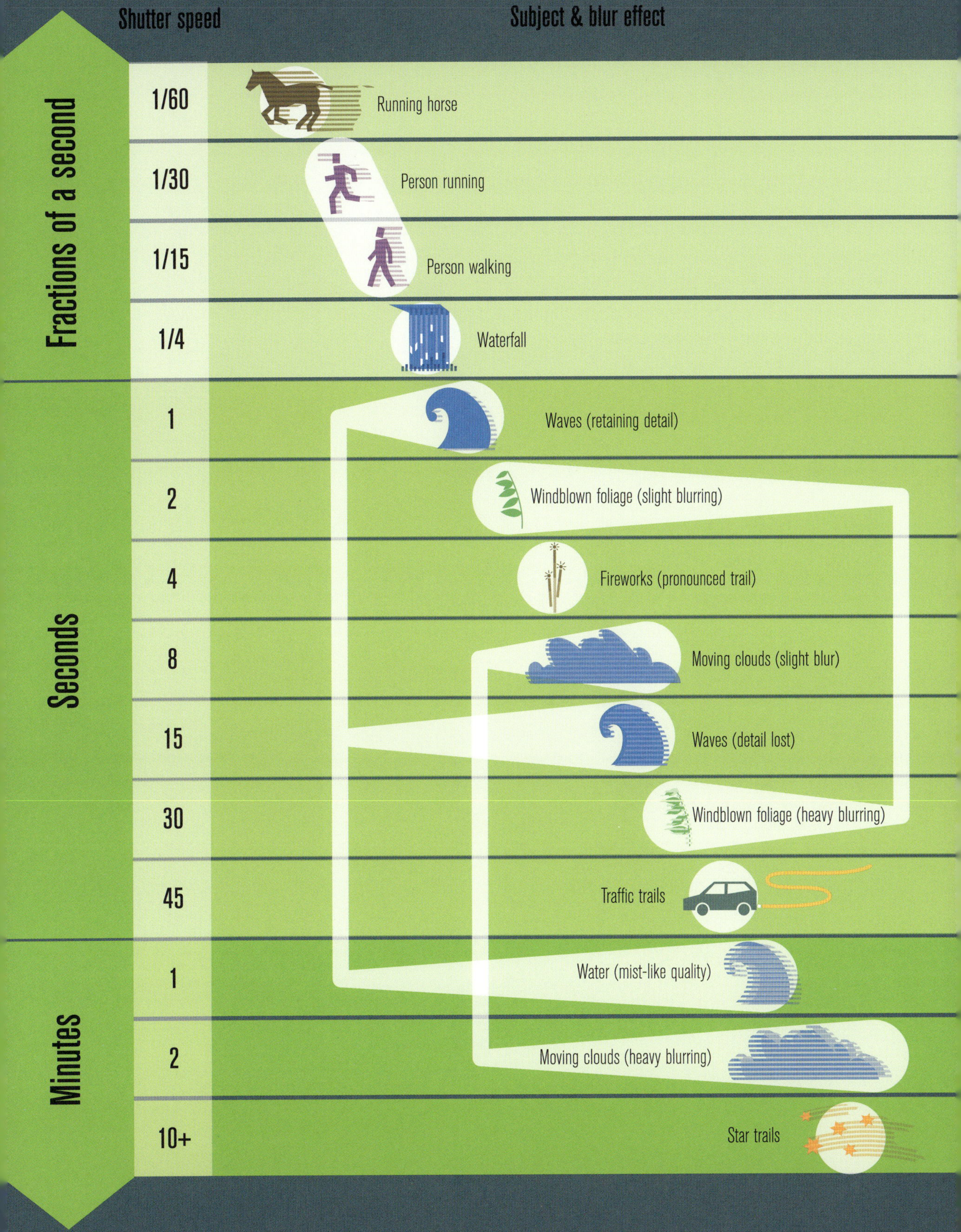

Fractions of a second

1/60	Running horse
1/30	Person running
1/15	Person walking
1/4	Waterfall

Seconds

1	Waves (retaining detail)
2	Windblown foliage (slight blurring)
4	Fireworks (pronounced trail)
8	Moving clouds (slight blur)
15	Waves (detail lost)
30	Windblown foliage (heavy blurring)
45	Traffic trails

Minutes

1	Water (mist-like quality)
2	Moving clouds (heavy blurring)
10+	Star trails

Panning

Freezing movement can make an image look static. Panning is a technique that helps to convey a sense of movement with subjects moving across the image space, while still retaining a degree of sharpness.

Follow the subject's movement with your camera in a smooth arc, and press the shutter-release button roughly half way through the arc—but keep the camera moving. If you get your timing right, the subject should be sharp and the background blurred. I used the panning technique for this shot after experimenting with different shutter speeds to see which was the most effective.

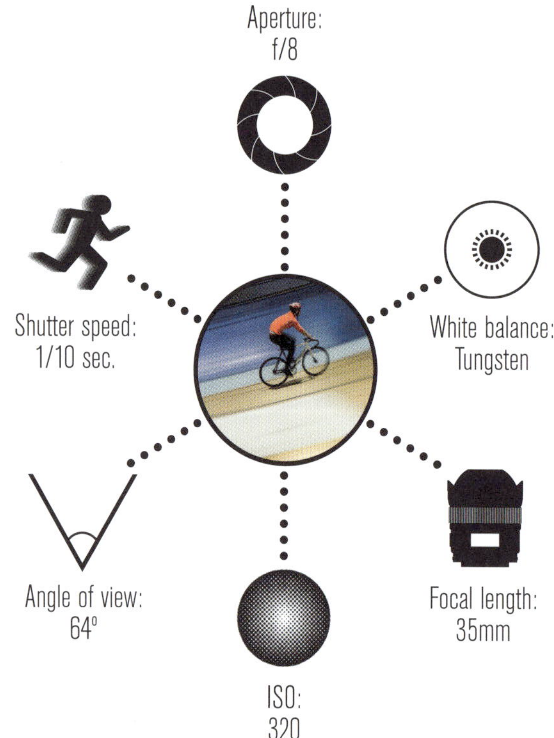

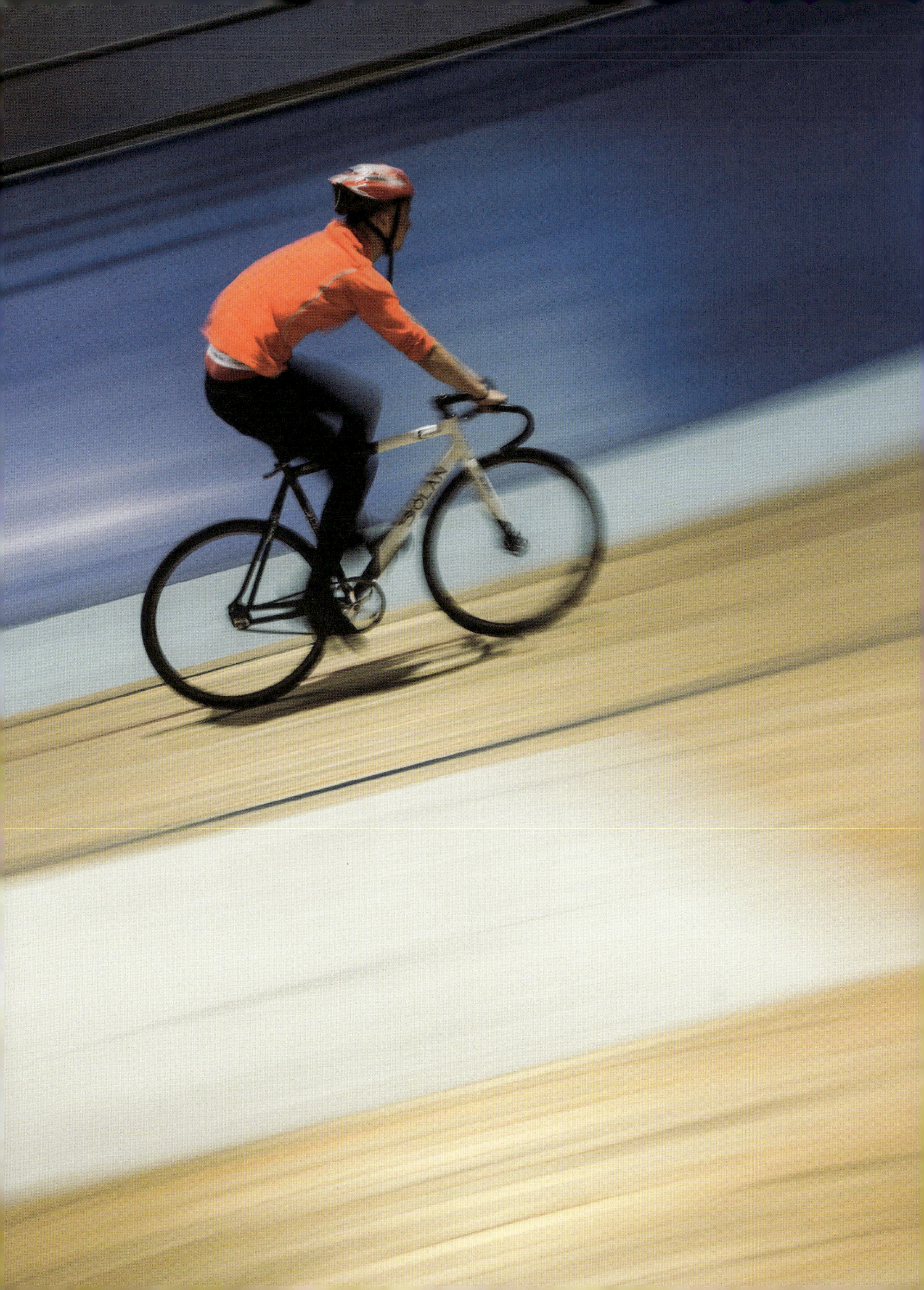

Aperture

The size of the lens aperture is shown as an f-stop value, with the range of apertures on a typical lens running f/2.8, f/4, f/5.6, f/8, f/11, f/16, and f/22. As the f-number gets bigger, the aperture becomes smaller, with each step up the scale indicating a halving of the amount of light passing through the lens.

As the f-number gets smaller, the aperture increases in size, doubling the amount of light passing through the lens. Cameras often allow you to set ½- or ⅓-stop values (f/4.8 is the ½-stop value between f/4 and f/5.6, for example).

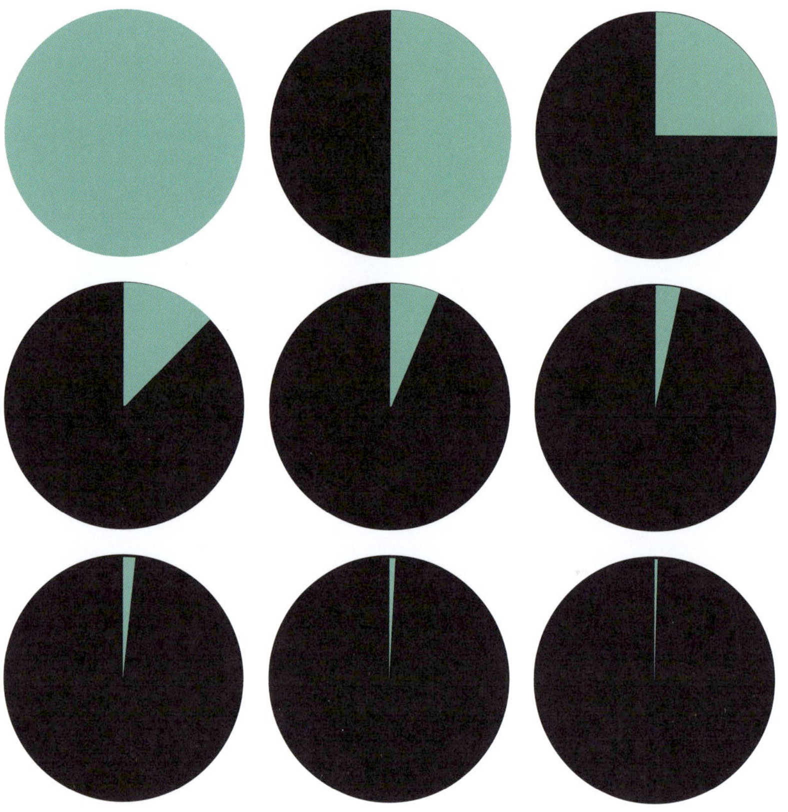

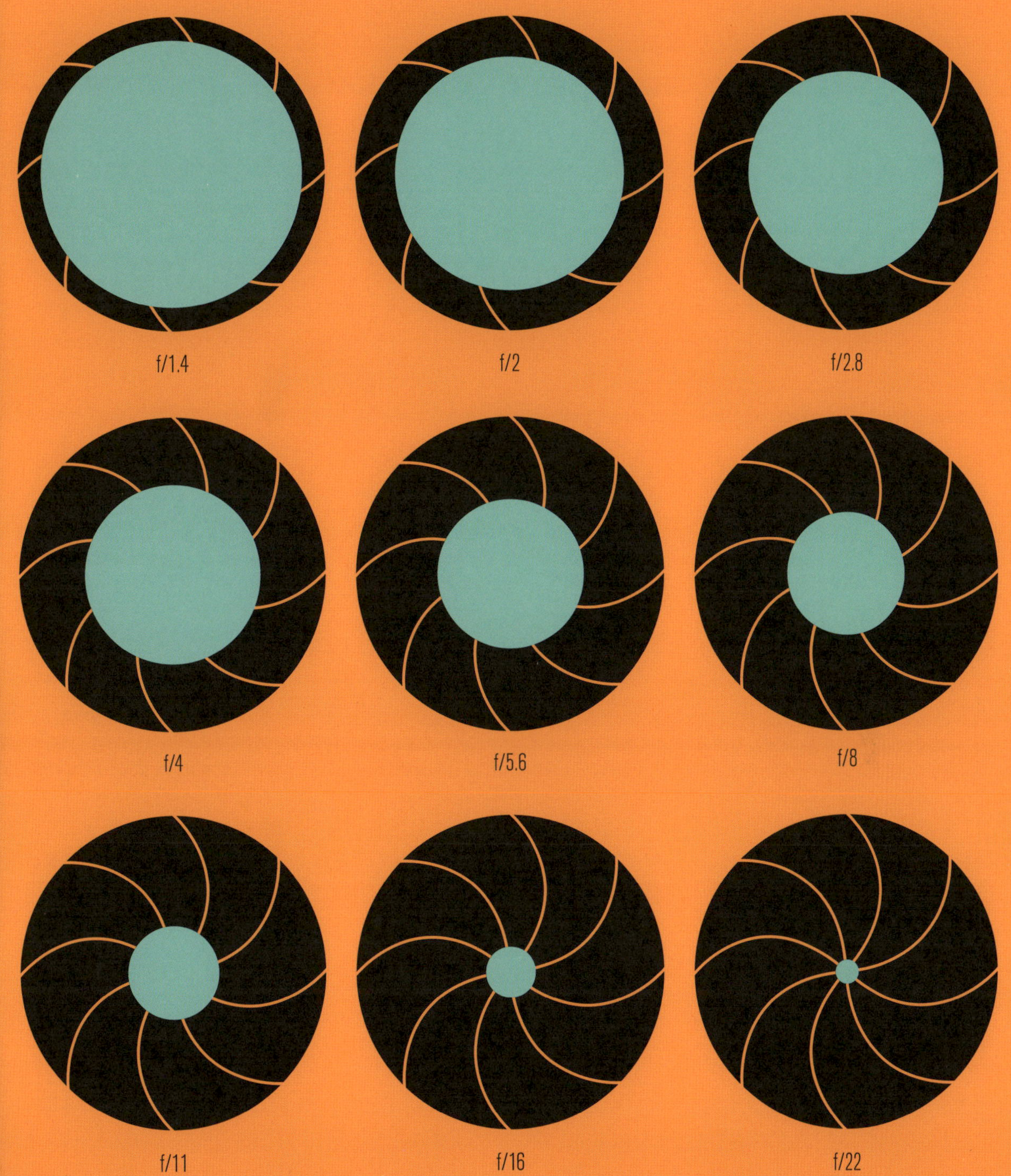

f/1.4
f/2
f/2.8
f/4
f/5.6
f/8
f/11
f/16
f/22

Depth Of Field

Depth of field describes the extent of sharpness through an image, from the sharpest point closest to the camera to the most distant point. Depth of field extends out from the focus point and always stretches twice as far back from the focus point than toward the camera.

Depth of field is controlled by aperture, focus distance, and focal length.

Aperture
Large apertures reduce depth of field; smaller apertures increase depth of field.

Focus distance
The greater the focus distance, the greater the amount of depth of field.

Focal length
The shorter the focal length of a lens (the wider it is), the greater the depth of field will be at any given aperture.

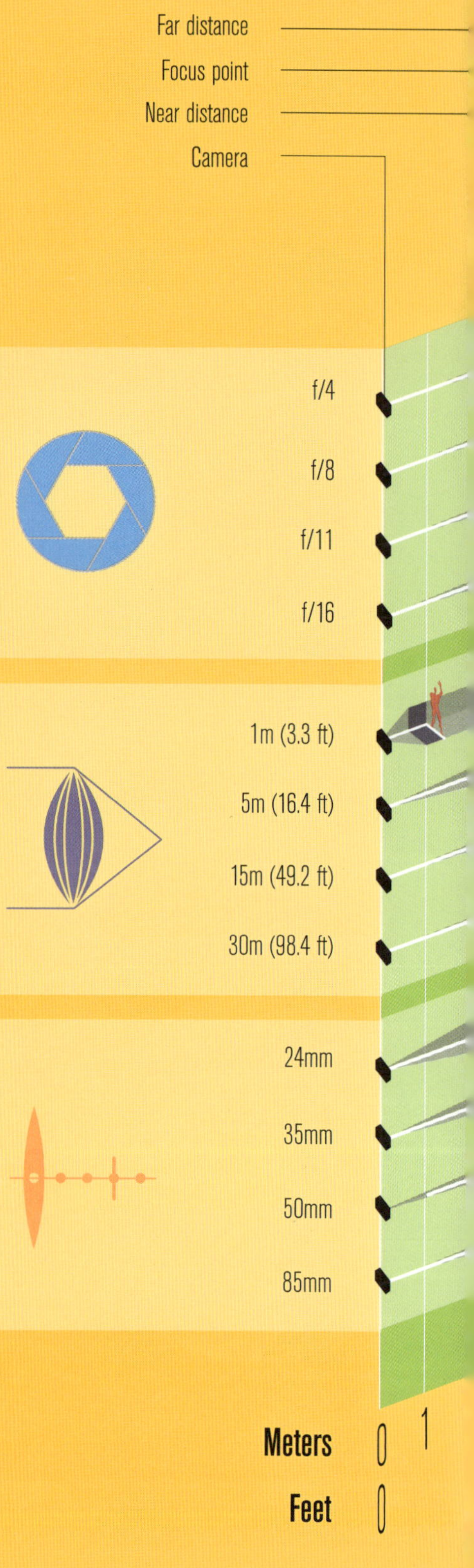

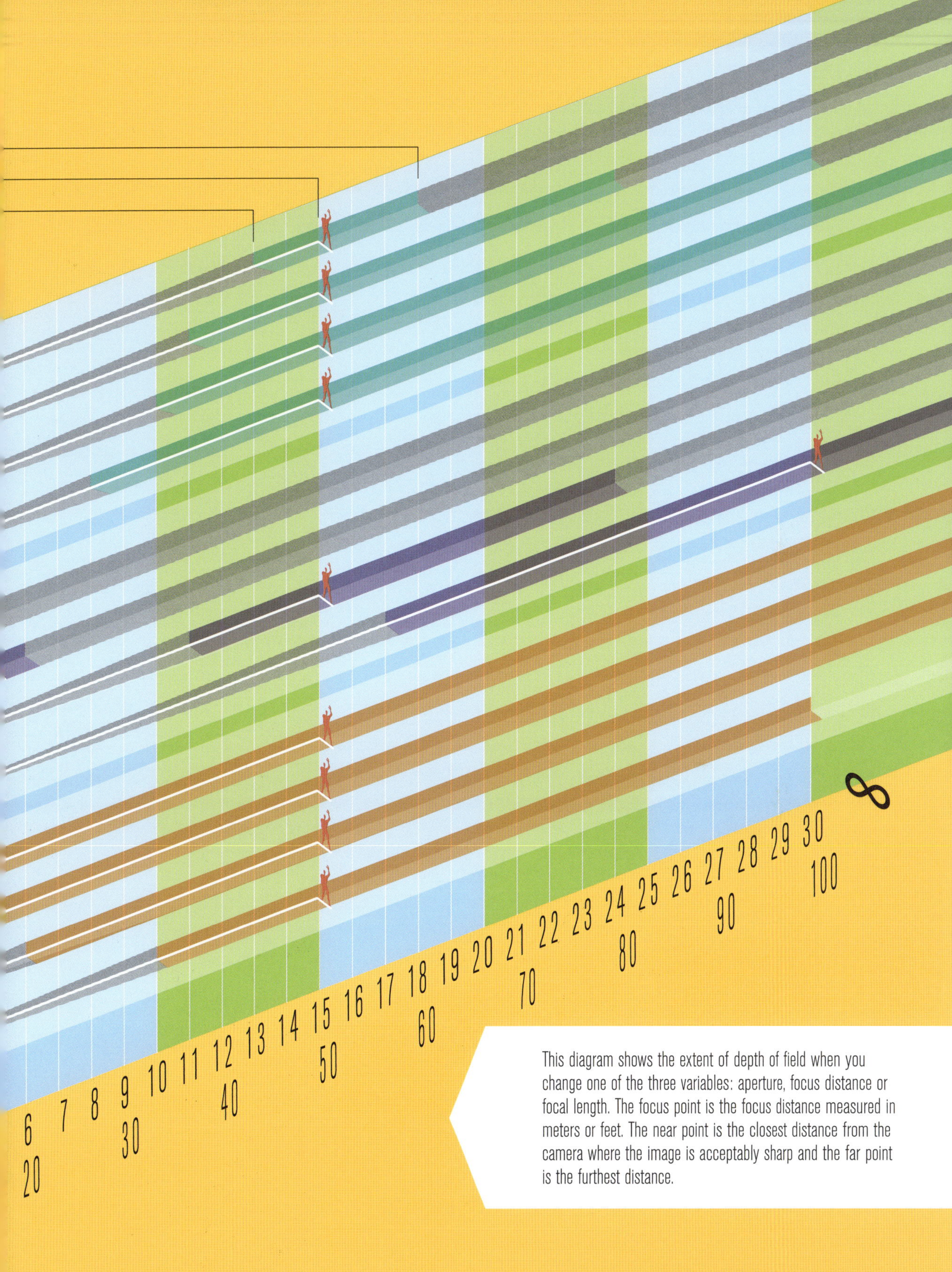

This diagram shows the extent of depth of field when you change one of the three variables: aperture, focus distance or focal length. The focus point is the focus distance measured in meters or feet. The near point is the closest distance from the camera where the image is acceptably sharp and the far point is the furthest distance.

Differential Focusing

Differential focusing is all about limiting the sharply focused area in a photograph, perhaps to make a subject stand out more easily from a complex background, or to direct the eye to a particular part of an image. The key to differential focusing is to focus precisely on your subject and set the aperture to its maximum value (which will minimize depth of field). The effect is more pronounced with a telephoto lens than a wide-angle lens, and subject distance also plays a part—the closer the camera is to the subject, the greater the effect.

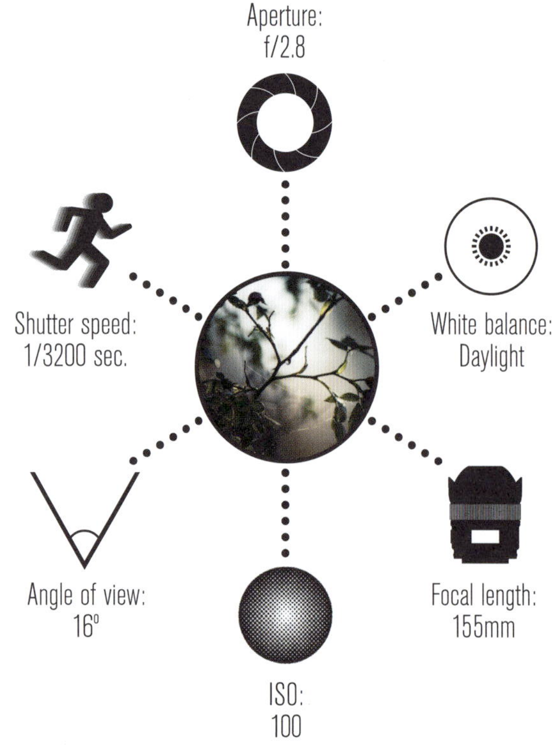

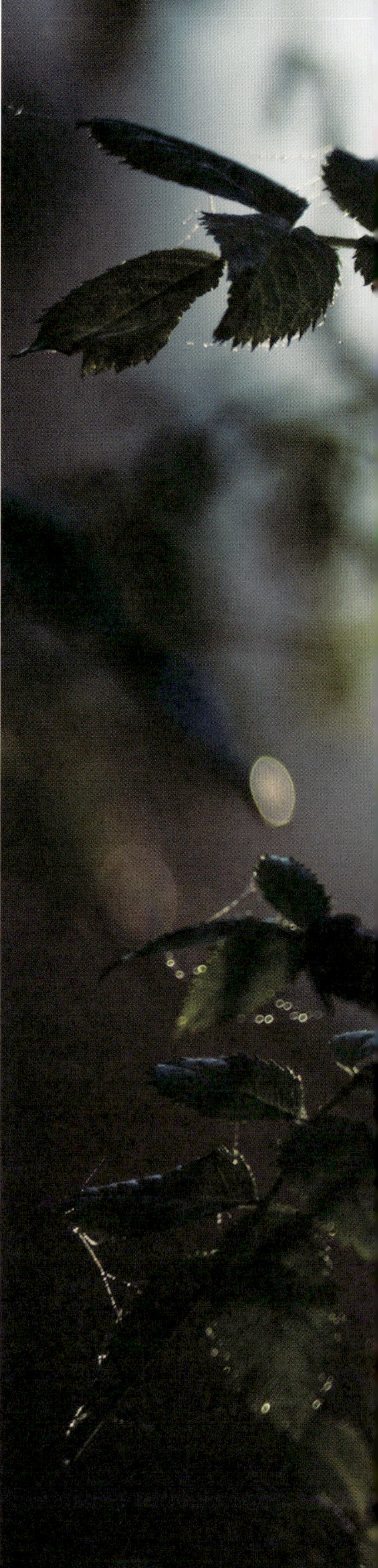

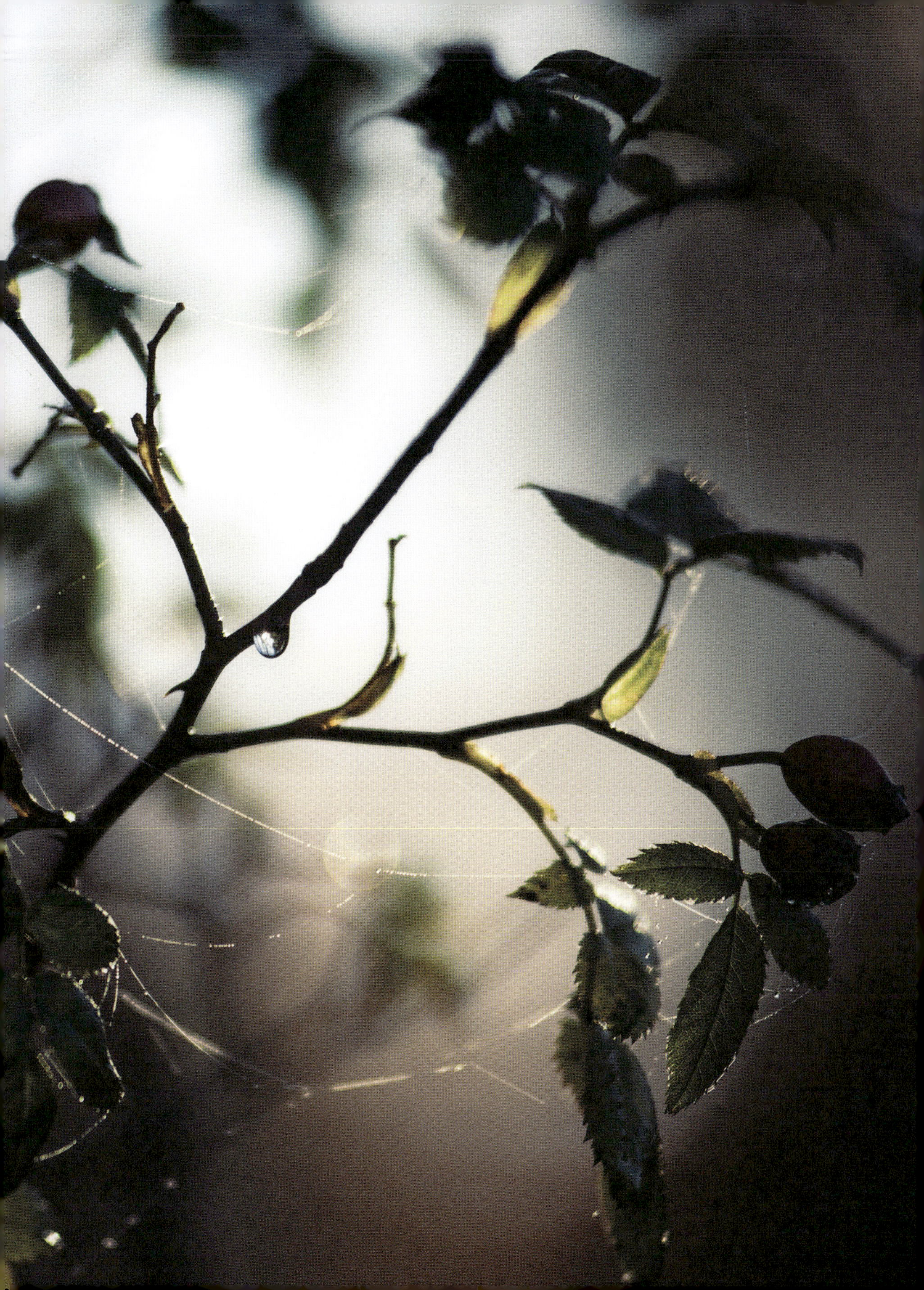

ISO

The ISO setting on a camera determines how much light is needed to make a successful exposure: the higher the ISO, the less light is required to make an image. This affects the required combination of shutter speed and aperture, so if you increase the ISO, you can use either a faster shutter speed or smaller aperture than when a lower ISO setting is selected.

You can either select an ISO manually on your camera or choose Auto ISO. When Auto ISO is selected the camera will dynamically change the ISO setting depending on the light levels of the scene you're shooting. Auto ISO is fixed and can't be altered when using a fully automatic shooting mode. When using filters such as ND filters, described in chapter 5, always use a fixed ISO setting.

This diagram shows the effect that changing the ISO has on how much light is needed for a pleasing exposure, how image quality is affected, the length of the shutter speed you'd need to use and how large the aperture would need to be.

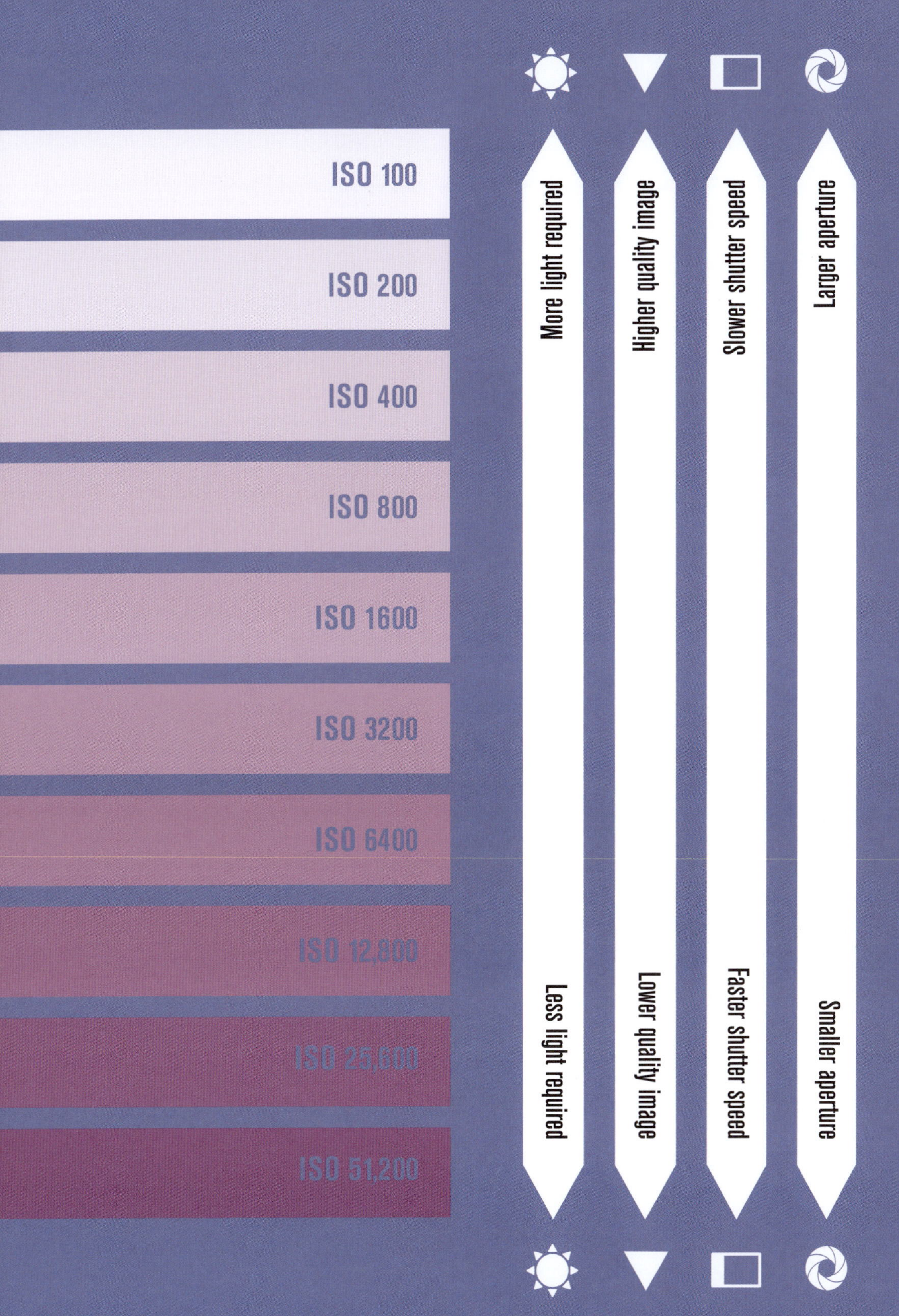

ISO 100
ISO 200
ISO 400
ISO 800
ISO 1600
ISO 3200
ISO 6400
ISO 12,800
ISO 25,600
ISO 51,200
More light required
Higher quality image
Slower shutter speed
Larger aperture
Less light required
Lower quality image
Faster shutter speed
Smaller aperture

Noise

Noise is seen as pixels of random brightness or color in a digital image. The camera's lowest ISO setting results in the least amount of noise, with noise increasing as the ISO value is raised. High levels of noise can smother fine detail in an image, reducing its clarity.

Photography often involves compromise. When selecting an ISO setting you need to trade off noise against either a faster shutter speed or smaller aperture. Using a high ISO will increase noise. However, this will be acceptable if it means that your subject isn't blurred (or you avoid camera shake), or if depth of field is sufficiently wide.

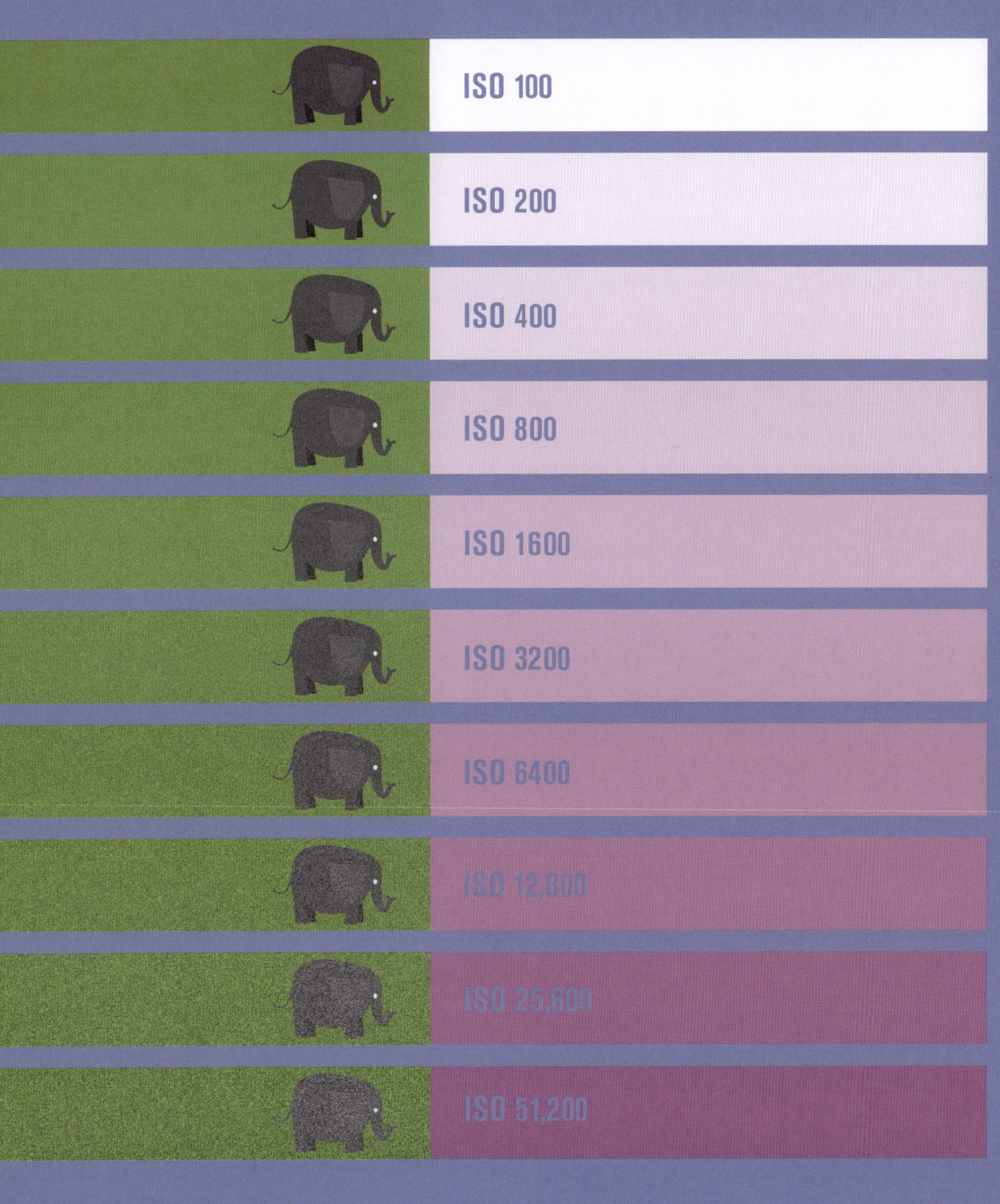

ISO 100
ISO 200
ISO 400
ISO 800
ISO 1600
ISO 3200
ISO 6400
ISO 12,800
ISO 25,600
ISO 51,200

Dynamic Range

The dynamic range of a camera is a ratio of the maximum intensity of light that can be recorded before the highlights burn out, to the minimum intensity of light recorded in the shadows before detail is lost to noise. In practical terms, the dynamic range of a camera determines how much of a scene's tonal range can be recorded successfully without detail loss. A very rough (but useful) rule is that the larger the photosites on a camera's sensor, the greater its dynamic range.

Full-frame cameras typically have a wider dynamic range than cameras with smaller sensors. This means that it's easier to capture a wider tonal range with a full-frame camera. It also means that using filters or techniques such as fill-in flash to reduce contrast are more necessary when using cameras with smaller sensors.

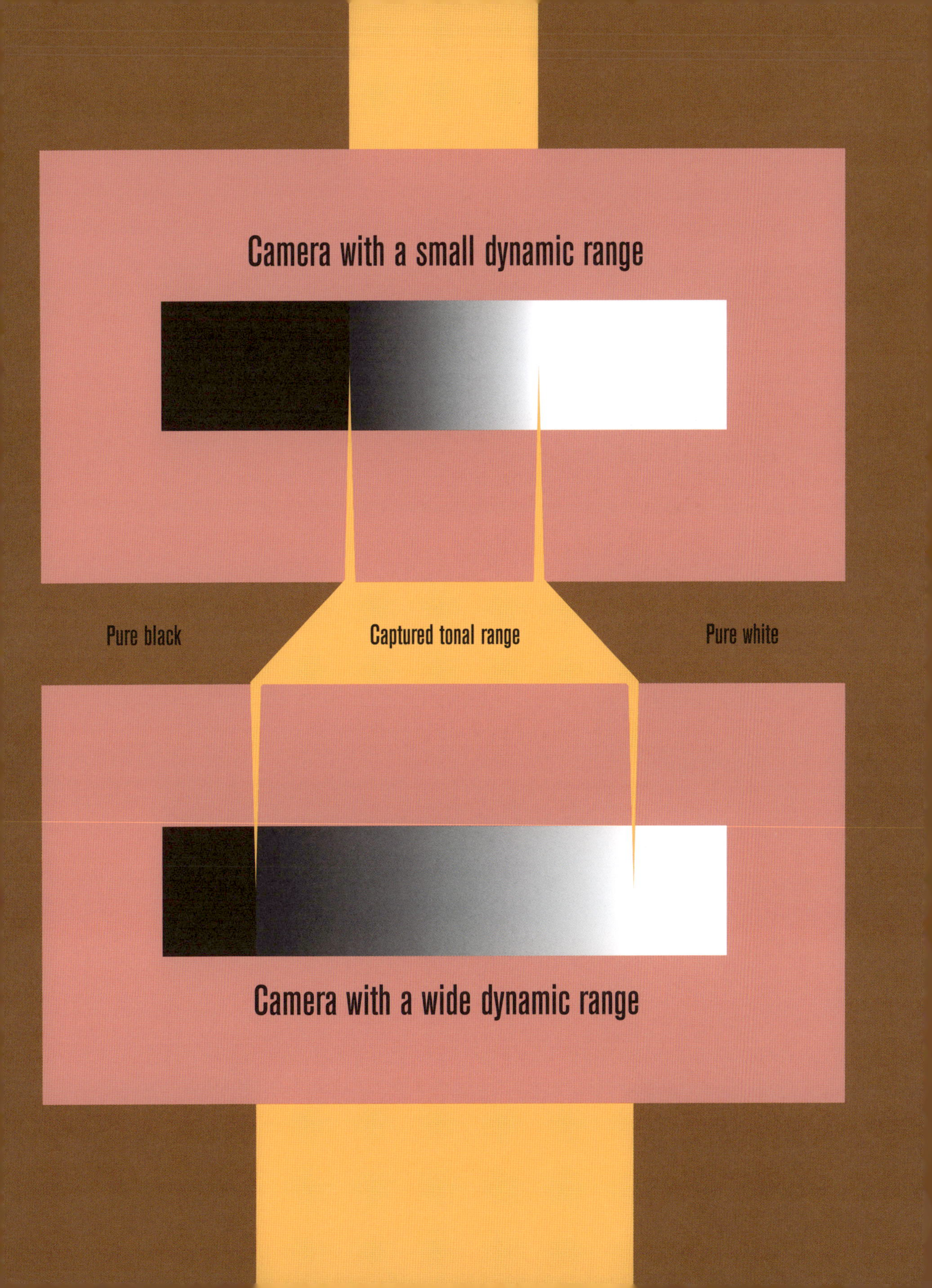

Camera with a small dynamic range
Pure black
Captured tonal range
Pure white
Camera with a wide dynamic range

Long-Exposure Noise

Long shutter speeds (typically shutter speeds that are 30 seconds or more) can also add noise to an image, due to the heat from the electronics of the camera corrupting the image data. For this reason long exposure noise is also known as "thermal noise." To reduce the visibility of thermal noise most cameras offer long exposure noise reduction.

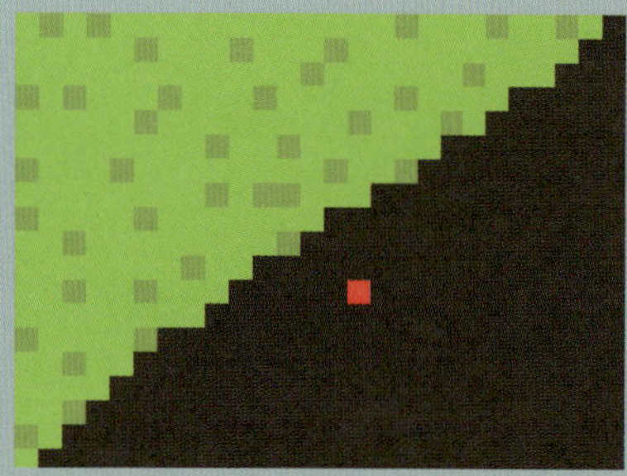

Hot Pixels

Thermal noise is seen as "hot pixels" scattered randomly across an image. These pixels are brightly colored (often red or cyan) and usually far brighter and more eye-catching than the "true" image pixels that surround them. They can be cloned out in postproduction, but this can be a time-consuming process if an image is heavily affected.

In-camera long-exposure noise reduction uses a technique known as "dark frame subtraction." After a long exposure is made, the camera shoots another exposure, this time with the shutter kept closed. From this "dark frame," the camera can detect where thermal noise is present and remove or subtract it from the first exposure. Long-exposure noise reduction effectively doubles the length of time it takes to shoot using long shutter speeds. However, although this can be slightly frustrating, it's far less frustrating than spending time cloning out thermal noise later.

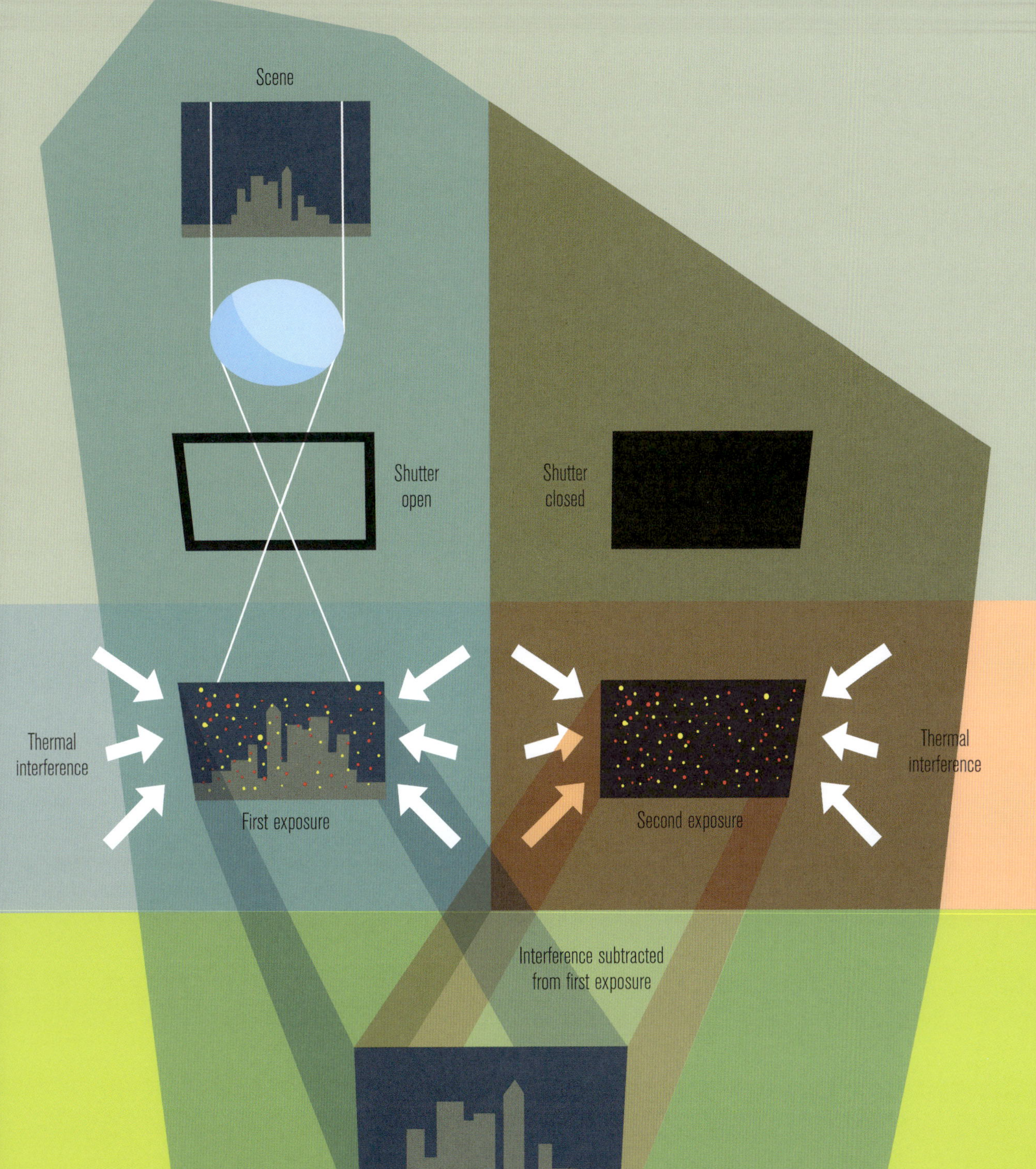

Scene
Shutter open
Shutter closed
Thermal interference
Thermal interference
First exposure
Second exposure
Interference subtracted from first exposure
Final image

The "Sunny 16" Rule

Although an exposure meter is useful, it's possible to set the correct exposure outside without one by following the "Sunny 16" rule. This rule states that on a sunny day, with the aperture set to f/16, the shutter speed should match (as close as possible) the ISO setting. So, you would use a shutter speed of 1/100 sec. if you were using ISO 100, 1/200 sec. with ISO 200, and so on. The rule can also be modified for different levels of brightness, such as when it's cloudy or if you're shooting in open shade.

A very rough-and-ready way to avoid the risk of camera shake is to match the shutter speed to the ISO setting. When using a 50mm lens (or full-frame equivalent) a shutter speed of 1/50 or faster is generally safe. Using the "Sunny 16" rule works well when using lenses smaller than 100mm for this reason. Increase the ISO to achieve faster shutter speeds when using longer lenses.

Match the weather condition you're shooting under to an image on this page. Then, with shutter speed at 1/ISO, set the aperture shown to the right of the image on your camera.

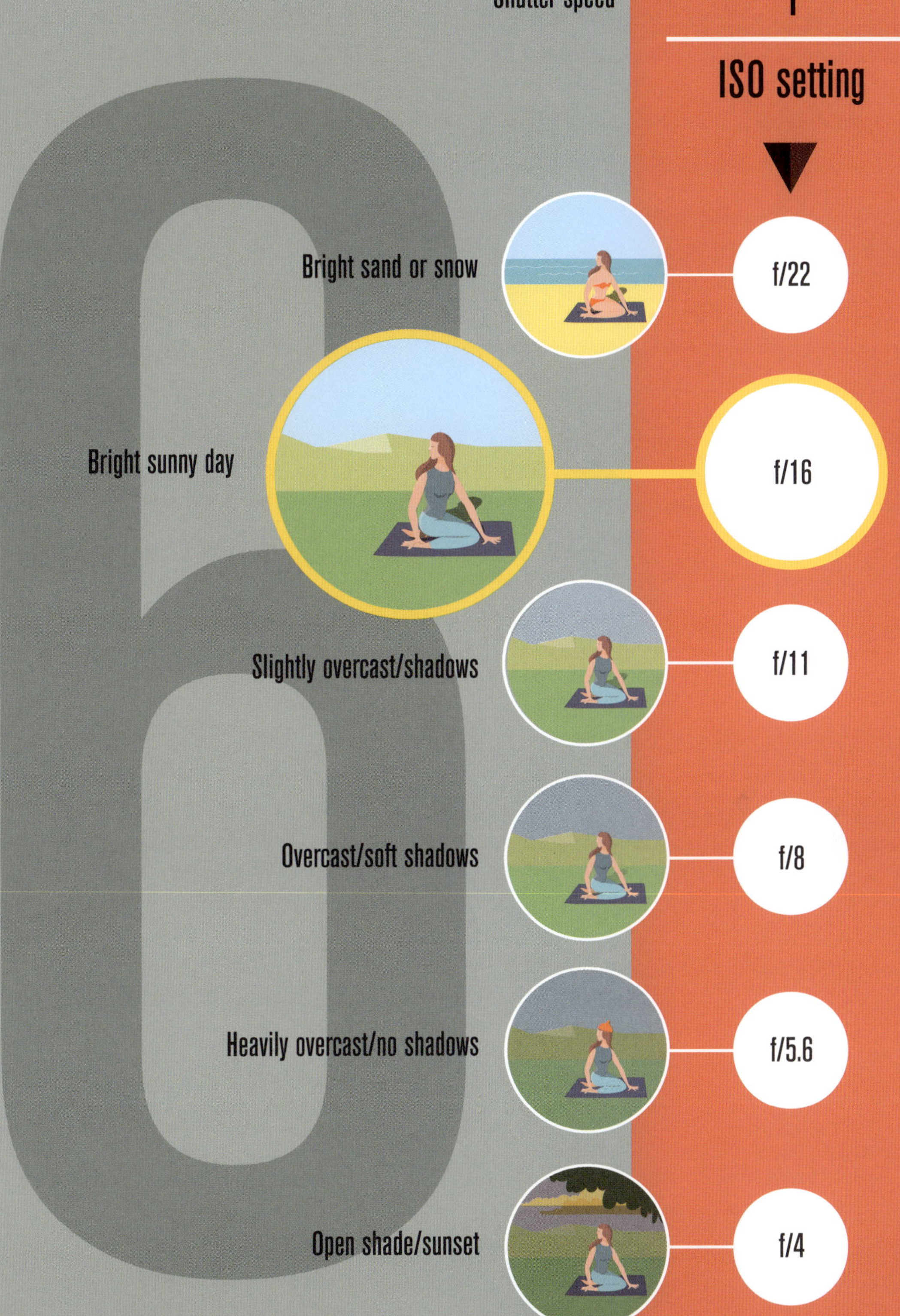

Shutter speed
1
ISO setting
Bright sand or snow
f/22
Bright sunny day
f/16
Slightly overcast/shadows
f/11
Overcast/soft shadows
f/8
Heavily overcast/no shadows
f/5.6
Open shade/sunset
f/4

Exposure Values

The reason the "Sunny 16" rule works is because the light levels (and therefore the required exposure settings) are similar under certain conditions. This forms the basis for exposure values (or EVs), which are a range of values and associated exposure settings that can be assigned to a wide range of lighting types. The lowest practical EV is -5, which describes the light levels when a scene is illuminated by a quarter moon; the highest EV in common use is 17.

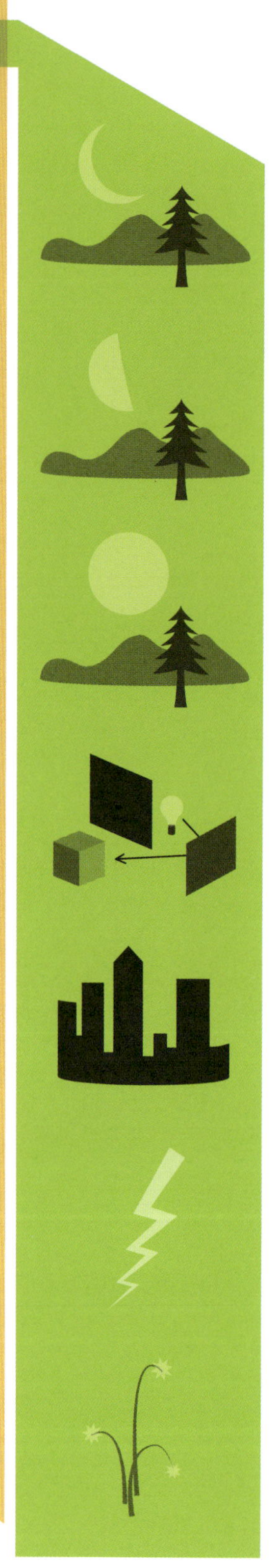

EV	f/4	f/8	f/16
4	1"	4"	15"
5	1/2	2"	8"
6	1/4	1"	4"
7	1/8	1/2	2"
8	1/15	1/4	1"
9	1/30	1/8	1/2
10	1/60	1/15	1/4

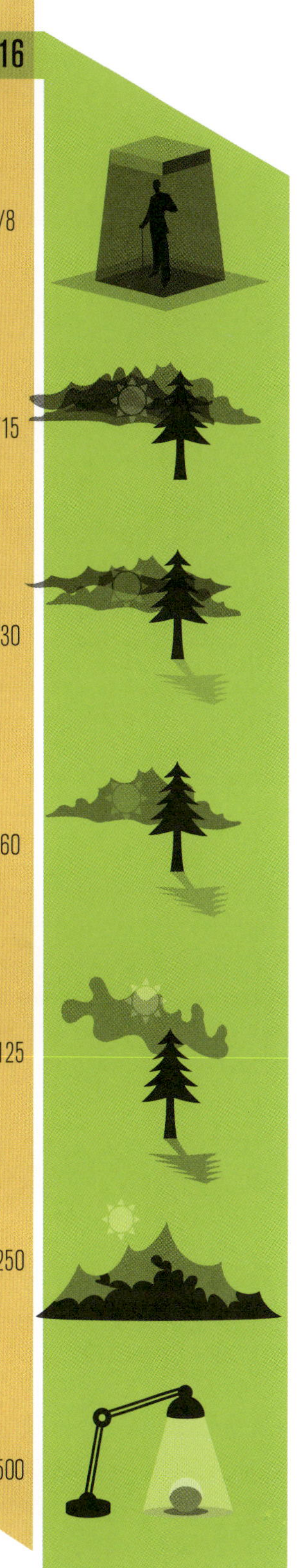

EV	f/4	f/8	f/16
11	1/125	1/30	1/8
12	1/250	1/60	1/15
13	1/500	1/125	1/30
14	1/1000	1/250	1/60
15	1/2000	1/500	1/125
16	1/4000	1/1000	1/250
17	1/8000	1/2000	1/500

Histograms

A histogram is a graph showing the distribution of brightness levels in an image. Histograms are read from left to right, with black at the extreme left edge and white at the extreme right edge. In the middle of the histograms are the midtones. The height of the histogram shows the number of pixels of a particular tone that can be found in the image. There's no right or wrong shape to a histogram, although the shape of a histogram can indicate that an image is under- or overexposed.

A histogram that is skewed completely to the left indicates that the shadows have been clipped and the image may be underexposed.

A histogram can be split into six rough zones: Black, Darks, Shadows, Midtones, Highlights, and White. Subjects such as grass and rock are midtones, but the intensity and hardness (or softness) of the light will determine how deep the shadows are or how bright the highlights are. High-contrast lighting can push those areas of the tonal range closer to black and white respectively, increasing the risk of clipping. The diagram on the right shows some of the different histogram readings you may encounter and what is required to fix your exposure.

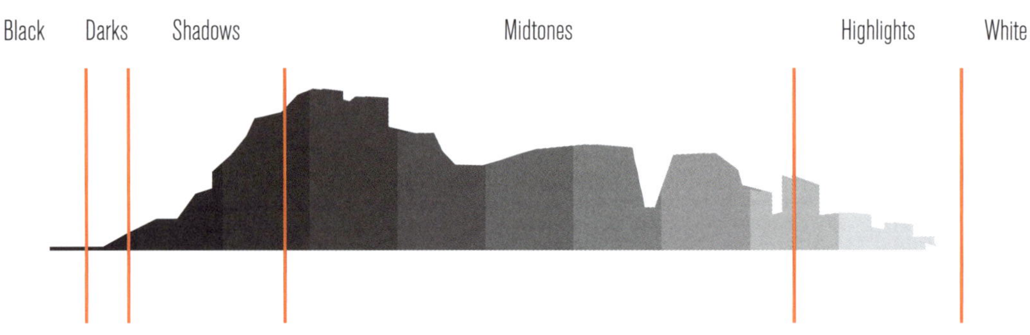

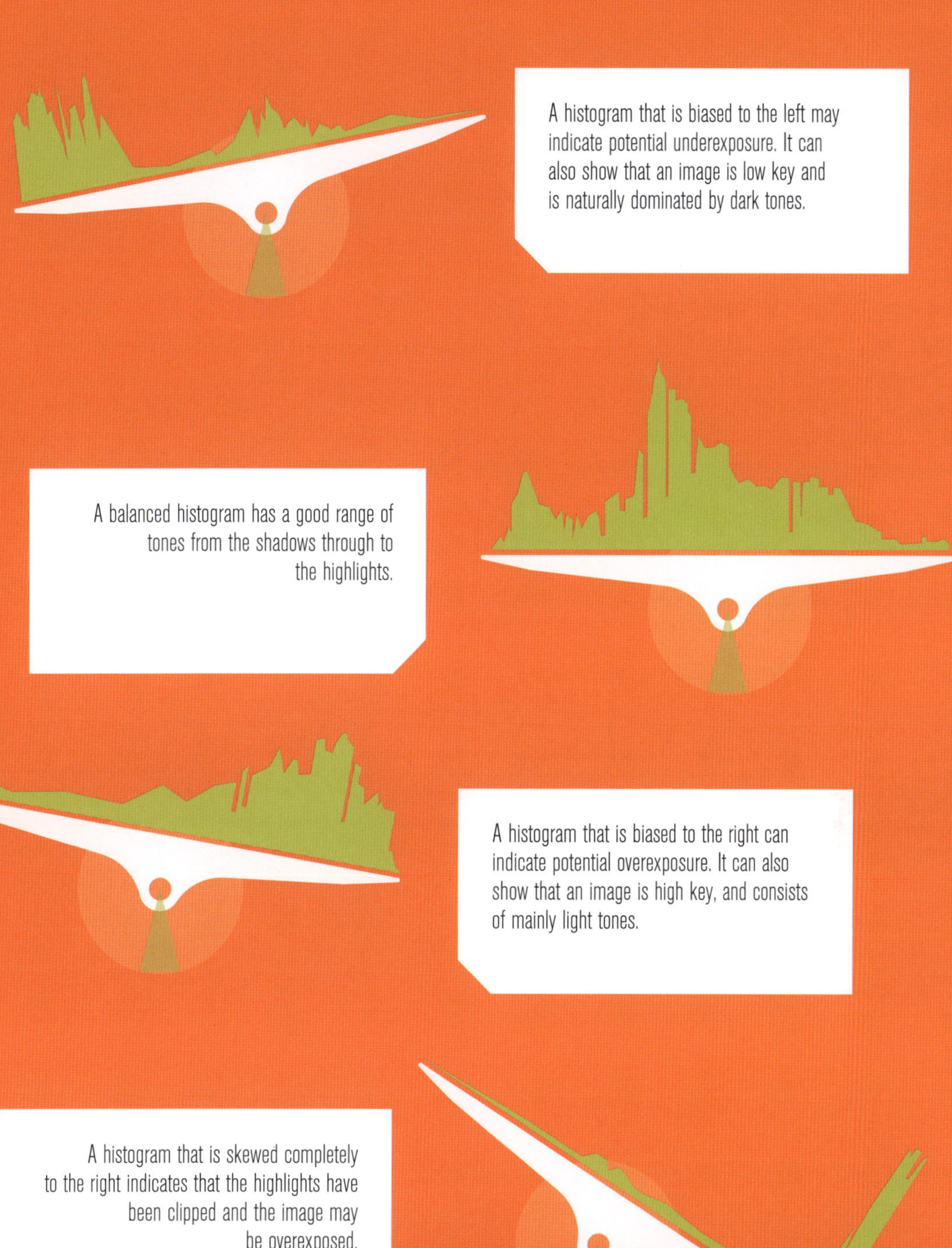

A histogram that is biased to the left may indicate potential underexposure. It can also show that an image is low key and is naturally dominated by dark tones.
A balanced histogram has a good range of tones from the shadows through to the highlights.
A histogram that is biased to the right can indicate potential overexposure. It can also show that an image is high key, and consists of mainly light tones.
A histogram that is skewed completely to the right indicates that the highlights have been clipped and the image may be overexposed.

File Formats

Cameras offer two choices for how still images are saved to the memory card: Raw and JPEG. A Raw file is unprocessed by the camera and contains all the data captured at the time of exposure; JPEGs are processed by the camera to produce a finished image. Both file types have advantages and disadvantages.

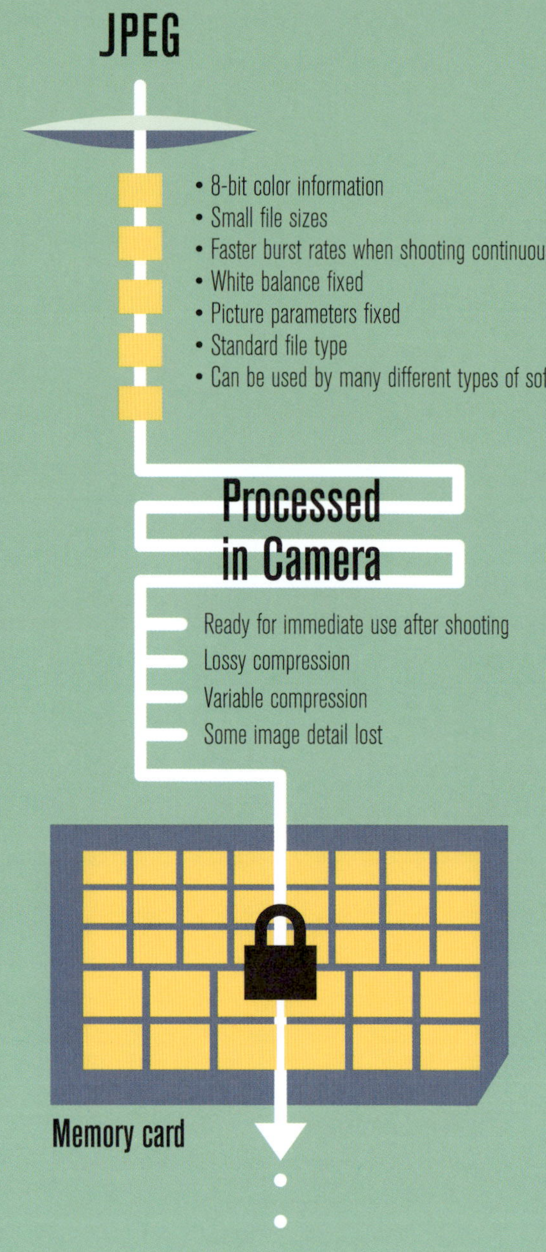

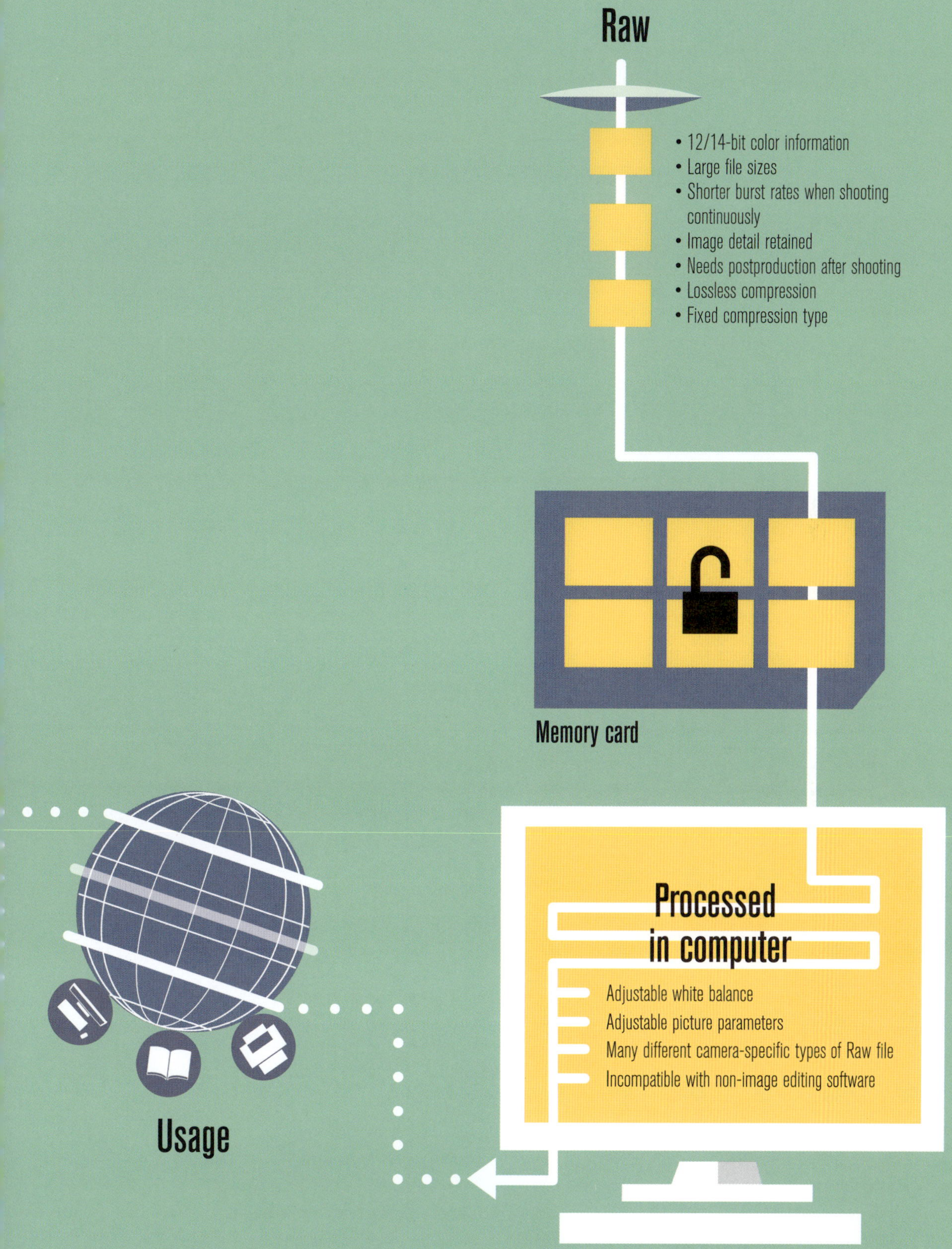

Raw

- 12/14-bit color information
- Large file sizes
- Shorter burst rates when shooting continuously
- Image detail retained
- Needs postproduction after shooting
- Lossless compression
- Fixed compression type

Memory card

Processed in computer

Adjustable white balance

Adjustable picture parameters

Many different camera-specific types of Raw file

Incompatible with non-image editing software

Usage

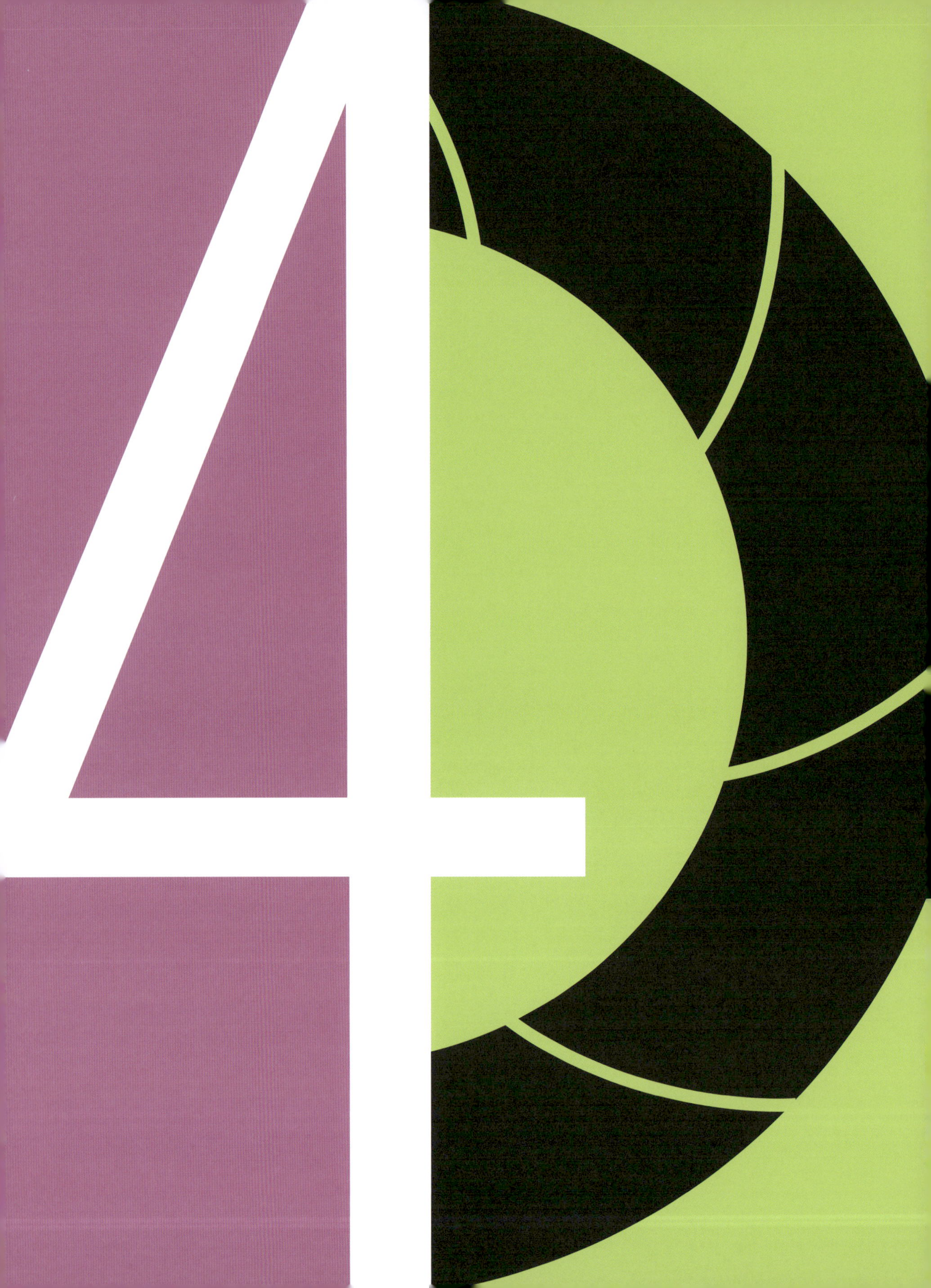

CONTROLLING EXPOSURE

MODERN DIGITAL CAMERAS ARE HIGHLY COMPLEX DEVICES AND ARE FAR MORE SOPHISTICATED THAN THEIR FILM-BASED PREDECESSORS. That complexity increases with each new model, with features continually added in an attempt to make you upgrade. What makes life more difficult is that different manufacturers generally use different words or terms to describe the same function found on every other manufacturer's cameras. Fortunately, the core features of cameras are similar and rarely change (largely because they work and therefore don't need to change). Once you have a grasp of the basics of how a camera works, you can use that knowledge when you (invariably) move to another camera.

There are two basic types of photographer. There are those photographers who enjoy the process of making a picture in-camera and who want to spend as little time tweaking their photos in postproduction as possible. Then there are those photographers for whom the picture-taking process is a chore to be got through, all so they have images to play with and adjust on their PC afterward. Both approaches are equally valid, although the "ideal" is arguably somewhere between the two extremes.

Whichever approach you favor, there's a lot to be said for getting the exposure (and other aspects of image making, such as white balance) right in-camera. Postproduction is a valuable and useful part of the picture-making process, but even if you shoot Raw, it's better to start with the optimum data possible.

However, in-camera exposure meters often seem to deliberately get in the way of achieving the correct exposure, and so produce less-than-optimal image data. This is because they make one basic assumption: that the scene being metered has an average level of reflectivity (equivalent to a midtone). Scenes that aren't "average" will therefore cause problems with exposure. A scene that is darker than average—a black cat curled up on a black cushion—will typically cause the camera's meter to overexpose, while a scene that is lighter than average—a brightly lit vista of snow—generally results in underexposure.

In both cases, the camera meter has simply created an exposure that matches the midtone ideal (by lightening black to a midtone and darkening white). Fortunately, cameras allow you to correct these exposure errors—the key is anticipating when they might occur and being ready to take preventative (or remedial) action.

Midtones, Shadows & Highlights

A midtone is equivalent to mid-gray and reflects approximately 18% of the light that falls onto it. However, midtones don't have to be gray—they can be any color as long as their level of reflectivity is 18%.

The shadows in a scene are the areas that are darker than a midtone (because their reflectivity is less than 18%), while the highlights are brighter than a midtone (their reflectivity is greater than 18%).

The tonal range of a scene is defined by the relative brightness difference between the deepest shadows, the midtones, and the brightest highlights. This has an influence on exposure settings and whether the tonal range fits into the dynamic range of a camera.

9%

4.5%

2.25%

0%

This diagram shows the percentage of light reflected by the range of tones that are commonly encountered when shooting. Being able to judge what subject areas are midtones is a useful skill to acquire. Typically, green grass is a midtone, as is the deepest blue of a sky.

Shadows

Reflectance
Highlights
100%
95%
72%
35%
18%
Midtones

Exposure Meters

There are two basic types of exposure meter: incident and reflective. Incident exposure meters (which includes handheld lightmeters) measure the amount of light falling onto a scene, while reflective exposure meters (the type found in cameras) measure the amount of light reflected by the scene. Both types of exposure meter has advantages and disadvantages.

Metering is the act of measuring how much light is required to create a photographic image. Understanding how it works and the advantages and disadvantages of both incident and reflective readings will help you to improve your chances of a succesful exposure.

Reflective lightmeter

Advantages
- Built into the camera (no need to buy more equipment)
- New meter readings easily taken and exposure altered automatically
- Takes account of filtration added to camera
- Can meter distant scenes accurately using spot metering (or a long focal length lens)

Disadvantages
- Assumes that a scene has an average 18% reflectivity
- Can be fooled by scenes that are darker or lighter than average

Incident lightmeter

Advantages
- Accurate
- Unaffected by scenes that are darker or lighter than average
- Can be used to manually meter flash

Disadvantages
- Meter readings need to be entered into the camera manually
- Can't meter light falling onto distant subjects easily
- New meter readings need to be taken if light levels change

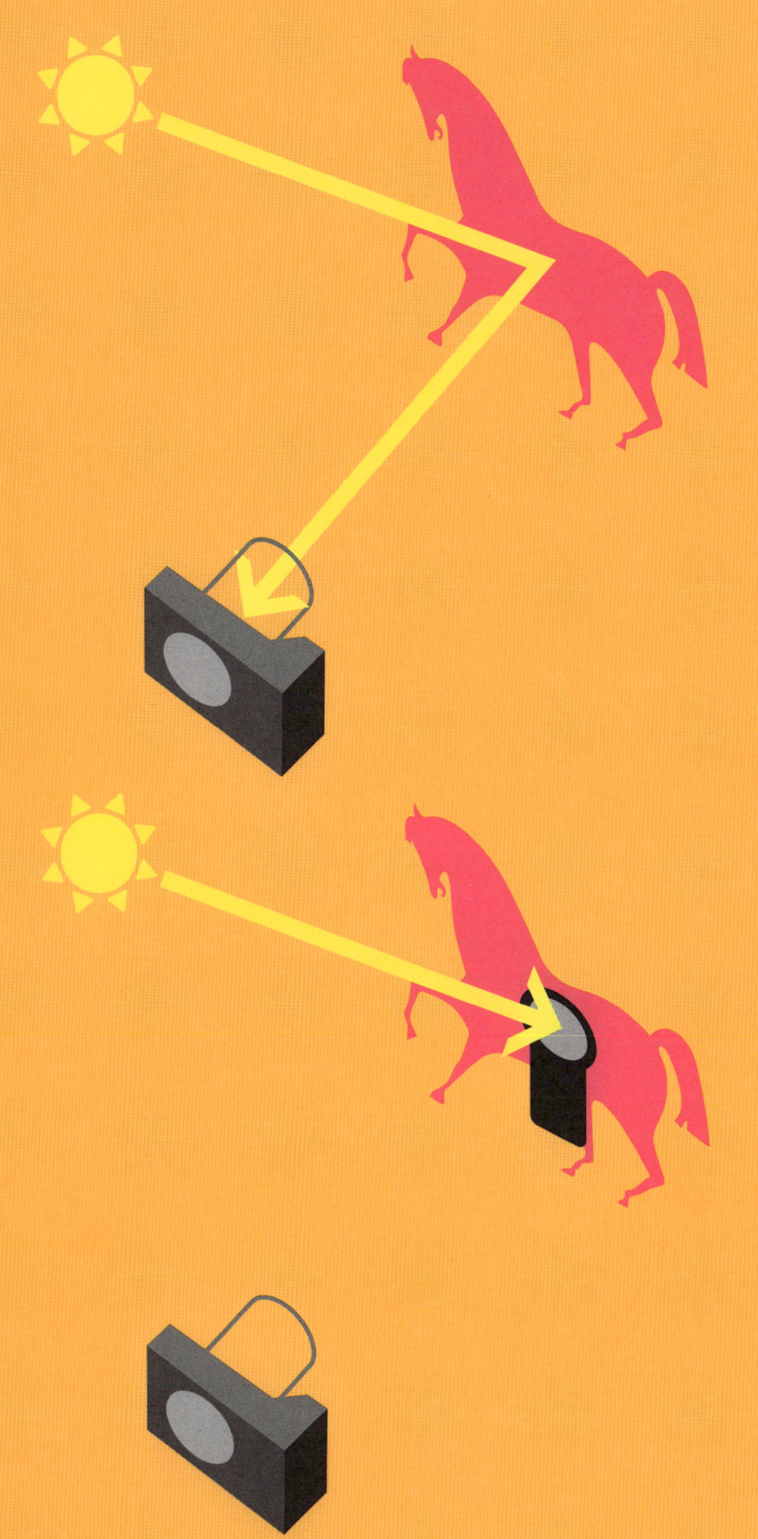

Metering Modes

Cameras typically offer three metering modes which alter the way in which the camera reads the light in a scene to determine the exposure.

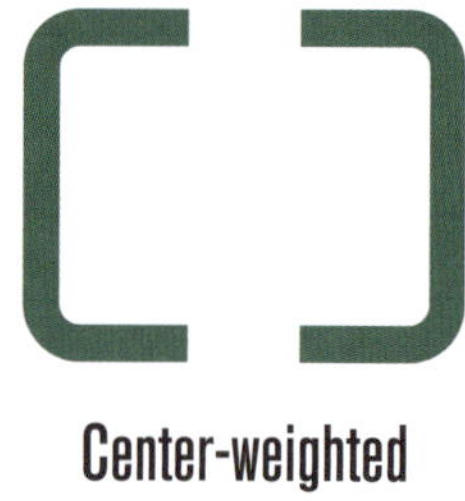

Center-weighted

Multi-zone

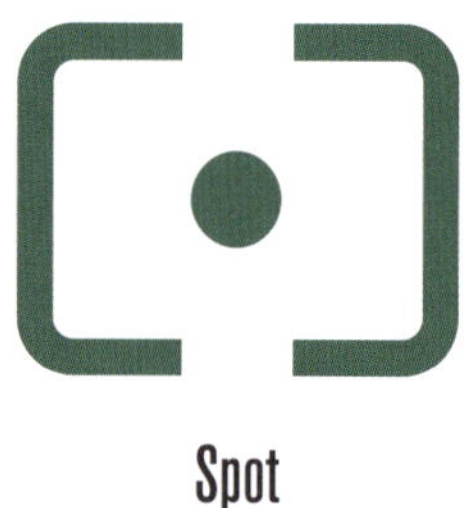

Spot

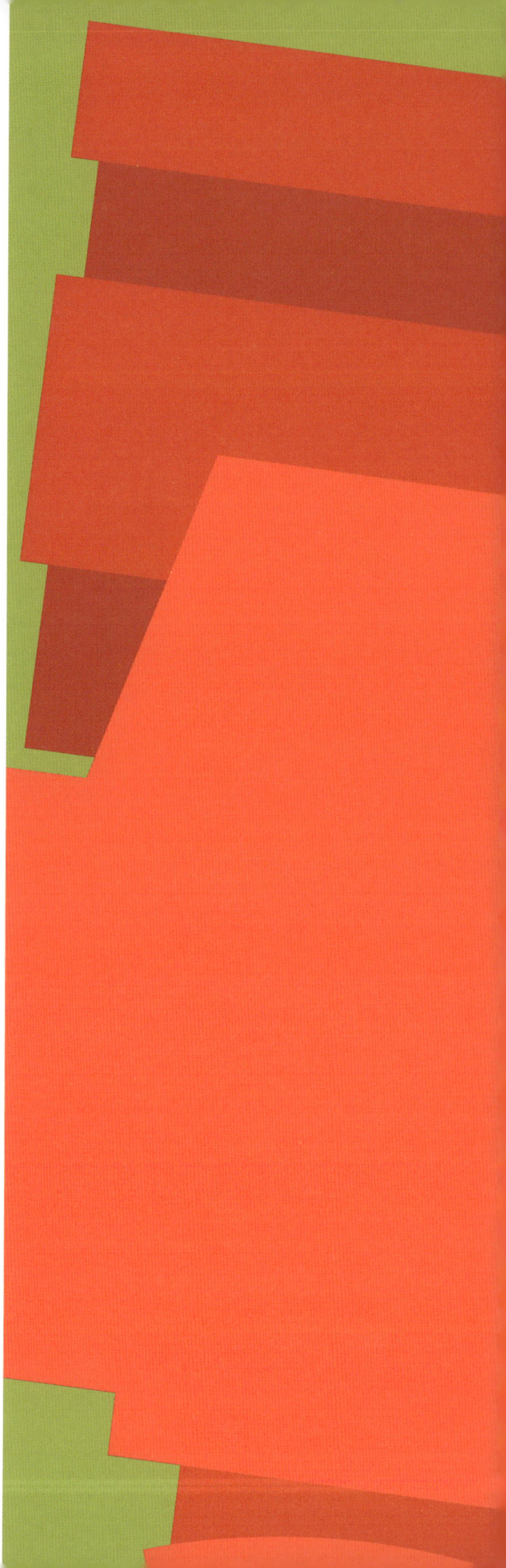

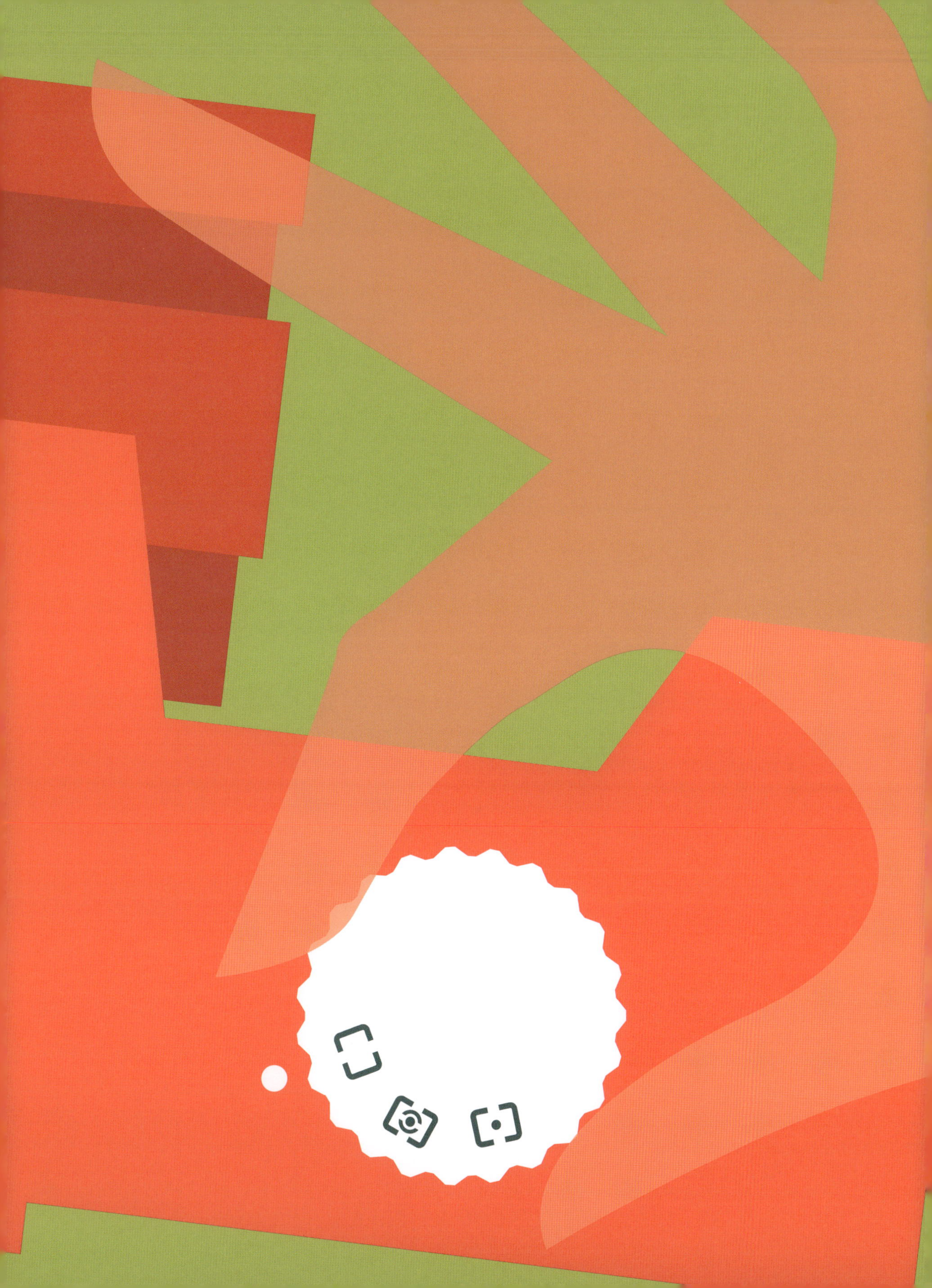

Metering Modes II

If you use a fully automatic shooting mode the metering mode will be set to multi-zone metering and cannot be changed. It's only when you shoot to less automated modes that you have a choice of metering modes.

Multi-zone metering breaks a scene into segments or zones, each of which is metered independently. The camera analyzes the metering data from each segment to calculate the final exposure settings.

Center-weighted metering also measures the entire scene, but the final exposure settings are biased toward a large zone at the center of the frame.

Spot metering restricts the camera's exposure metering to a small zone. This is usually set at the center of the frame, but some cameras allow you to link the spot metering area to an autofocus point.

Camera manufacturers use different names and icons when describing metering modes. This diagram shows the metering mode names and icons for the most common camera systems.

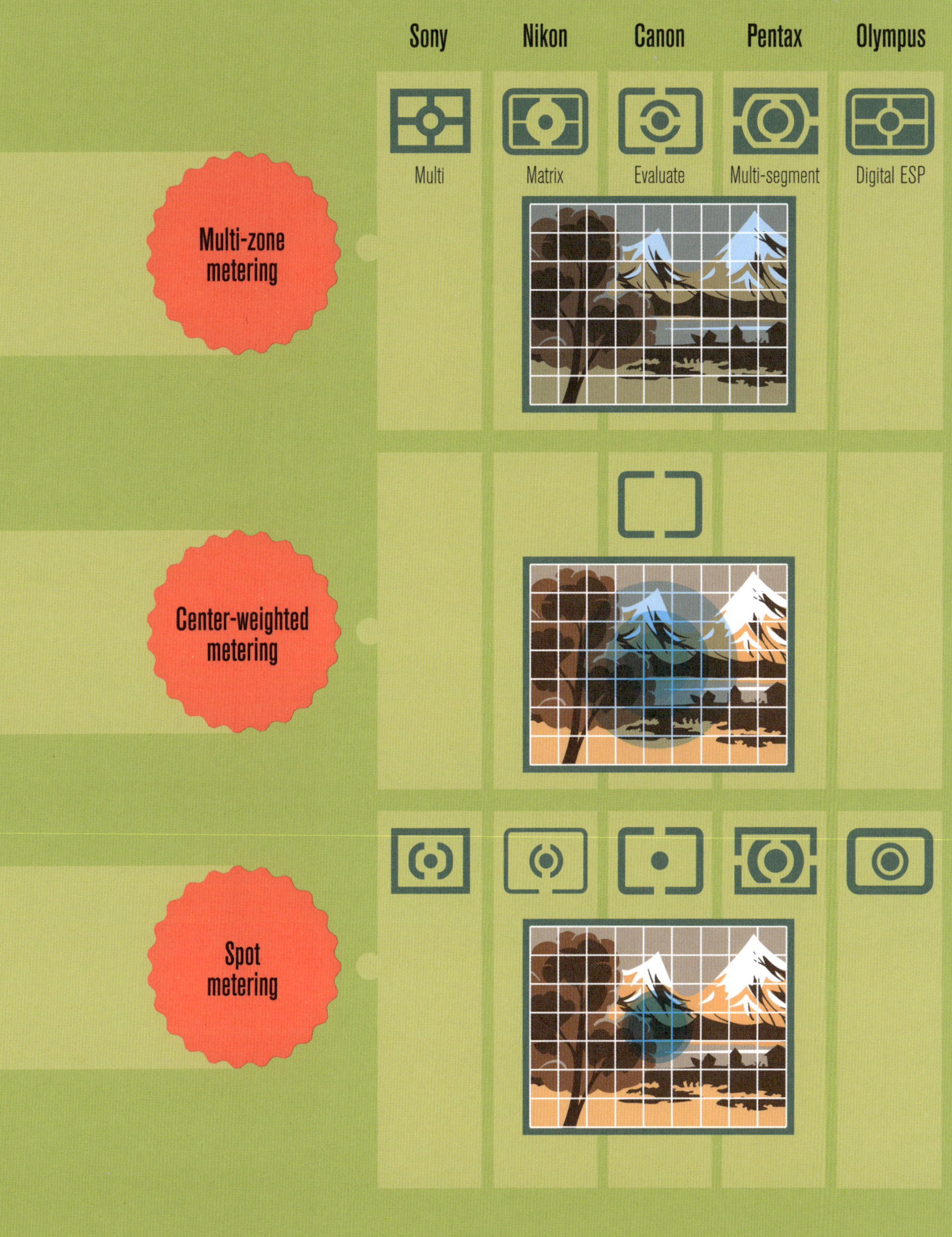

Sony
Nikon
Canon
Pentax
Olympus
Multi
Matrix
Evaluate
Multi-segment
Digital ESP
Multi-zone metering
Center-weighted metering
Spot metering

Spot Metering

Spot metering is perfect when you need to meter very precisely from a small area of a scene. This is often necessary at concerts, when performers are spotlit against a dark background; the large areas of black around the subject can fool multi-zone metering into overexposing. Spot metering from the performer will make the exposure reading more accurate and require less use of exposure compensation.

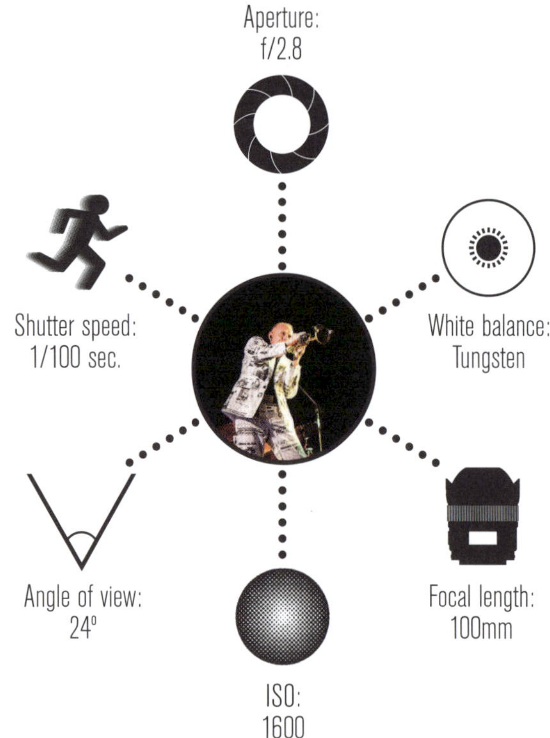

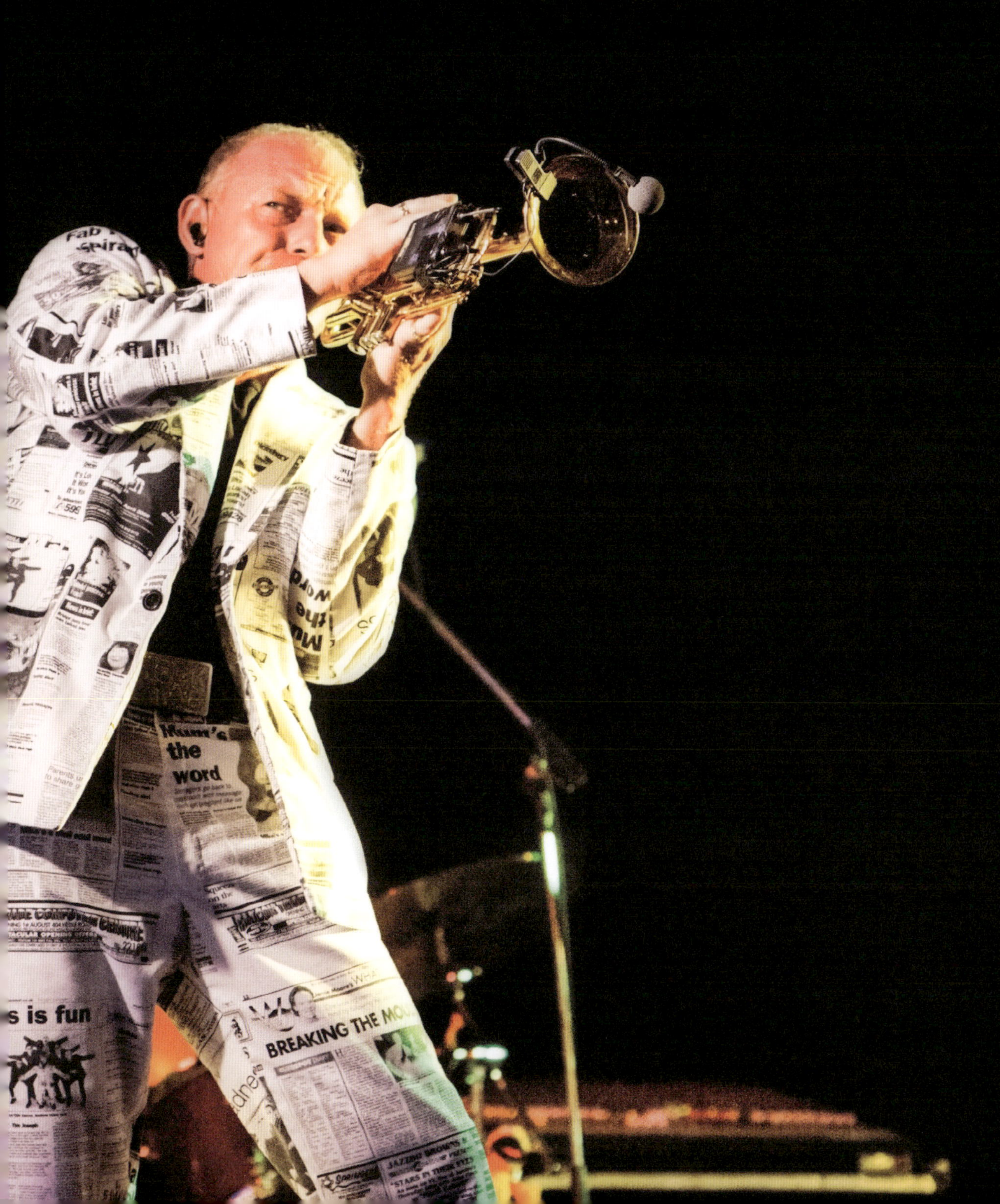

Picture Parameters

Most cameras let you choose from a range of picture parameters presets, including settings such as Portrait or Landscape. You can usually create your own presets as well, adjusting the level of color saturation, sharpness, and contrast in an image to suit your own tastes.

The picture parameter you choose is fixed when you shoot JPEG. However, if you shoot using Raw you can undo and alter the picture parameter in postproduction. This applies even when you use an extreme picture parameter such as Monochrome.

There are typically three variables that change as you swap between the different picture parameters on your camera: contrast, sharpness and color saturation. This diagram shows how these three variables differ across the various picture parameters typically found on cameras.

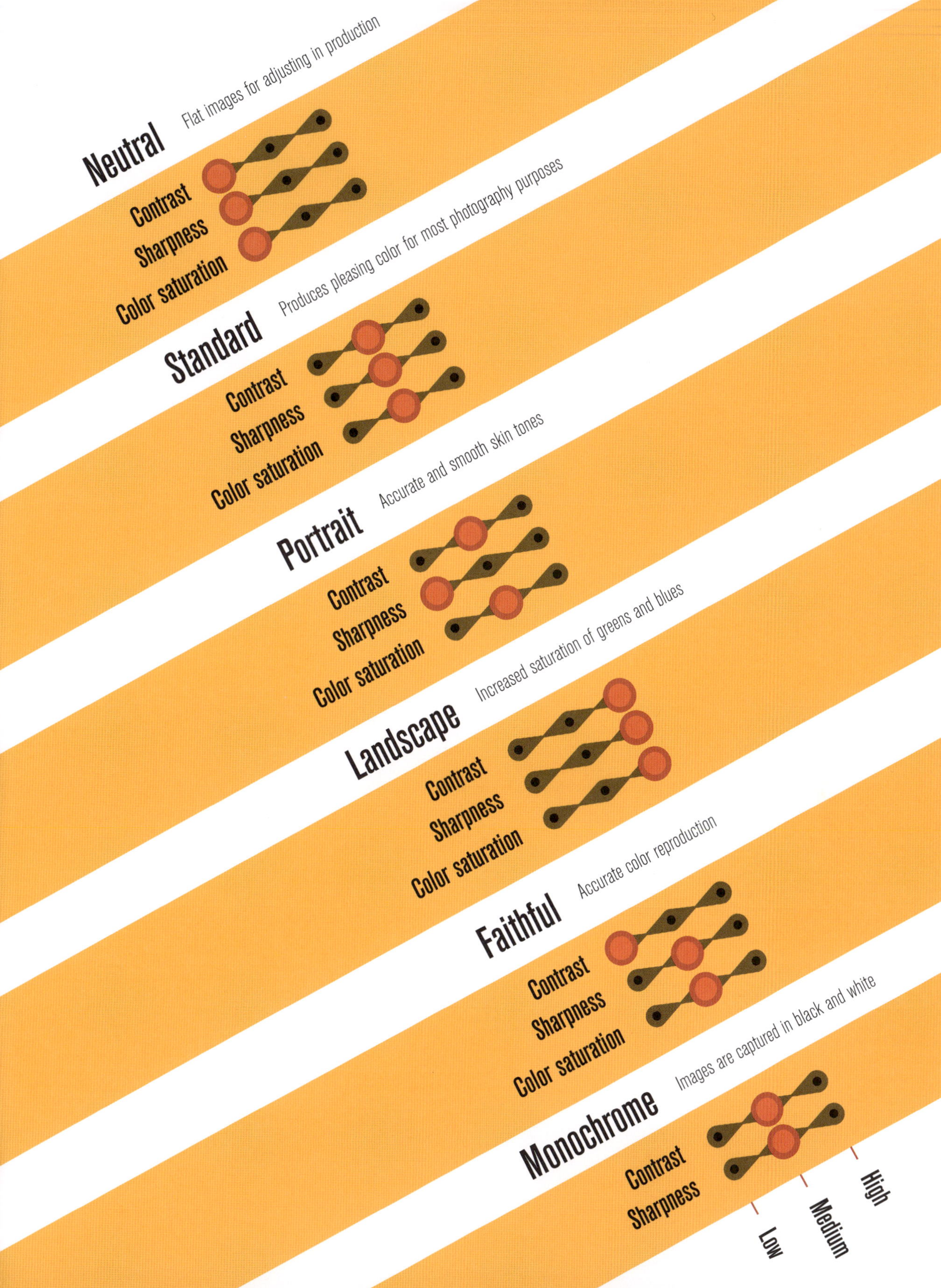

Neutral
Flat images for adjusting in production
Contrast
Sharpness
Color saturation

Standard
Produces pleasing color for most photography purposes
Contrast
Sharpness
Color saturation

Portrait
Accurate and smooth skin tones
Contrast
Sharpness
Color saturation

Landscape
Increased saturation of greens and blues
Contrast
Sharpness
Color saturation

Faithful
Accurate color reproduction
Contrast
Sharpness
Color saturation

Monochrome
Images are captured in black and white
Contrast
Sharpness

Low
Medium
High

Exposure Modes

The exposure mode you choose determines how much control you have over exposure. The more automated the mode, the fewer options you will have when it comes to making changes to your exposure. This means there's less risk of error, but also less scope for creative exposure adjustments.

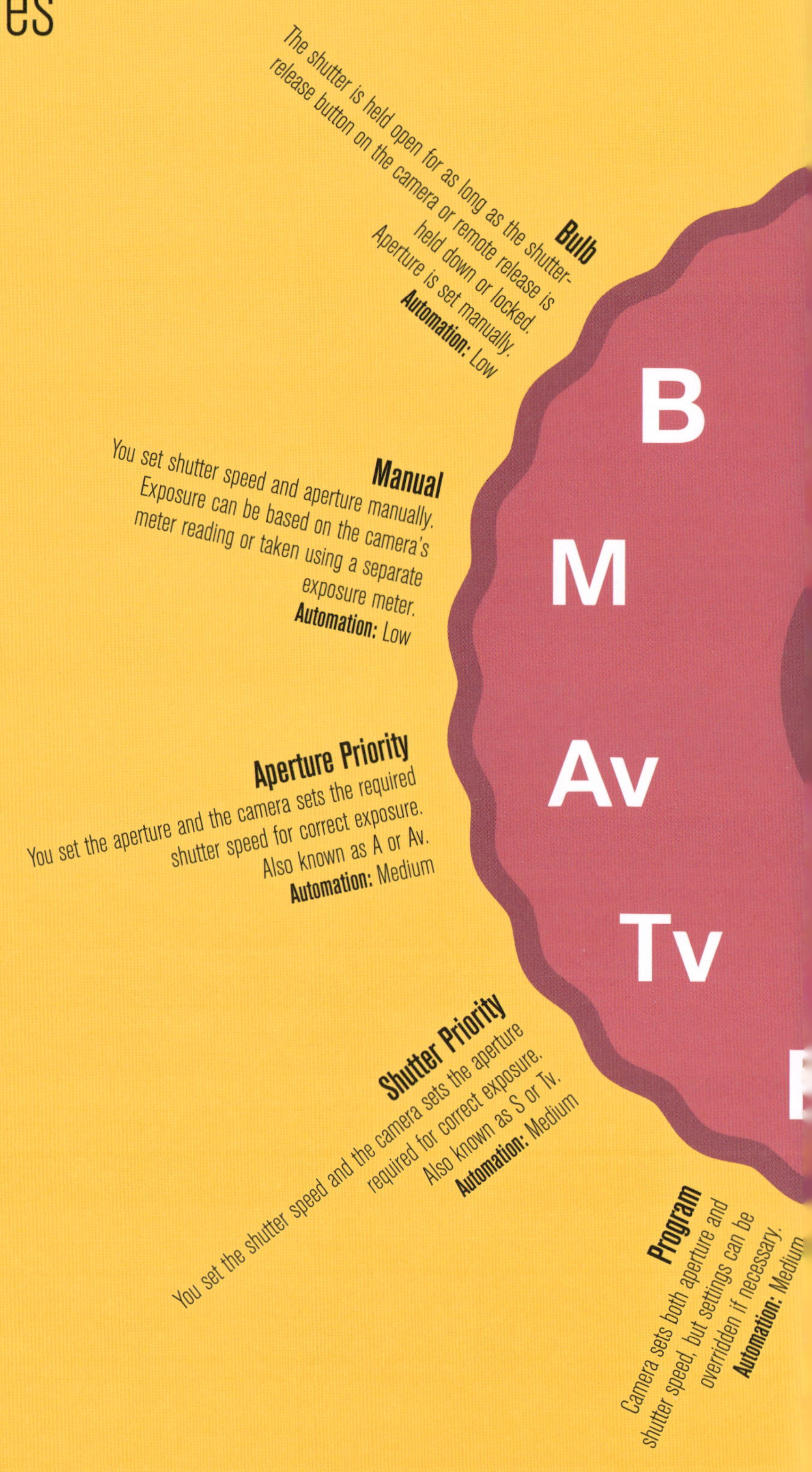

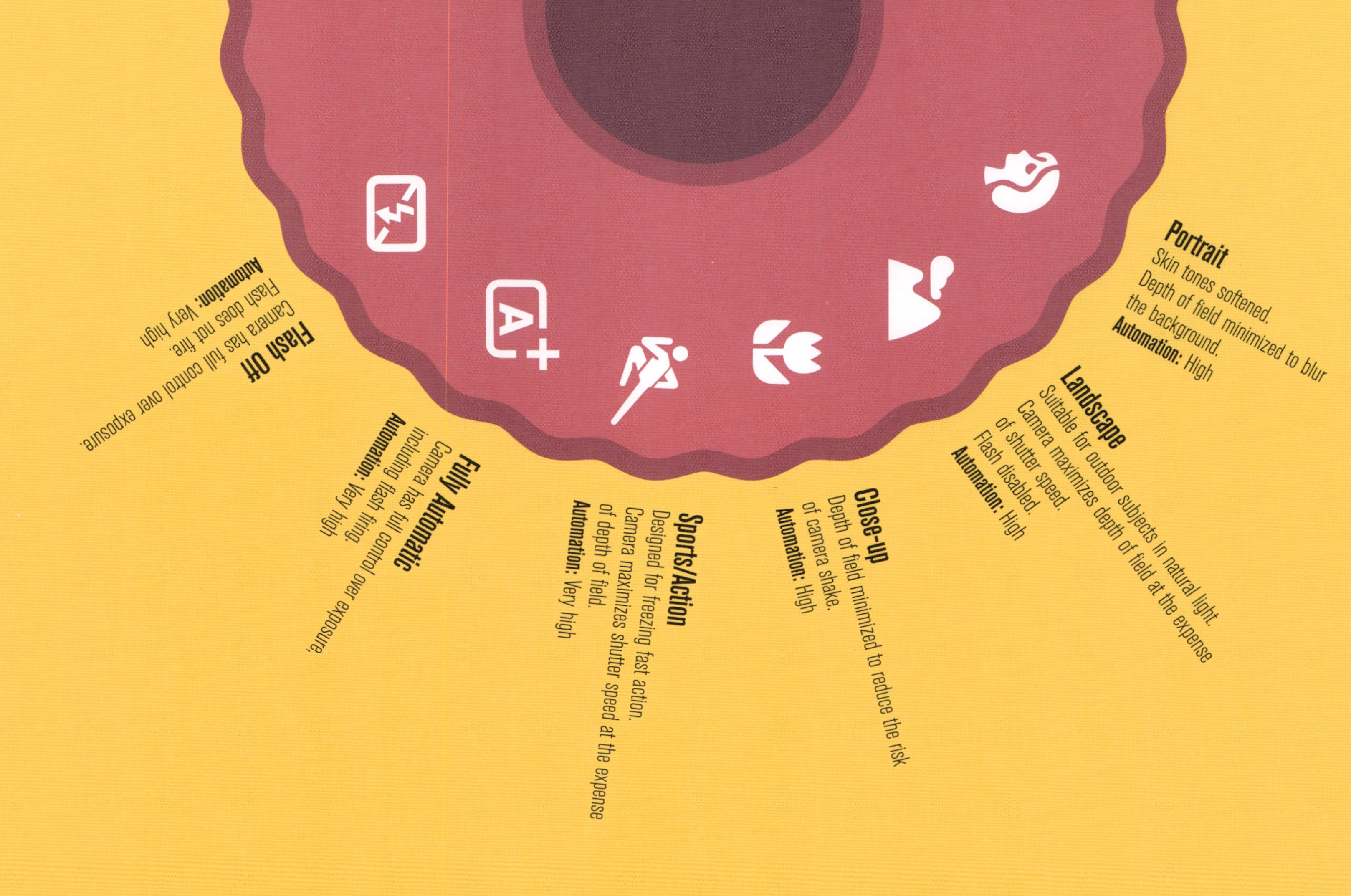

Portrait
Skin tones softened.
Depth of field minimized to blur
the background.
Automation: High

Landscape
Suitable for outdoor subjects in natural light.
Camera maximizes depth of field at the expense
of shutter speed.
Flash disabled.
Automation: High

Close-up
Depth of field minimized to reduce the risk
of camera shake.
Automation: High

Sports/Action
Designed for freezing fast action.
Camera maximizes shutter speed at the expense
of depth of field.
Automation: Very high

Fully Automatic
Camera has full control over exposure,
including flash firing.
Automation: Very high

Flash Off
Camera has full control over exposure.
Flash does not fire.
Automation: Very high

Exposure Compensation

In certain exposure modes (typically Program, Shutter Priority, and Aperture Priority) you can override the exposure suggested by the camera by applying exposure compensation in fractions of stops or in whole stops.

Exposure compensation is generally needed to correct for any exposure errors made by the camera metering. Predominantly dark-toned scenes generally need negative compensation, lighter-toned scenes usually require positive compensation.

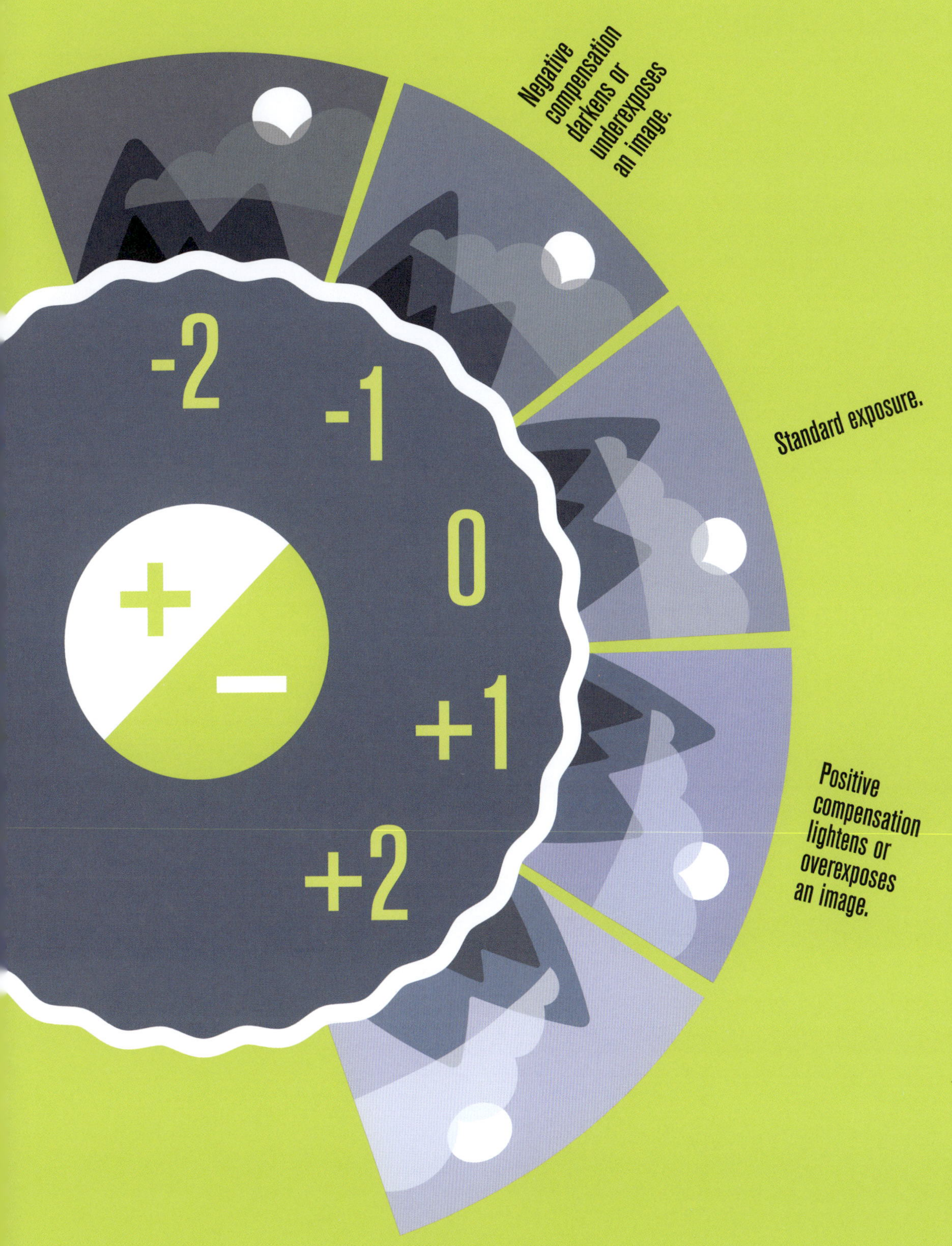

Negative compensation darkens or underexposes an image.
Standard exposure.
Positive compensation lightens or overexposes an image.
-2
-1
0
+1
+2
+
−

Bracketing

Bracketing is the technique of shooting two or more images using different camera settings. Bracketing is usually associated with exposure; where a sequence of bracketed exposures produces a number of images that vary in brightness. The technique is typically used as a way of ensuring that you have one exposure that's "correct" (the incorrect variations can then be discarded) or when shooting to produce HDR (high-dynamic-range) images.

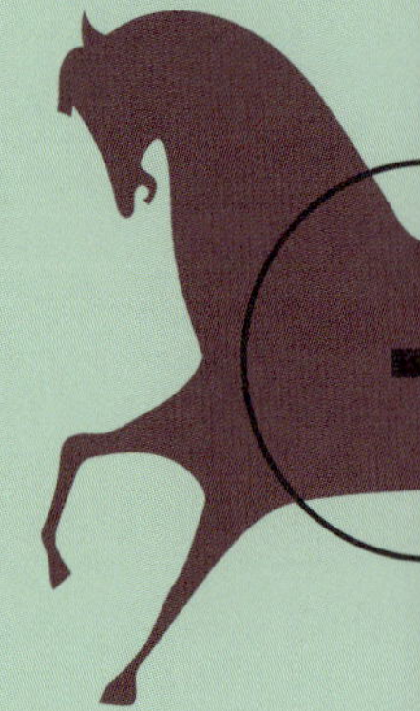

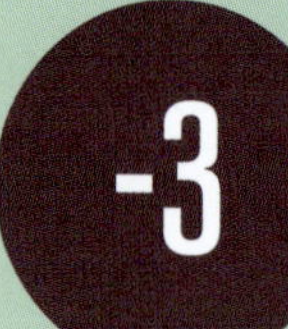

The bracketing order on a camera is usually 0 – +. This means that the first exposure is "correct," the second underexposed, and the third overexposed.

The bracketing range can be set so the exposure variation is as small or as large as necessary.

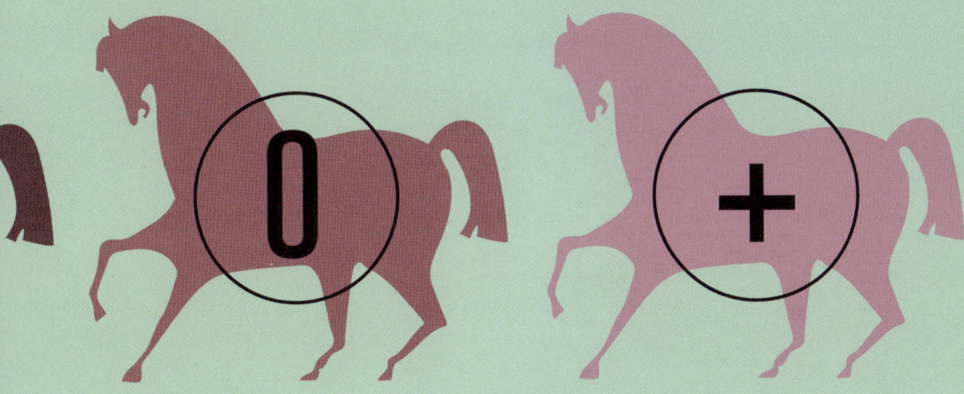

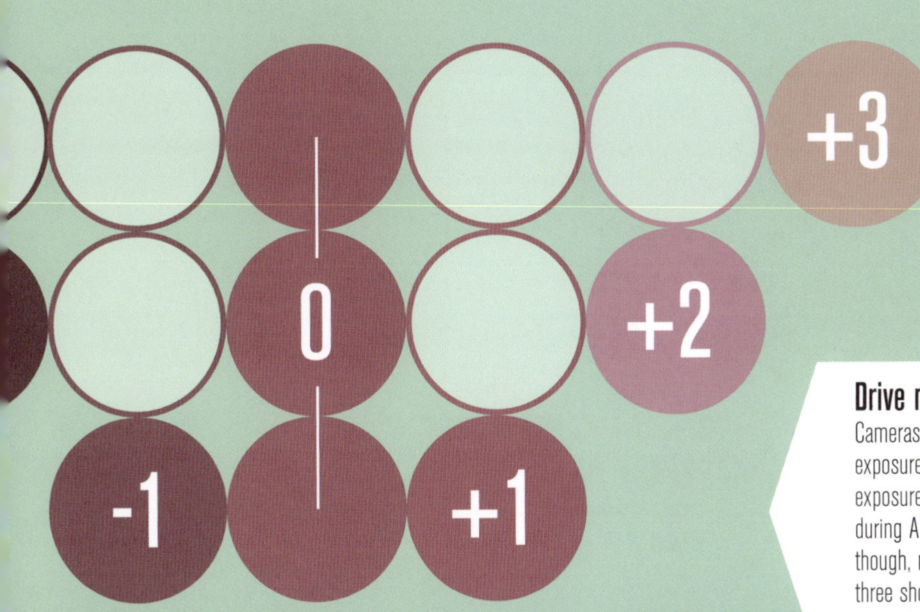

Drive mode

Cameras can be set to automatically bracket exposure using a mode known as AEB. The exposure range and number of frames shot during AEB vary between cameras. Typically, though, most cameras can shoot at least three shots using different exposure settings, with a bracketing range of ±1–3 stops.

Sequences

Bracketing is useful when you're shooting high-contrast scenes with a wide range of brightness levels. This means you can either choose the best exposure after shooting or use the bracketed sequence to produce an HDR image in postproduction. The latter option was the one chosen for this image, which was created by blending three bracketed shots.

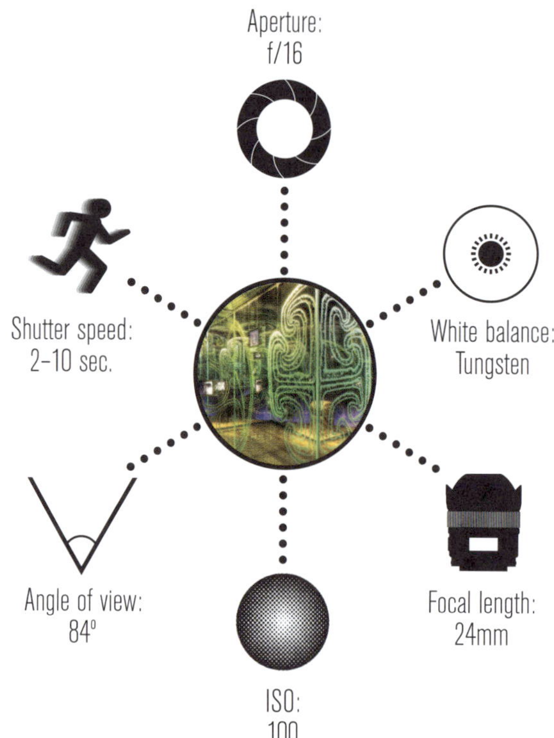

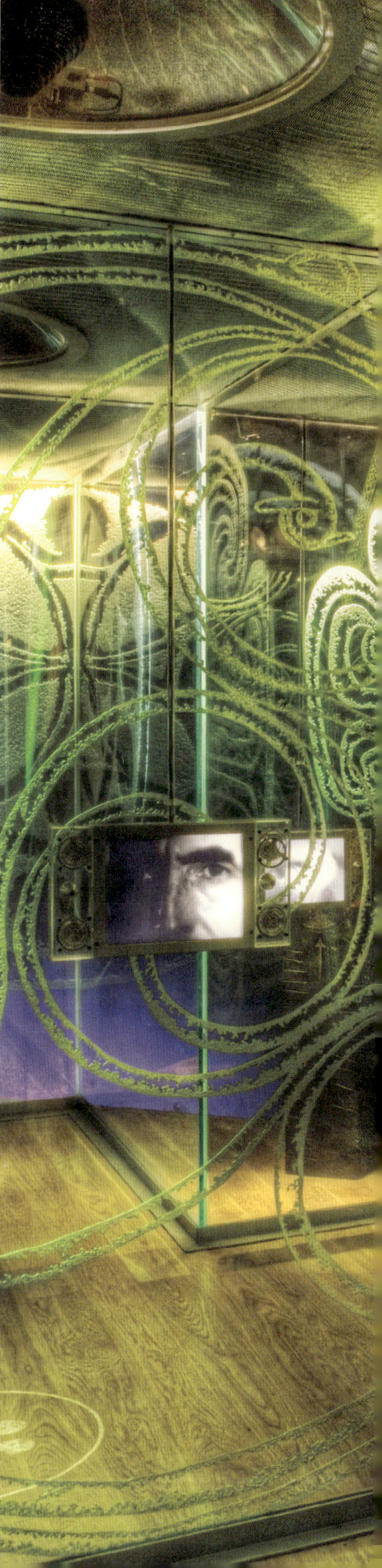

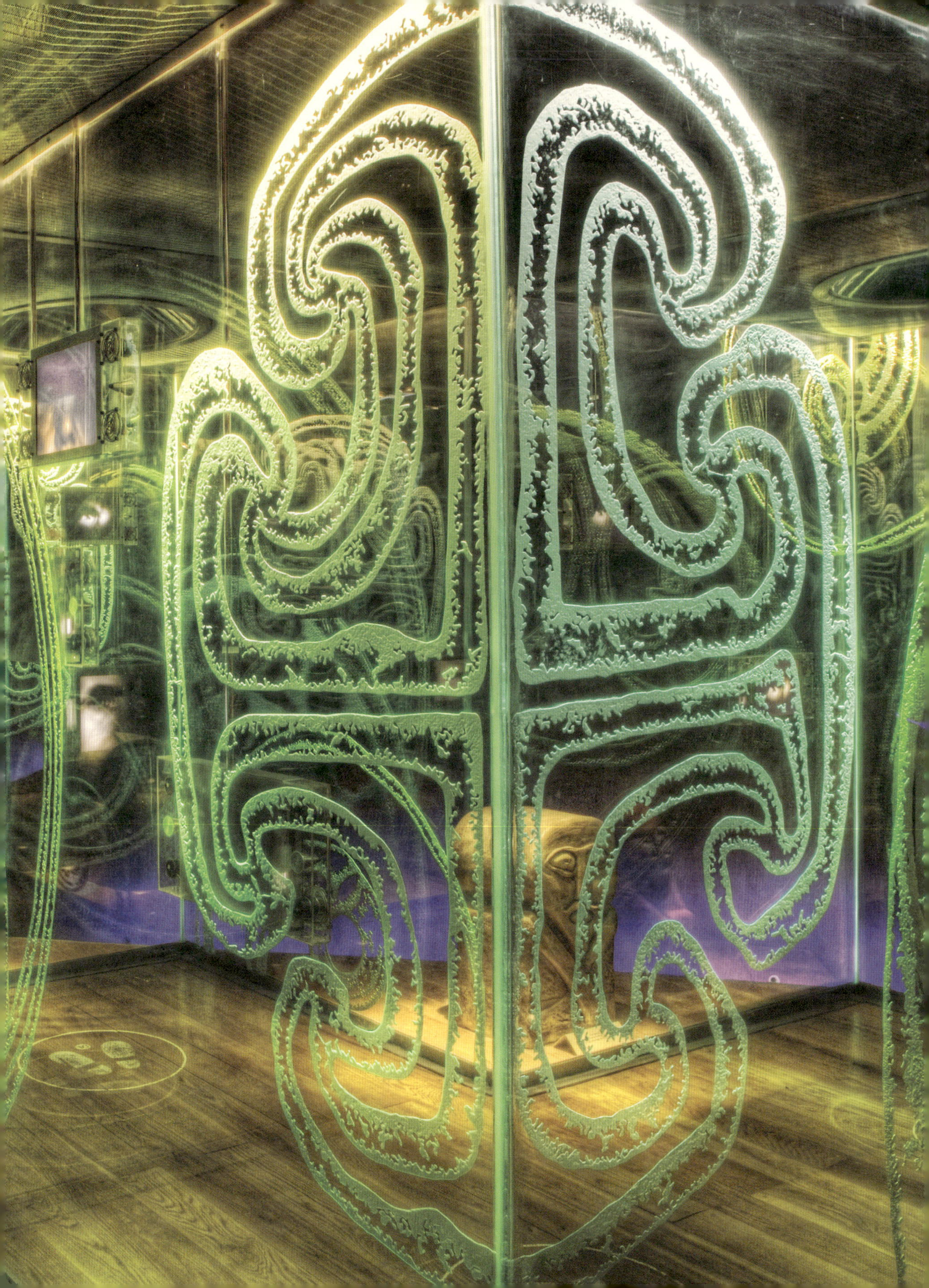

Video

Video footage is shot at a number of frames per second—24, 25, 30, 50, or 60 fps—which is referred to as the "frame rate." Each of those frames is exposed at a shutter speed selected by you or your camera. The ideal shutter speed setting is one that's twice the number of frames per second: this is known as a "180° shutter angle." Shooting at higher or slower shutter speeds than the ideal produces interesting effects, but the resulting footage often isn't easy to watch.

Typically you only get full control over the shutter speed used to shoot video when the camera is set to Manual exposure mode. Automatic shooting modes will often adjust the ISO or aperture setting in order to maintain a 180° shutter angle.

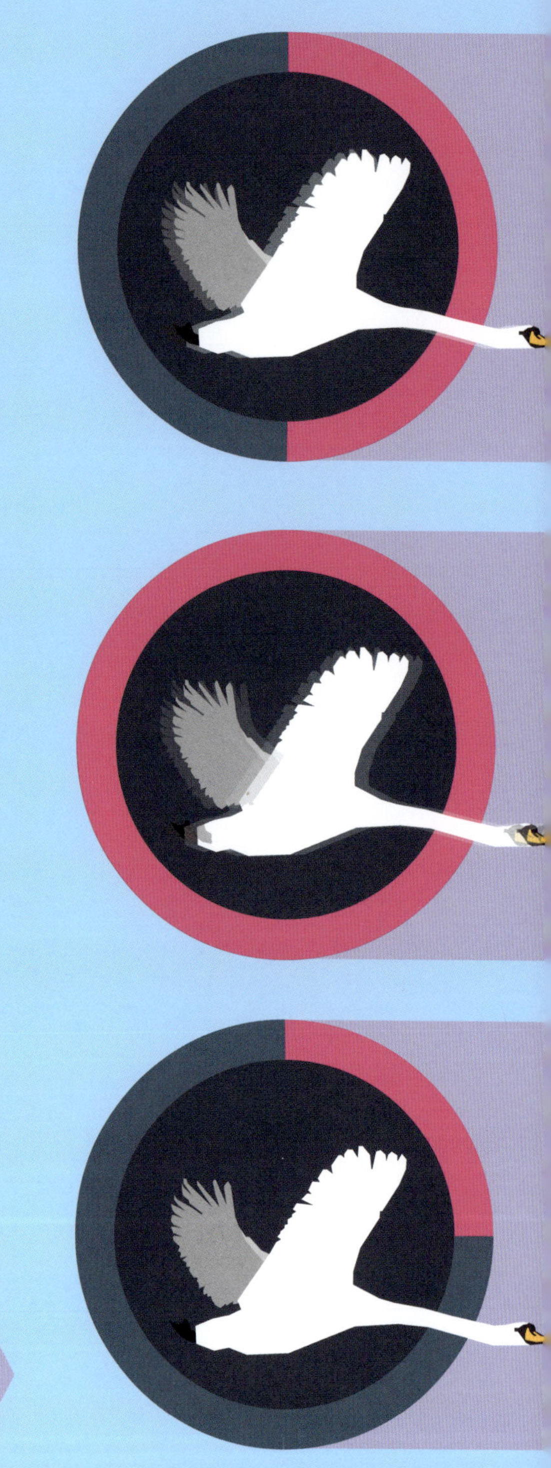

These images show how long the shutter is open and closed—due to the shutter speed used—compared to the selected frame rate per second.

180⁰ angle

Footage shot with the shutter speed set twice as fast as the frame rate has a natural quality. This is due to blur making movement appear smoother.

360⁰ angle

If you shoot using a shutter speed that matches (or is slower than) the frame rate, blur becomes excessive, making the footage look smeared.

0–135⁰ angle

Footage shot with the shutter speed more than twice as fast as the frame rate has a sharp, staccato feel. This is effective for short action scenes, but can be tiring to watch over a long period.

Shutter closed

Shutter open

HDR

High Dynamic Range (or HDR) photography is a technique used in high-contrast scenarios when it would be otherwise impossible to record detail in both the highlights and shadows simultaneously. An HDR image is typically created by merging a sequence of bracketed photos, using either an in-camera HDR option, or specialized HDR software in postproduction.

Creating an HDR image means making a number of decisions throughout the shooting process. Follow this diagram, starting at A and ending at H, altering how you shoot based on the options presented at each stage.

A

Assess the scene. Not every photograph needs to be HDR, so take a test shot of your subject and check the histogram. A histogram that's clipped at both ends means that HDR will be useful.

B

Fit your camera to a tripod. Keeping your camera steady when shooting an HDR sequence will prevent alignment errors later on.

C

To produce your HDR images in-camera you need to switch on HDR mode. This is either a specific shooting mode or is turned on via the menu system.

D

For HDR images that will be created during postproduction, select Raw: this gives you greater flexibility than JPEG.

E

Set the bracketing range. The range needed will depend on the relative brightness of the shadows and highlights: the greater the difference, the wider the bracketing range will need to be.

F

Shoot. Ideally, both the camera and subject should be static. If your subject moves too much as you shoot, you may need to restart.

G

Merging images. There are many ways that your exposures can be merged to produce an HDR image, and different software packages offer different options. Experiment until you produce a result that you like—there's no right or wrong answer!

H

Export your HDR image. If you want to print out your HDR image, or post it online, you'll need to export it as a JPEG.

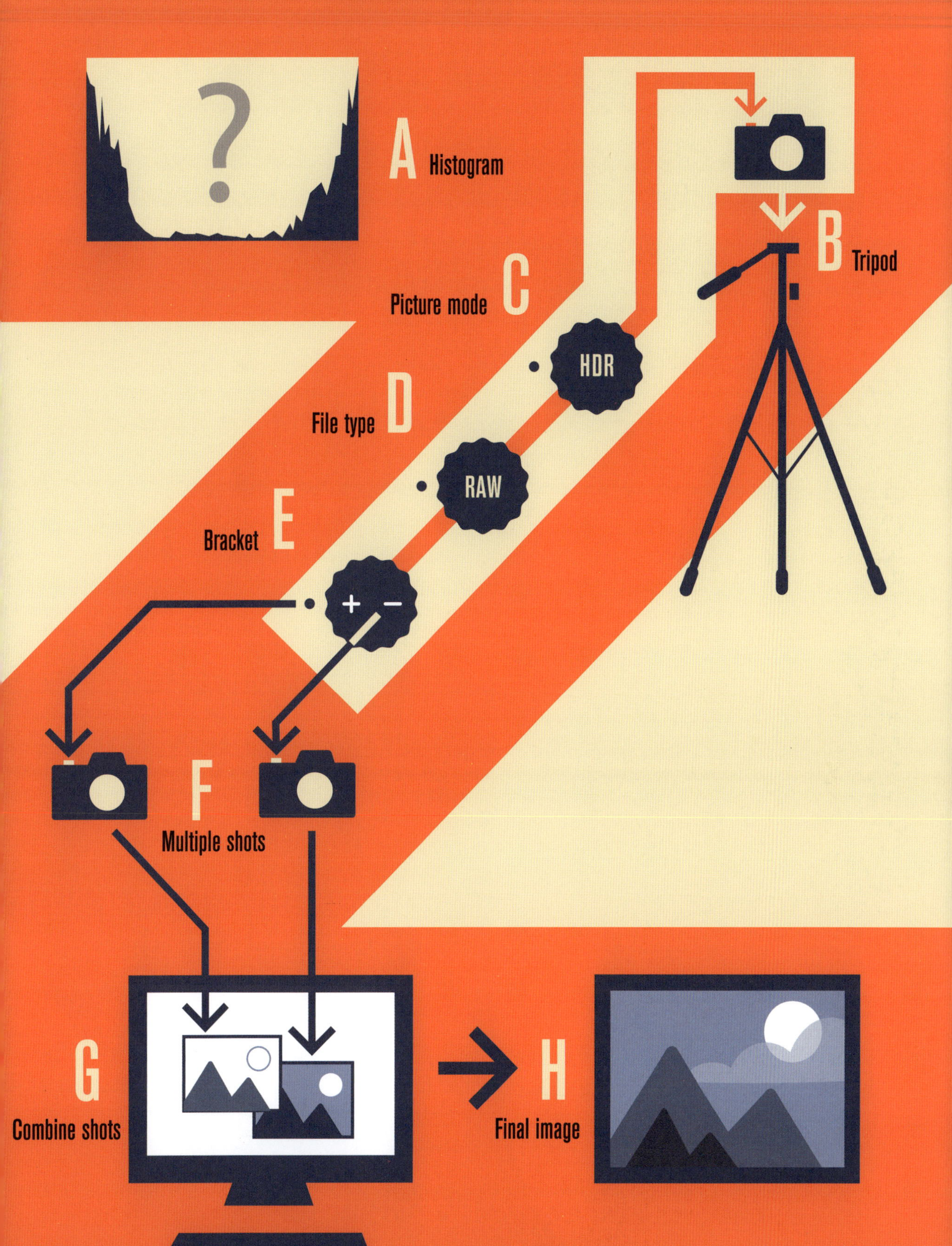

?
A Histogram
B Tripod
C Picture mode
HDR
D File type
RAW
E Bracket
+ −
F Multiple shots
G Combine shots
H Final image

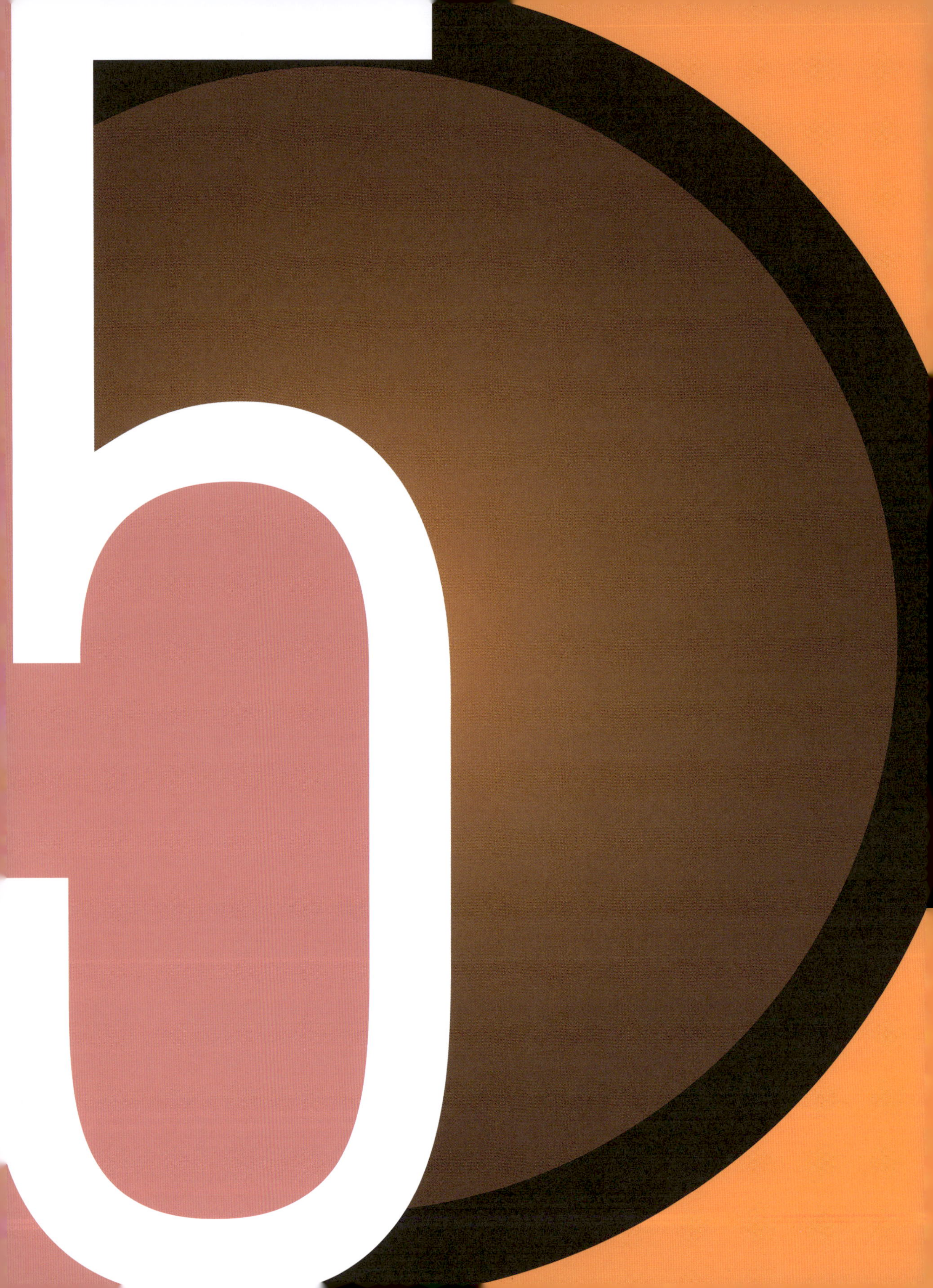

FILTERS

A FILTER IS A SHEET OF GLASS OR OPTICAL PLASTIC THAT AFFECTS ANY LIGHT THAT PASSES THROUGH THE FILTER.

This can be a change in the color of the light or a reduction in its intensity. Digital photography has made some types of filter redundant. Altering the color of an image can often be achieved more easily in postproduction than at the time of shooting. However, there are filters that are still invaluable and that are worth adding to a camera bag.

There are two main ways to fit a filter to a camera lens. Round filters screw directly to the filter thread on a lens. Square filters slot into a filter holder, which is fitted to the lens via an adapter ring screwed to the filter thread. Both methods have advantages and disadvantages. Because of this some photographers mix and match their filter types.

The big advantage of the round filter is its cost. The cost of buying a few useful round filters is far less than buying the equivalent square filters, particularly when you factor in the cost of the filter holder too. You can also leave round filters attached to your lenses. This means there is less set-up time if you use the same filter on a regular basis. Round filters are usually robust too: the metal ring that surrounds the filter offers some protection to the glass of the filter.

The downside to the round filter is simple: there is a wide range of filter thread sizes found on lenses (from a minuscule 30.5mm all the way up to a massive 127mm). If you own two or more lenses you may find yourself needing to buy the same filter in different sizes more than once.

Square filters and their filter holders are an initially more expensive option than round filters. However, once you have invested in a filter holder, the cost for every subsequent filter will seem easier to bear. The adapter rings needed to fit the holder to a lens are generally easily obtainable and cheap. If you own multiple lenses, each with a different filter thread size, the cost saving compared to owning many round filters can be considerable. There are also some types of filters that are only usable in square form, such as neutral density (ND) graduated filters. The disadvantages to square filters are their size and relative fragility compared to round filters. Square filters have no metal surround so it is all too easy to drop a square filter and chip it or even smash it entirely.

Filters aren't necessary for all types of photography, though. Photographers who mainly shoot portraits seldom need to use filters, for example, and nor do many photographers who enjoy shooting macro images. However, for certain genres of photography, filters are almost essential. Landscape photography is one such area, as it often involves shooting in less-than-ideal light.

Filter Thread Sizes

There is a wide range of filter thread sizes used on different lenses from different manufacturers. Most lens makers tend to have one "main" filter thread size that's common to a lot of their lenses, but it will not extend through their entire range: lenses with a large maximum aperture typically demand larger diameters, for example.

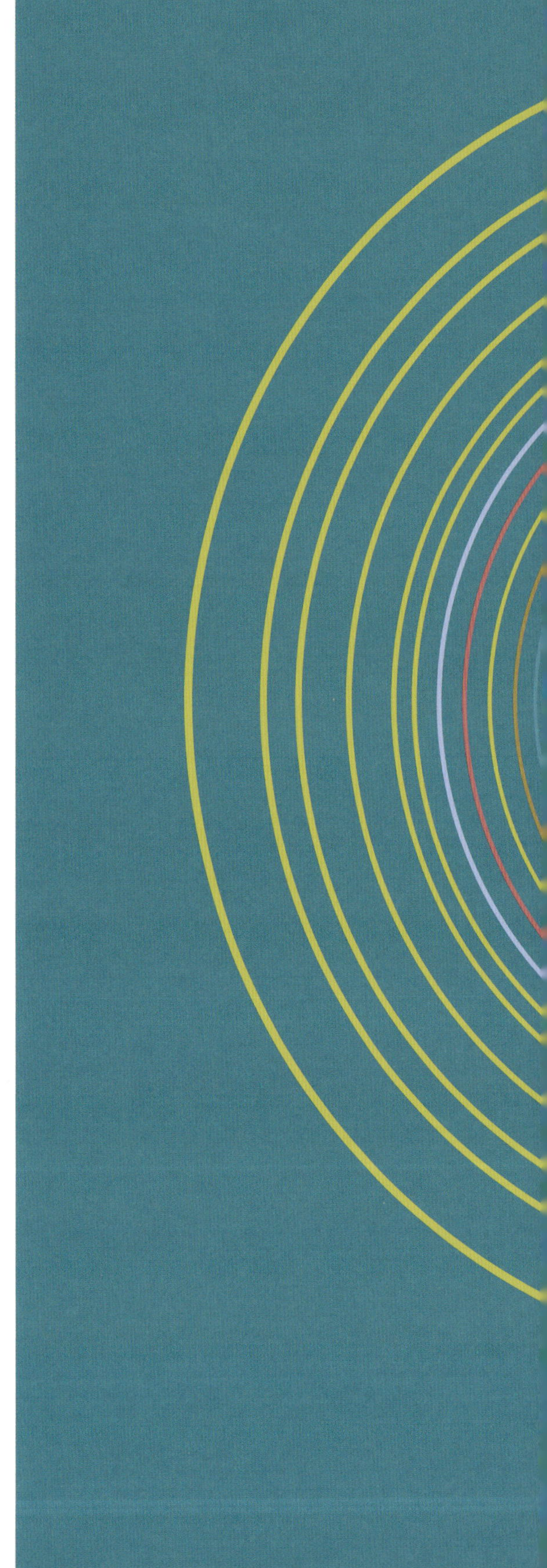

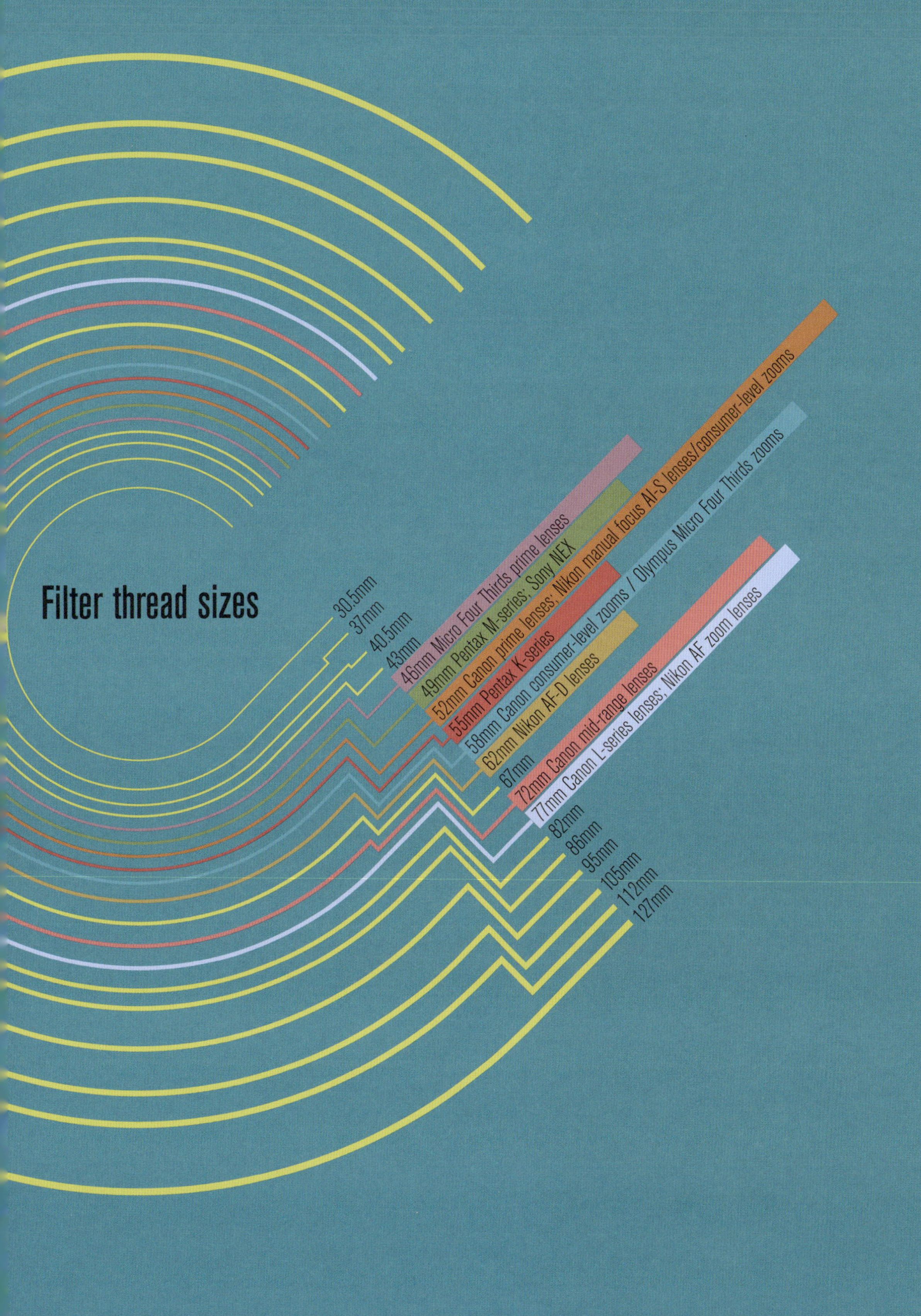

Filter thread sizes
30.5mm
37mm
40.5mm
43mm
46mm Micro Four Thirds prime lenses
49mm Pentax M-series; Sony NEX
52mm Canon prime lenses; Nikon manual focus AI-S lenses/consumer-level zooms
55mm Pentax K-series
58mm Canon consumer-level zooms / Olympus Micro Four Thirds zooms
62mm Nikon AF-D lenses
67mm
72mm Canon mid-range lenses
77mm Canon L-series lenses; Nikon AF zoom lenses
82mm
86mm
95mm
105mm
112mm
127mm

Filter Holder Sizes

There are a number of different filter holder systems to choose from, and these determine the size of the filters you can use. In turn, this influences what camera systems and lenses are compatible without the need to use stepping rings.

It's possible to adapt a filter so that it fits a lens with a different thread size through the use of a stepping ring. A "step-up" ring lets you fit a filter to a lens with a smaller thread size, while a "step-down" ring lets you fit a filter to a lens with a larger thread size.

The main drawback to using a step-down ring is the increased risk of mechanical vignetting. This is seen in an image as darkened corners caused by the stepping ring or filter intruding into the picture space.

Filter holder sizes

● Filter holder size

○ Filter adaptor ring sizes

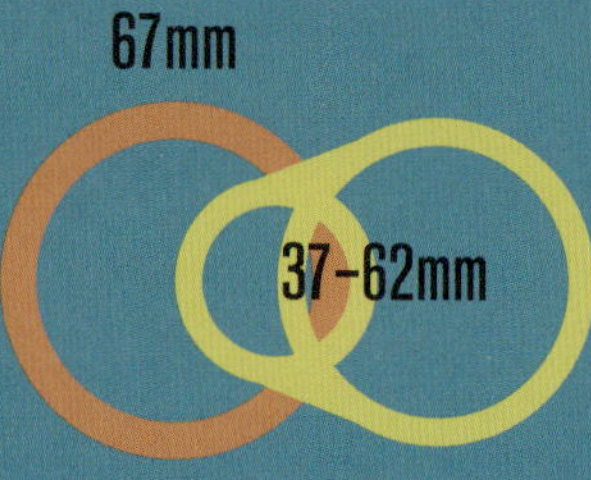

Suitable for: Compact cameras

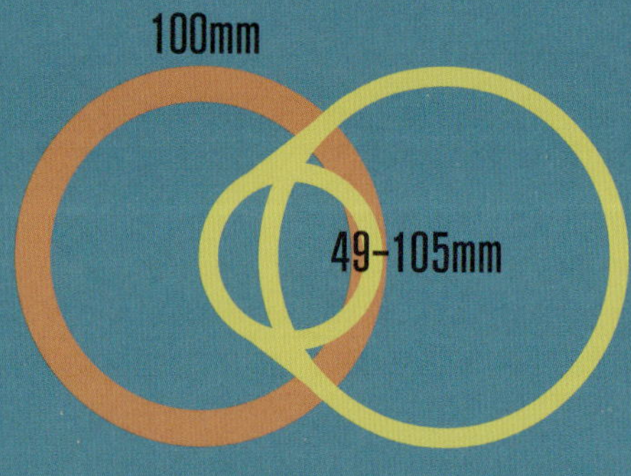

Suitable for: Mirrorless/DSLR

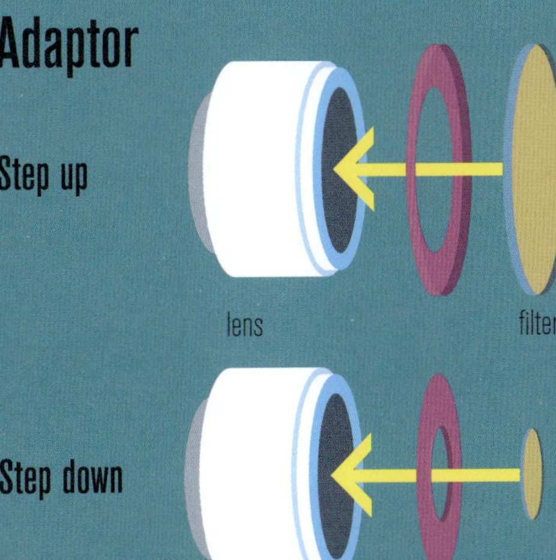

Adaptor
Step up
Step down
lens
filter

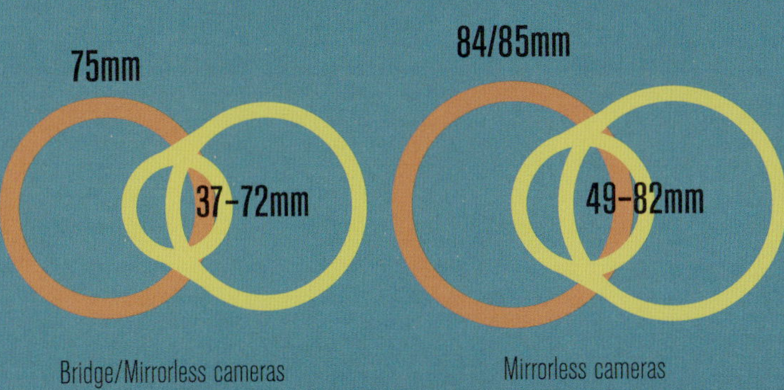

75mm
84/85mm
37–72mm
49–82mm
Bridge/Mirrorless cameras
Mirrorless cameras

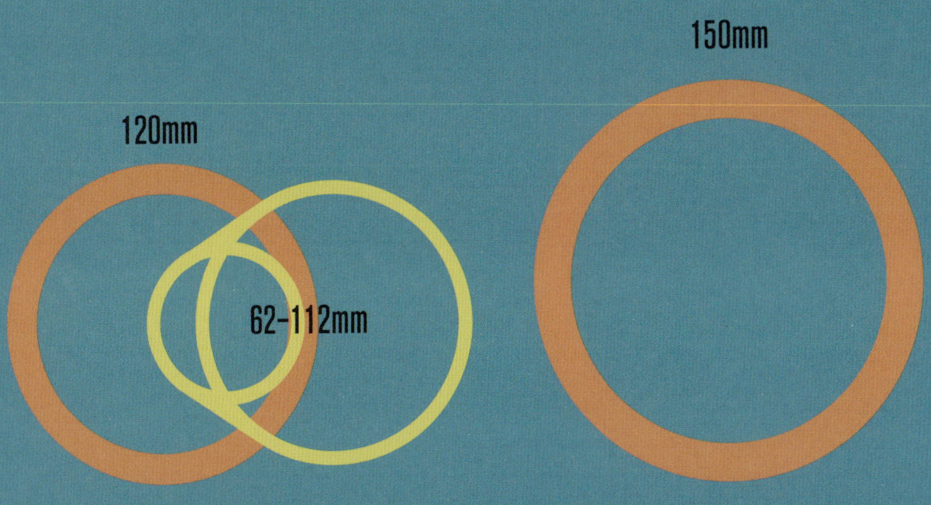

150mm
120mm
62–112mm
DSLR/Medium format
Wide-angle lenses with projecting front lens elements

Filter Types

There are five main filter types, each used for a specific purpose. It's possible to mix and match filters to achieve several different corrections or effects in an image.

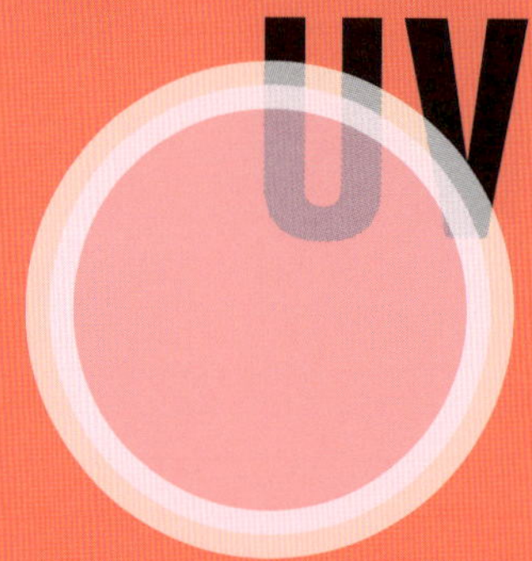

UV/skylight

Compensates for the blue cast of ultraviolet light. As they have no effect on exposure, UV and skylight filters are often fitted to protect the front elements of a lens.

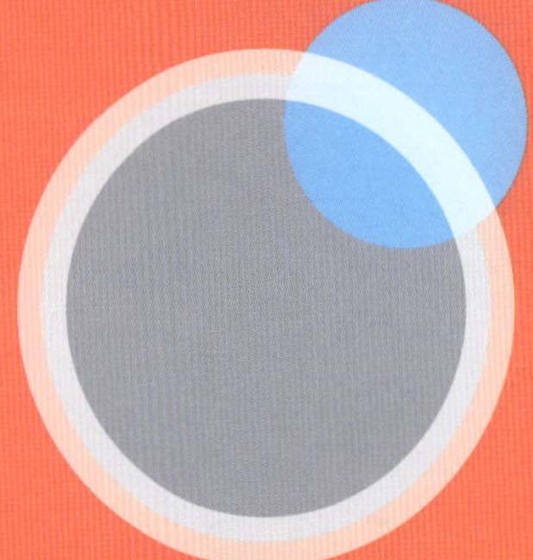

Neutral density (ND)

Reduces the amount of light reaching the sensor. Used for exposure control. Graduated ND filters are used to balance the exposure across an image.

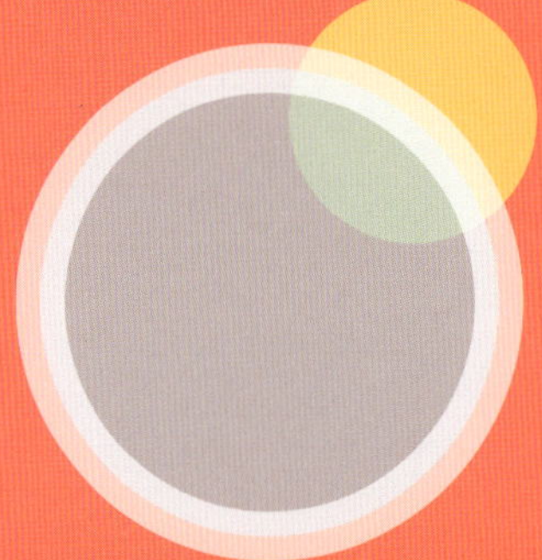

Polarizing filter

Reduces glare on non-metallic surfaces and deepens the blue of sky.

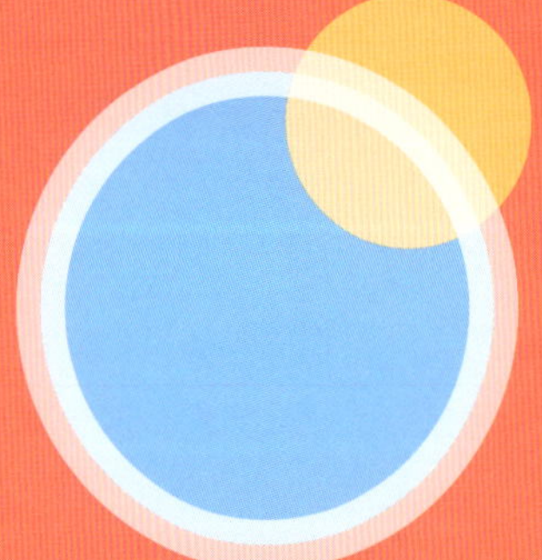

Color correction

Used to neutralize the color temperature of a light source. In digital photography this can now be achieved by adjusting white balance.

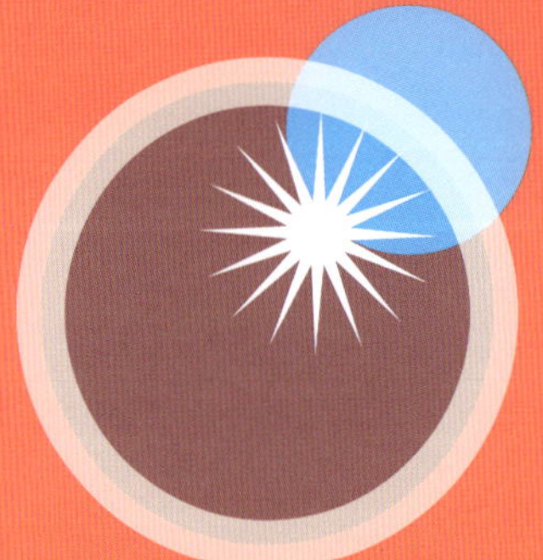

Effect

Creates an effect that would not be possible to achieve in-camera without the use of a filter, such as soft-focus or star-burst.

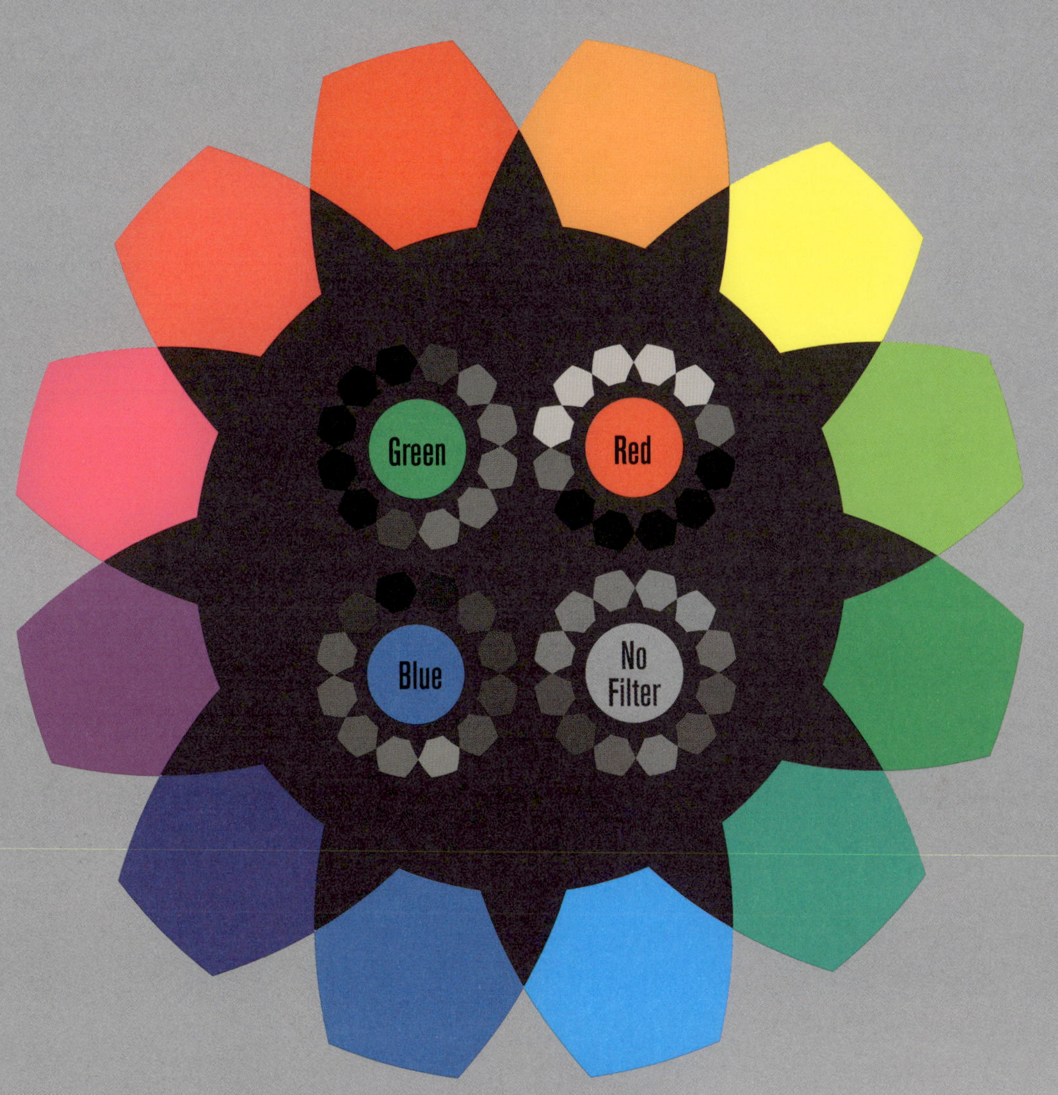

Plain color filters

Plain colored filters help to separate colors with the same reflectivity in a black-and-white image. A colored filter lightens colors similar to itself and darkens those colors that sit on the opposite side of a color wheel.

Filter Factors

The more dense and opaque a filter is, the less light reaches the camera's sensor. This means that an increase in exposure is often necessary when using filters: the filter factor tells you what adjustment is required.

When an automatic (or semi-automatic) exposure mode is used, your camera will adjust the exposure automatically to compensate for any filter you fit. However, in Manual exposure mode you need to remember to adjust the exposure yourself to avoid underexposed results.

This diagram shows how much exposure adjustment in stops (the figure within the orange circle) will need to be made when a particular filter type is fitted to a camera. If more than one filter is fitted (such as a polarizer and ND 0.3), add all the relevant figures together to calculate the exposure adjustment.

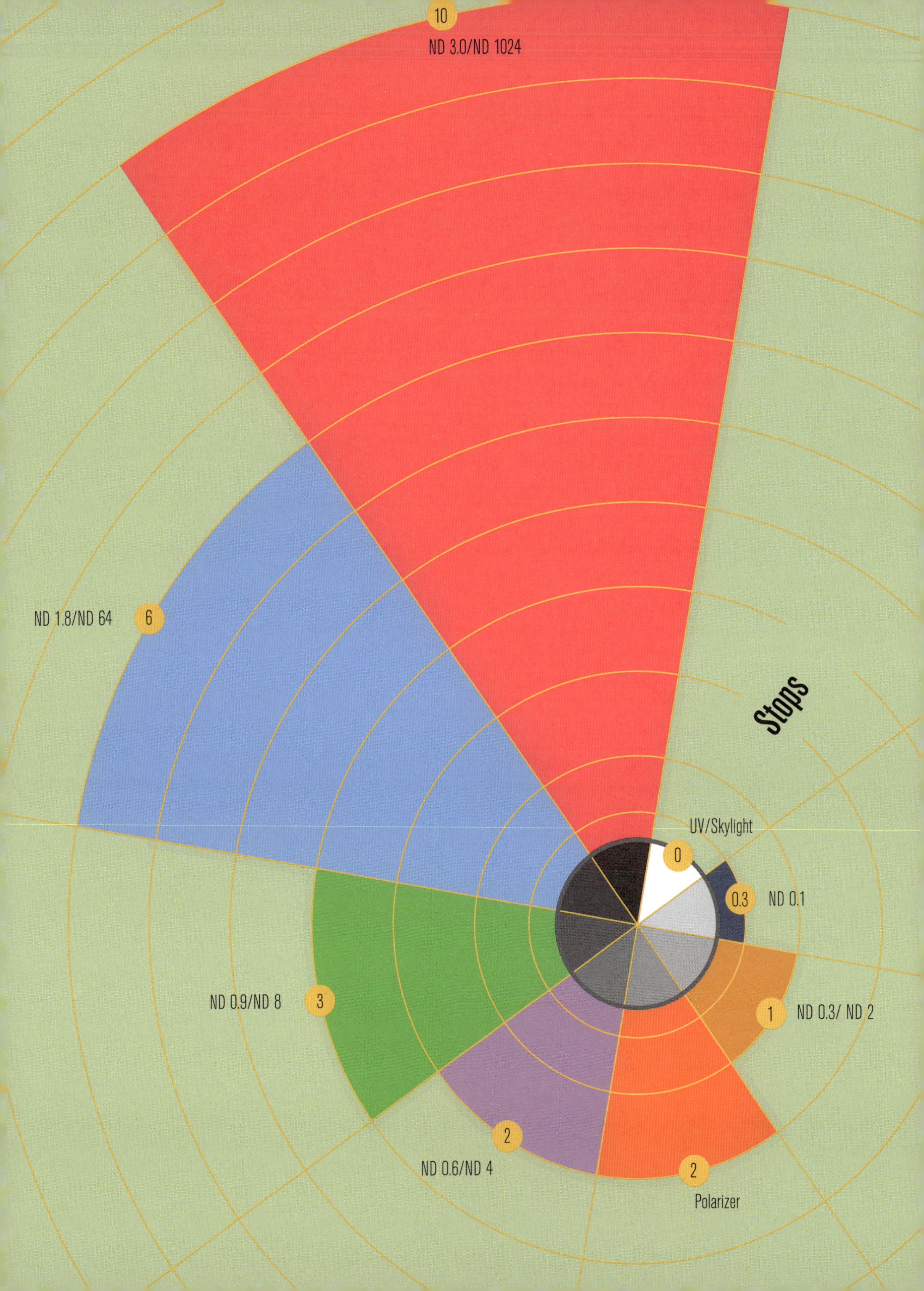

10
ND 3.0/ND 1024
ND 1.8/ND 64
6
Stops
UV/Skylight
0
0.3
ND 0.1
ND 0.9/ND 8
3
1
ND 0.3/ ND 2
2
ND 0.6/ND 4
2
Polarizer

Neutral Density Filters

Neutral density (ND) filters are designed to reduce the amount of light reaching the sensor inside the camera. This means you can use either a slower shutter speed or a wider aperture to create a particular effect.

Graduated ND filters

A close relation of the ND filter is the graduated ND filter (or "ND grad"). ND grads have a semi-opaque top half and a clear bottom half and are used to balance exposure across an image. They are available in different strengths, such as 1-, 2-, or 3-stops, and you would usually have a selection of different ones, as the greater the difference in exposure between two halves of an image, the stronger the filter you would need to use. ND grad filters can also be bought either with a soft or hard transition between the semi-opaque and clear areas: soft ND graduated filters are ideal when there is an irregular boundary between the dark and light areas in a scene.

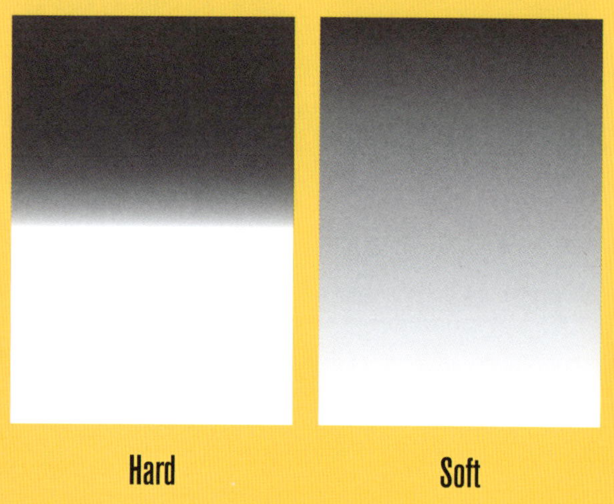

The outer orange wheel in this diagram shows the range of shutter speeds, measured in thousandths of a second, seconds (''), minutes ('), and hours. The four inner wheels show the adjustment to the shutter speed that will need to be made when an ND filter of a particular strength is fitted to a camera.

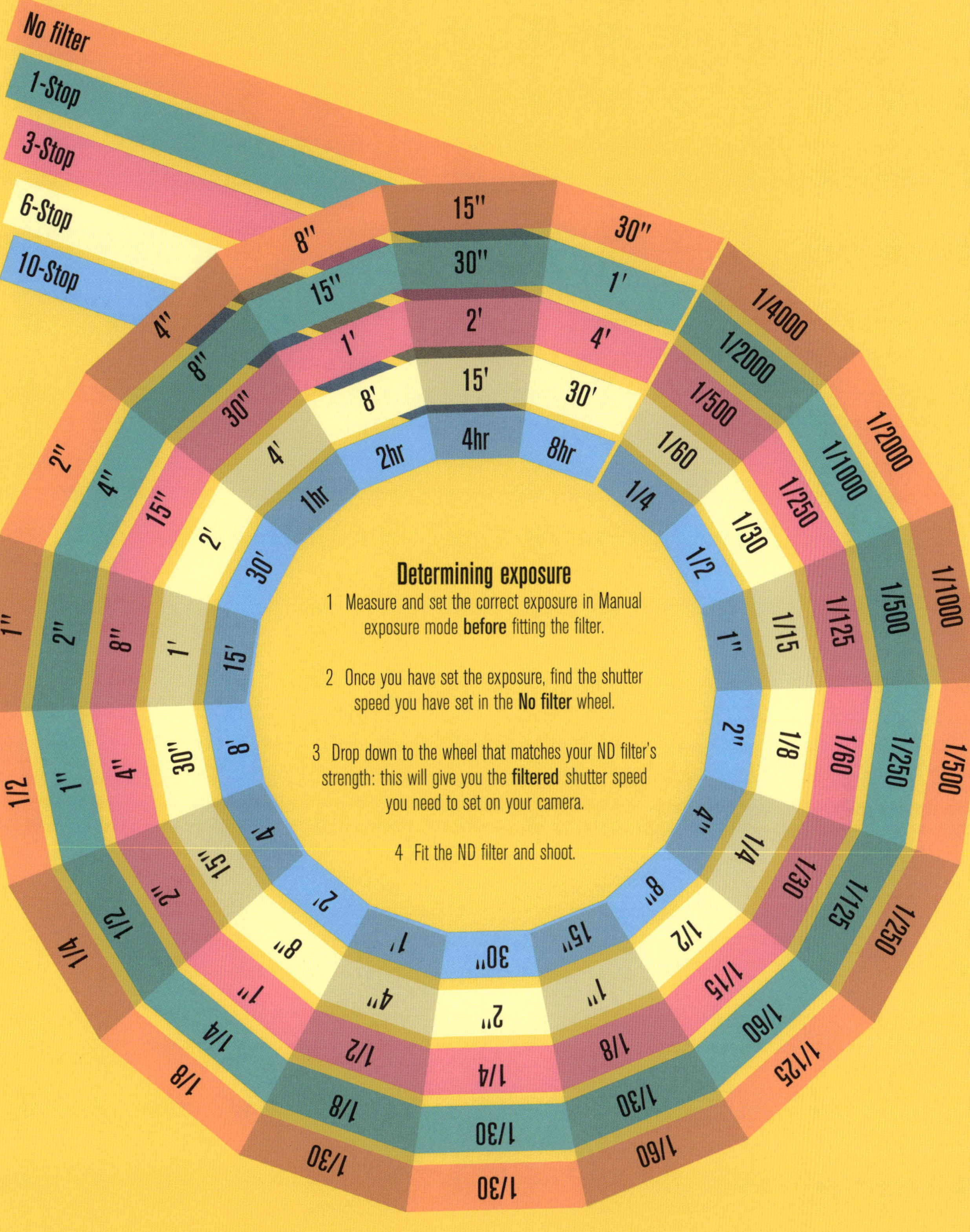
No filter
1-Stop
3-Stop
6-Stop
10-Stop

Determining exposure

1 Measure and set the correct exposure in Manual exposure mode before fitting the filter.

2 Once you have set the exposure, find the shutter speed you have set in the No filter wheel.

3 Drop down to the wheel that matches your ND filter's strength: this will give you the filtered shutter speed you need to set on your camera.

4 Fit the ND filter and shoot.

Polarizing Filters

A polarizing filter controls the plane of polarization of light that passes through the filter. It's not necessary to understand the science of how the filter works, but it is useful to know what it does: it can cut out reflections on non-metallic surfaces, letting you see through any glare, and it can also deepen the blue of skies. However, in both instances the filter only works at a narrow range of angles. An adjustment ring on the filter lets you rotate it and vary the strength of the effect.

Reducing glare and reflections

Polarizing filters work best to reduce reflections when they're at an angle of approximately 35º. Note that polarizing filters won't cut out reflections when aimed directly at a non-metallic surface.

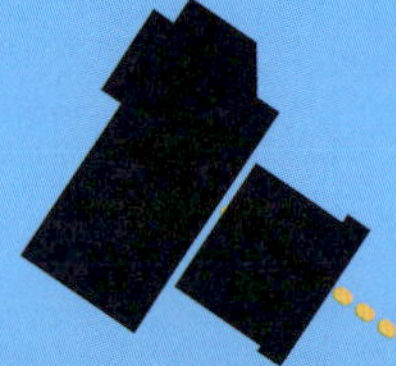

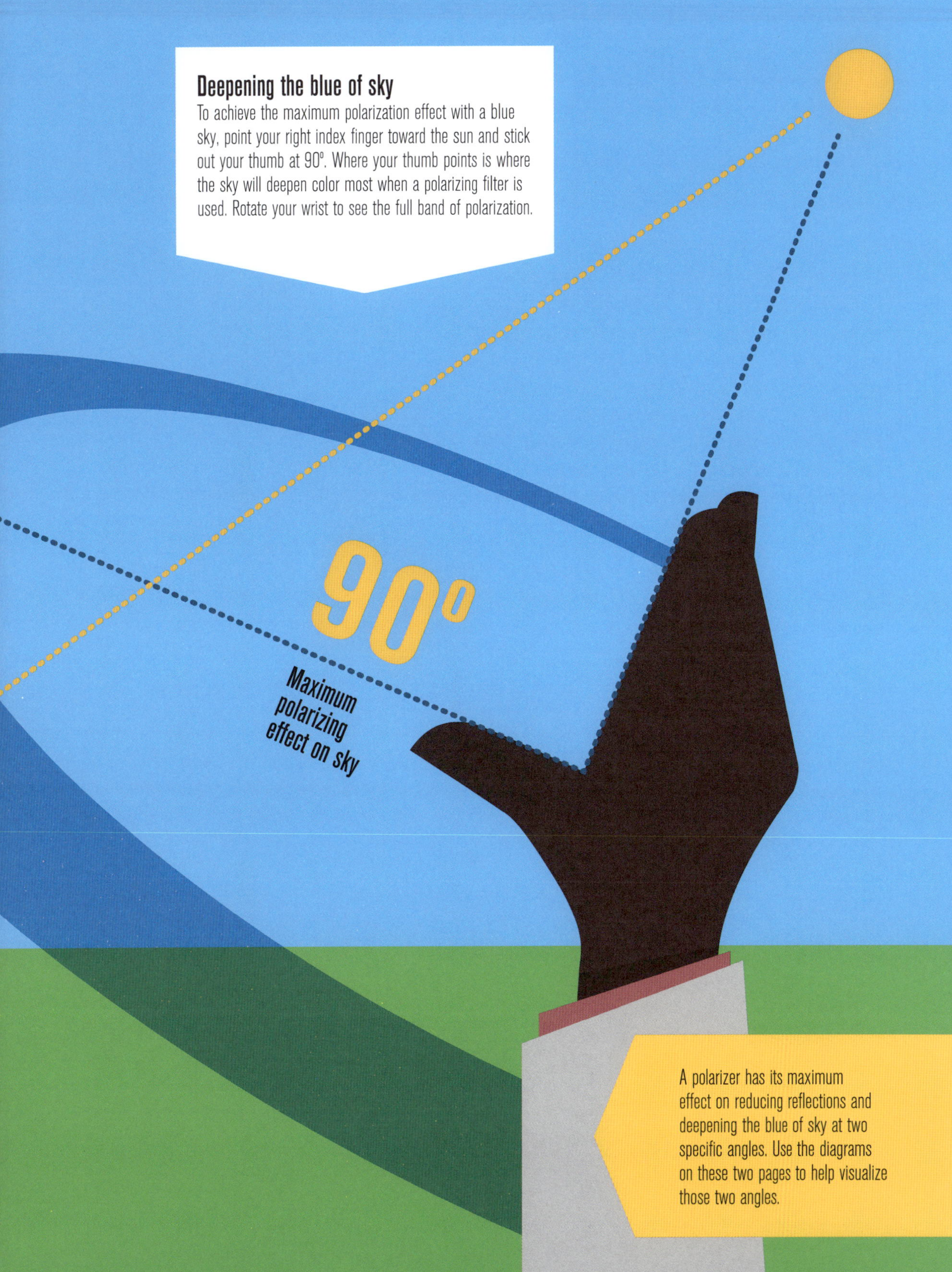

Deepening the blue of sky
To achieve the maximum polarization effect with a blue sky, point your right index finger toward the sun and stick out your thumb at 90º. Where your thumb points is where the sky will deepen color most when a polarizing filter is used. Rotate your wrist to see the full band of polarization.

90º
Maximum polarizing effect on sky

A polarizer has its maximum effect on reducing reflections and deepening the blue of sky at two specific angles. Use the diagrams on these two pages to help visualize those two angles.

Black & White

Most cameras let you switch to a black-and-white (or monochrome) picture parameter. If you use colored filters you can adjust the tonal range of your images as described previously. However, most cameras have options that mimic the effects of colored filters, making the use of physical filters unnecessary. Another way to create black-and-white images is to convert color images in postproduction. In many ways this is the best option of all, as you'll have greater scope for adjusting the tonal range.

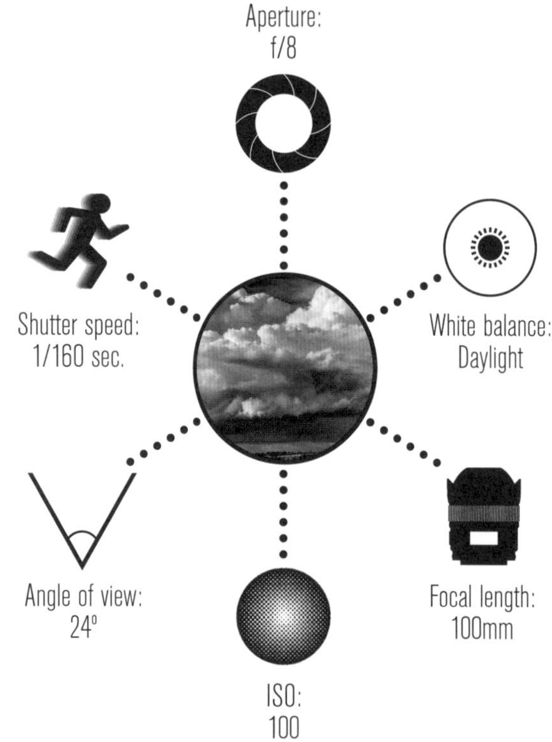

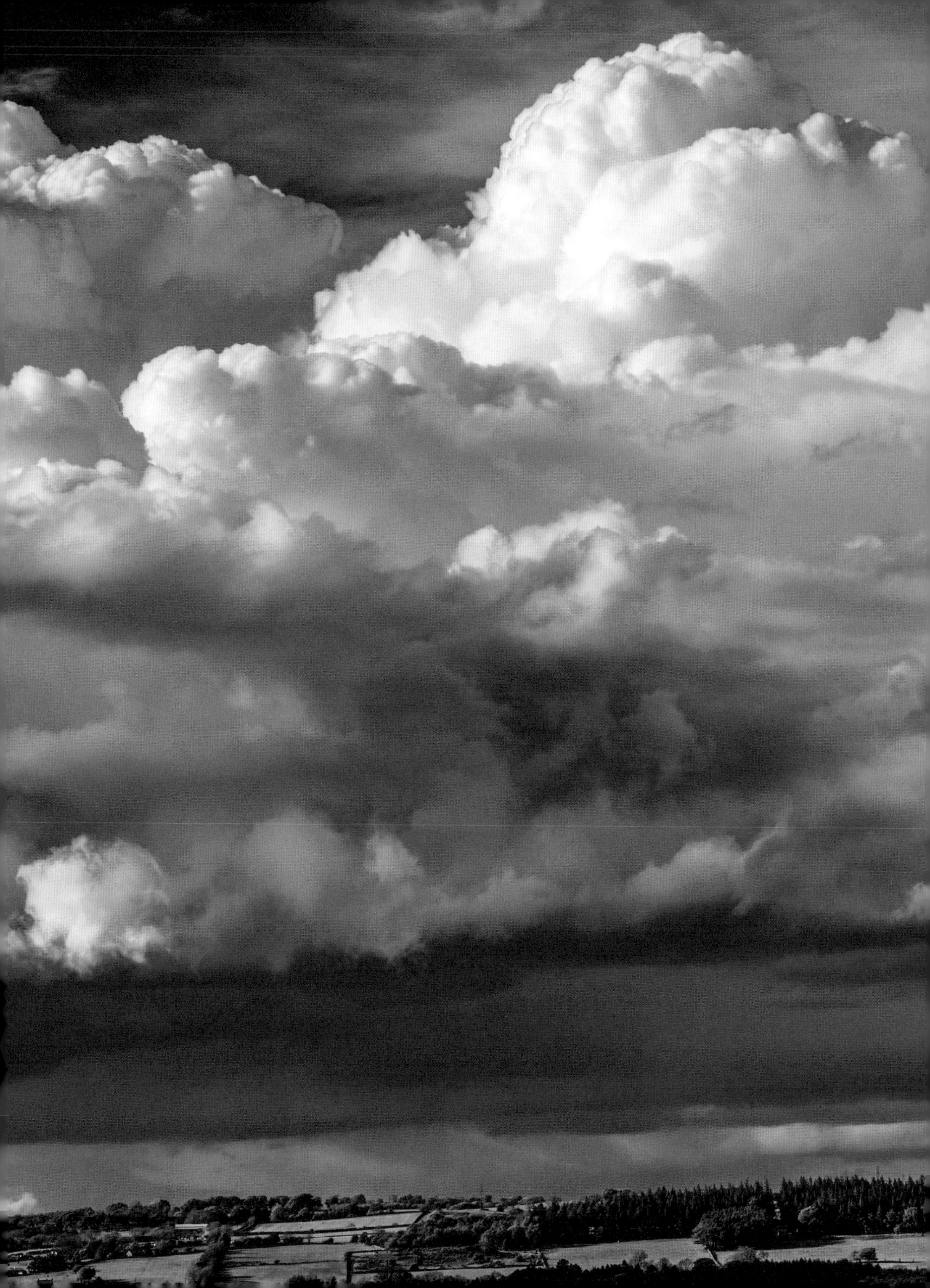

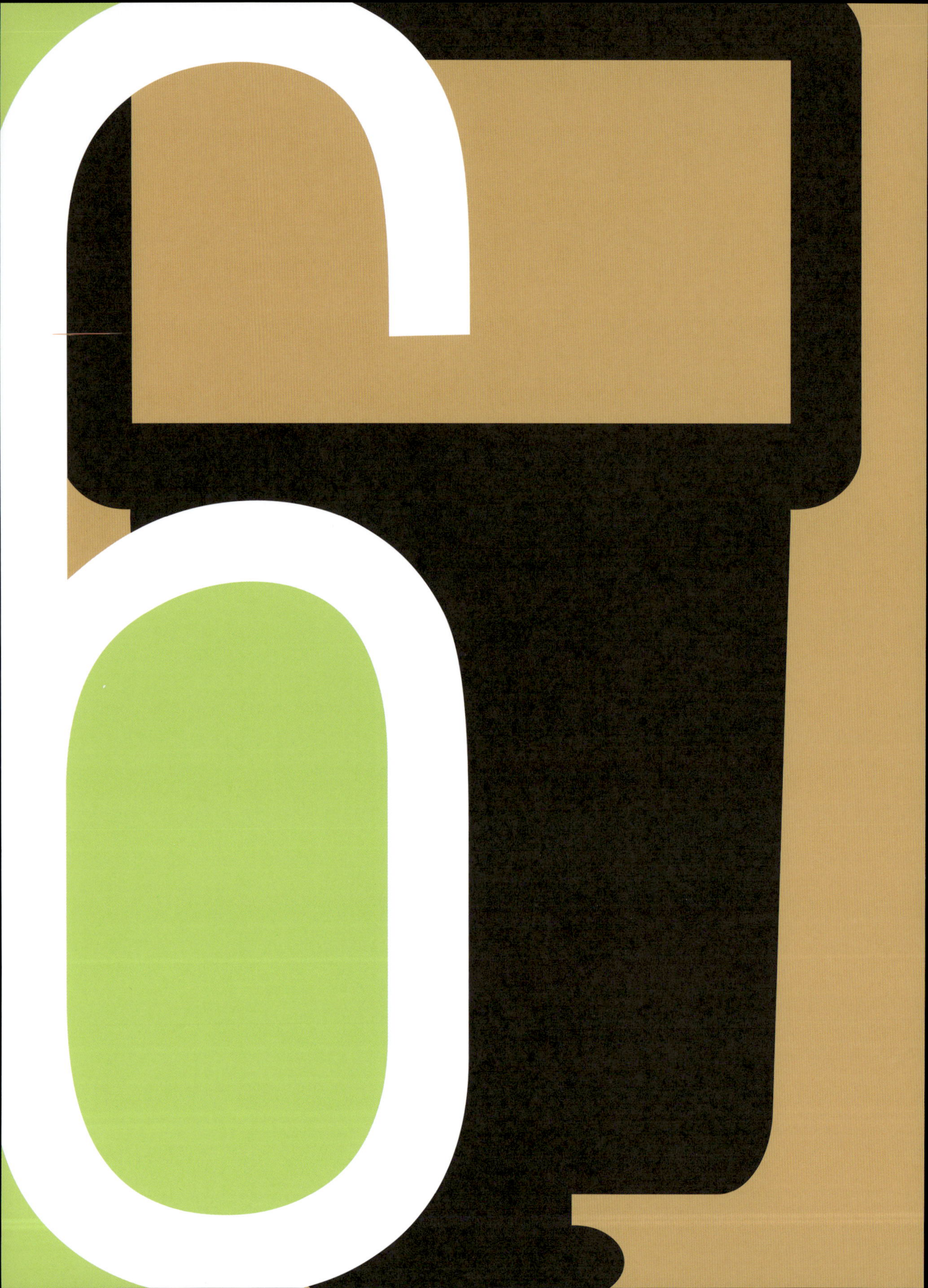

FLASH

THERE ARE TIMES WHEN EXTRA LIGHT NEEDS TO BE ADDED TO A SCENE TO CREATE AN IMAGE THAT WORKS.

The most convenient way to add light is to use flash. Cameras often have built-in flashes or can fire an external flash via a hotshoe, but all flash units work in a similar way. The light-emitting head contains a flash tube. This is a xenon-filled chamber that emits a burst of light when an electrical charge is applied. The power for this charge comes from a capacitor, which is recharged by a battery once the flash has fired. However, this does not mean that a flash has to be fired at maximum power every time it is used: the power can be reduced to enable different aperture or ISO settings to be used. Cell phone cameras use LED's to provide the light for their flash.

There are two ways to set flash exposure: TTL and Manual. TTL stands for "through-the-lens," and is an automatic mode that leaves the flash exposure decisions to the camera. In TTL mode a pre-flash is fired when the shutter-release button is pressed down. This pre-flash is used to calculate the amount of flash illumination necessary for a satisfactory exposure. The power of the flash is then modified when the "main" exposure is made. When 1st curtain flash sync is used the main flash follows the pre-flash so quickly that they are essentially simultaneous. Although TTL is an automatic flash mode it is usually possible to override the exposure by applying flash exposure compensation.

Manual flash requires you to set flash exposure yourself based on the flash-to-subject distance, the aperture you want to use, and the flash's power. As manual flash exposure is more involved than TTL, it is more suited to a slower paced way of working, such as shooting in a studio rather than a social occasion. It can also help if you work with a handheld lightmeter that is capable of taking flash exposure readings.

Unlike a regular exposure, the shutter speed you use has no effect on flash exposure (although it will have an effect on the exposure of areas of a scene *not* lit by flash). However, both the aperture and ISO settings will have an effect on flash exposure, and the effective range of a flash can be increased by using a larger aperture or setting a higher ISO value. To reduce the effective range of a flash (which may be necessary if your subject is overexposed) you can decrease the size of the aperture or reduce the ISO value.

Inverse Square Law

When you fire a flash, the light spreads out from it. This means two things: the light covers a larger area the farther it travels, and the intensity of the light diminishes with distance. How these things happen is governed by a law of physics known as the "inverse square law," which states that the intensity of a point light source (such as a flash) is inversely proportional to the square of the distance (or $1/\text{distance}^2$). Or, to put it more simply, an object one measurement unit away from the flash will receive four times more light than an object at twice the distance.

The practical implications of the inverse square law is that a flash has to emit more light to successfully illuminate objects that are further away. However, flashes don't have unlimited power, so beyond a certain distance it will be impossible to illuminate an object. At this point, the object is said to be beyond the effective range of the flash.

At twice the distance from the flash, light is spread over four times the area. This means that for a specific area of coverage the intensity of the light falling on that area is quartered.

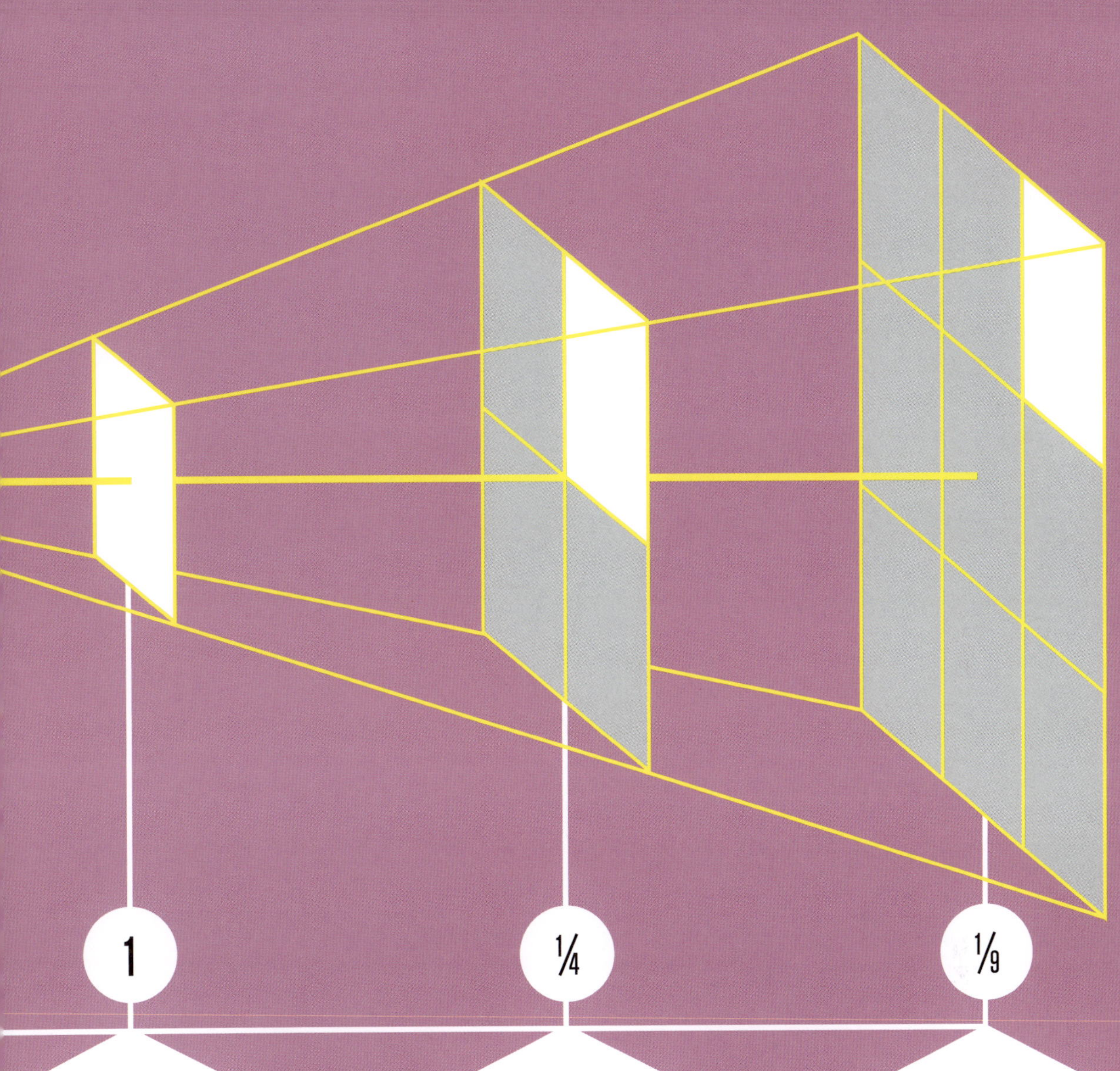

1
¼
⅑
DISTANCE = 1
BRIGHTNESS = 1
100%
0 stops difference
DISTANCE = 2
BRIGHTNESS = 1/4
25%
-2 stops difference
DISTANCE = 3
BRIGHTNESS = 1/9
11%
-3.17 (-3) stops difference

Guide Numbers

The guide number (or GN) of a flash indicates its power to throw light over a distance measured in meters or feet: the higher the guide number, the more powerful it is. The GN can be used to calculate either the effective range of the flash at a particular aperture, or the aperture needed to illuminate a subject at a given distance (using the formulae below).

The ISO setting you use also has an effect on the effective range of your flashgun. As you increase the ISO the effective range of the flashgun also increases. Use the graphics on the following two spreads to calculate the effective range of a flashgun by matching the GN of your flashgun to the aperture and ISO setting you've selected on your camera.

$$\text{Aperture} = \frac{\text{GN}}{\text{distance}}$$

$$\text{Distance} = \frac{\text{GN}}{\text{aperture}}$$

The diagrams on this and the following page shows the effective flash distance for flashguns with four different guide numbers: 12, 27, 43 and 60. To use the diagram find the guide number that matches (or is close to) your flashgun. Select an ISO setting and follow the distance scale across until you find the required aperture to work out the effective distance of the flash at these settings.

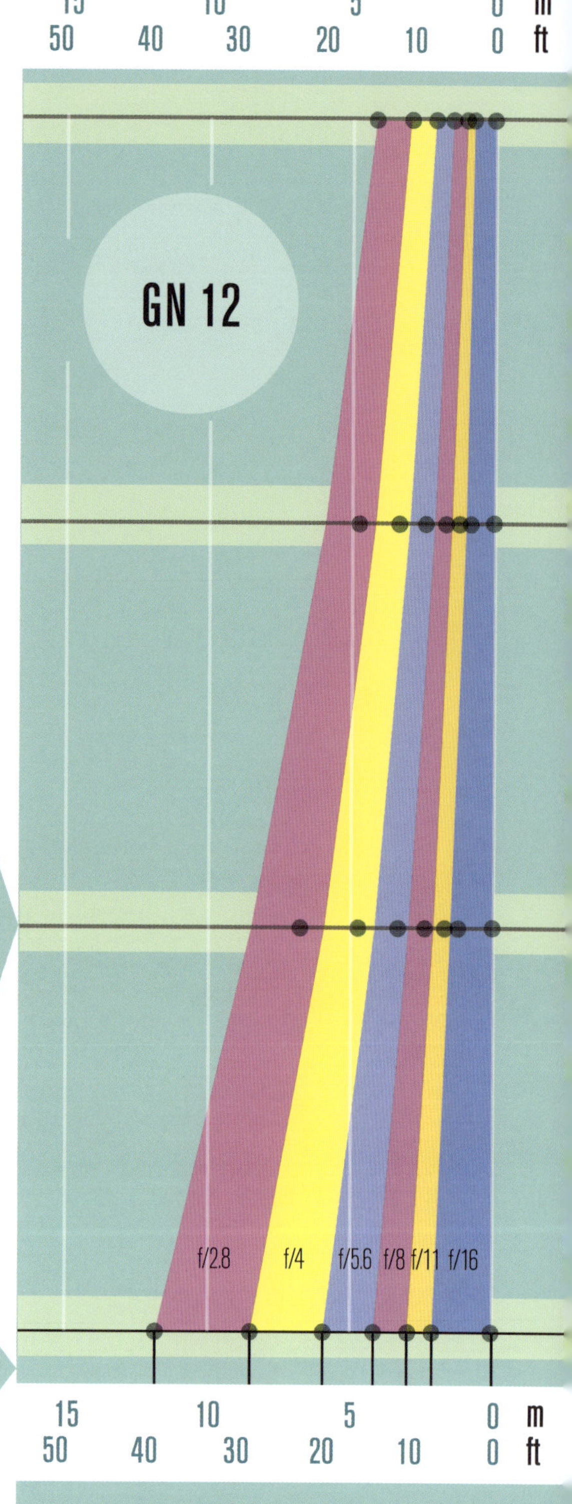

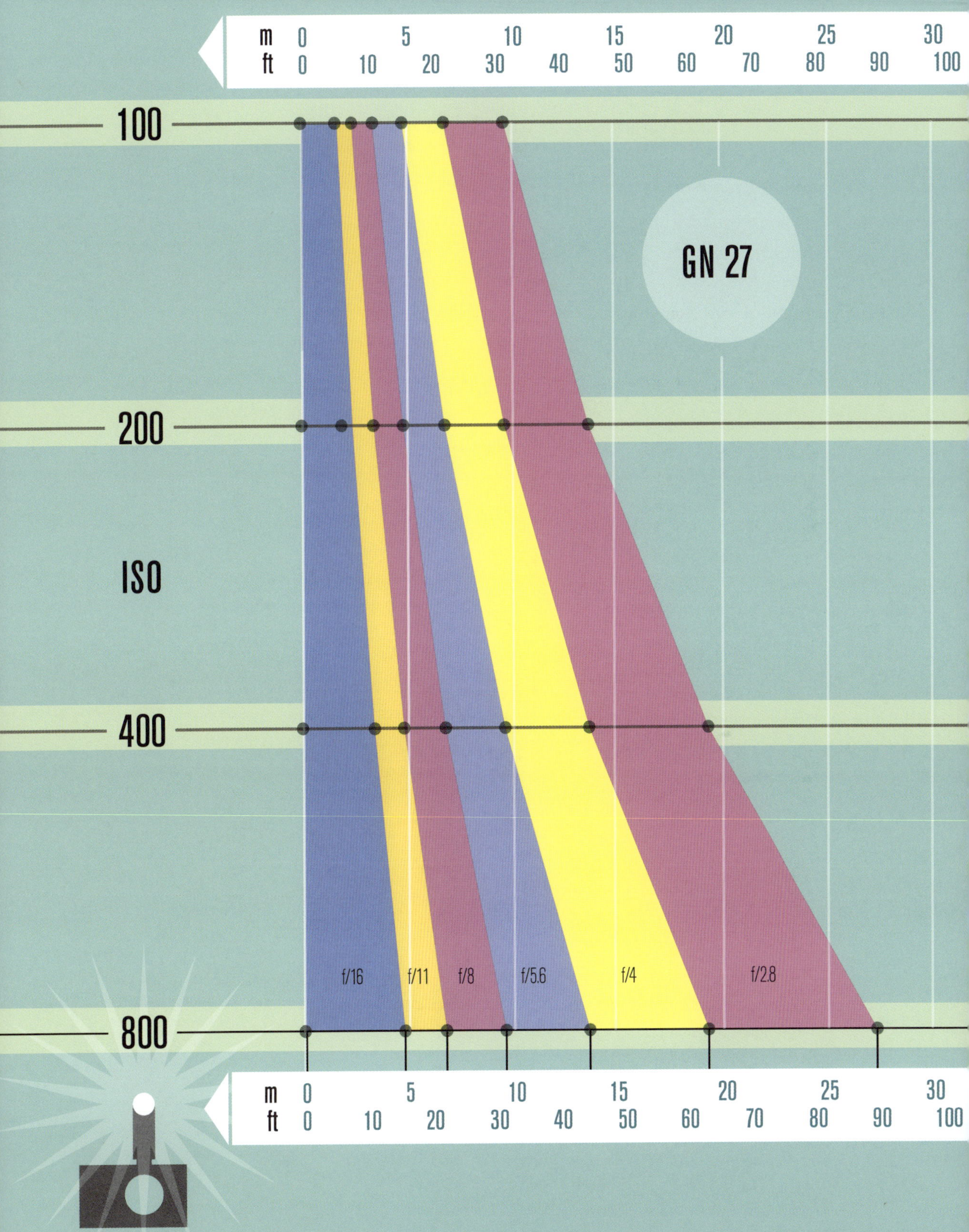

m
ft
0
0
5
10
10
20
15
30
20
40
25
50
30
60
70
80
90
100
100
200
ISO
400
800
GN 27
f/16
f/11
f/8
f/5.6
f/4
f/2.8

Guide Numbers II

Guide numbers are more important when you want to manually set flash exposure. In TTL mode, as long as your subject is within the effective range of the flash at a given aperture, the camera will calculate the amount of flash light needed for a satisfactory exposure. If you own a smartphone then there are apps that will make flash exposure calculation a far less painful affair.

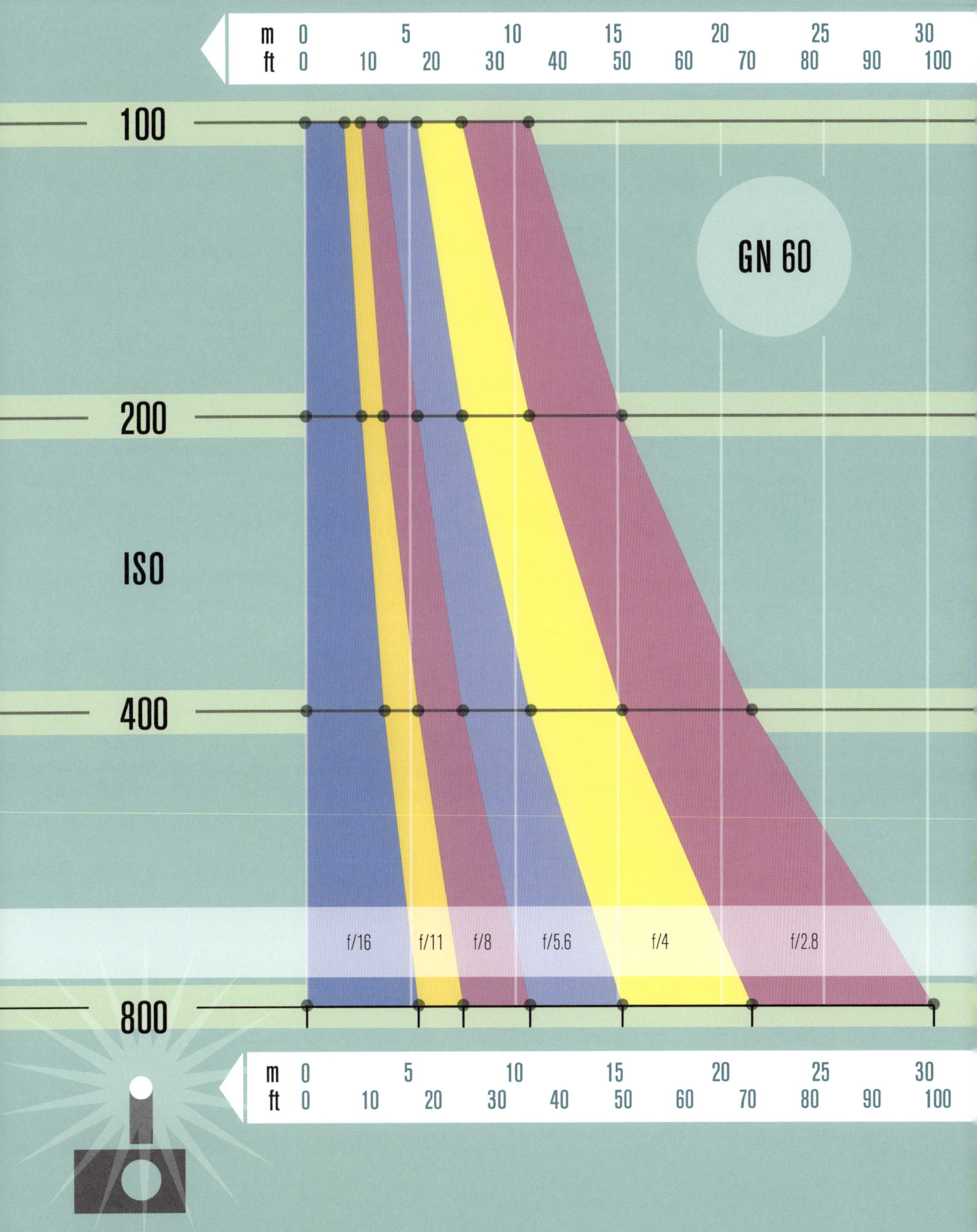

m 0 5 10 15 20 25 30
ft 0 10 20 30 40 50 60 70 80 90 100
100
200
ISO
400
800
GN 60
f/16 f/11 f/8 f/5.6 f/4 f/2.8
m 0 5 10 15 20 25 30
ft 0 10 20 30 40 50 60 70 80 90 100

Flash Sync Speed

The flash sync speed is the fastest shutter speed possible on a camera with a focal plane shutter. The flash sync speed varies between camera models but is typically in the region of 1/160–1/250 sec. If a shutter speed faster than the sync speed is selected, the image will only be partially lit by light from the flash.

Flash only illuminates the entire frame when the sensor is exposed to light in its entirety. This only happens at the sync speed, or at shutter speeds longer than the sync speed.

When the shutter speed is faster than the sync speed, only a small section of the sensor is exposed to light from the flash.

This diagram shows why shooting at the sync speed or slower is necessary with standard flash. It's only when the camera is shooting at the sync speed or slower that sensor is fully exposed to light from the flash. When a shutter speed faster than the sync speed is used the sensor is never totally exposed to light from the flash at any point during the exposure.

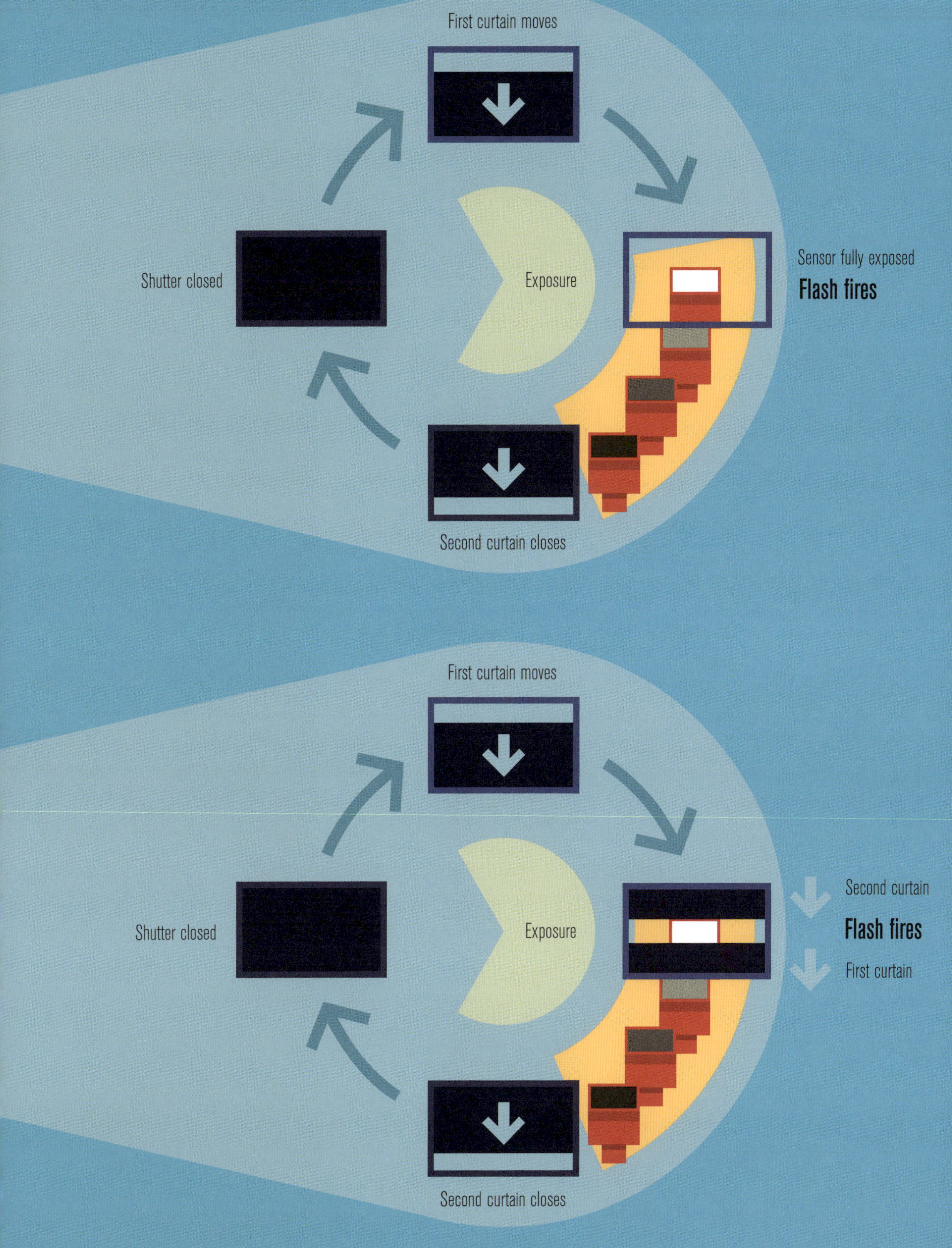

First curtain moves
Shutter closed
Exposure
Sensor fully exposed
Flash fires
Second curtain closes
First curtain moves
Shutter closed
Exposure
Second curtain
Flash fires
First curtain
Second curtain closes

Slow Sync Speed

It isn't necessary to use the camera's sync speed every time flash is used. In fact, in many situations it's preferable to use a slower shutter speed, as this allows you to set the exposure for areas of a scene that are *not* illuminated by the light from the flash. In this scene, the foreground was lit using two off-camera flashes, which were hidden from view of the camera. The shutter was held open for 30 seconds, which was long enough to record the stars in the sky above.

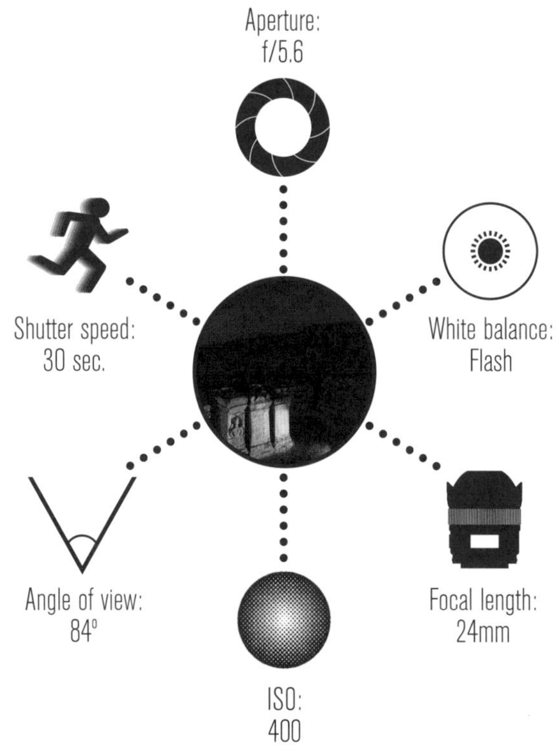

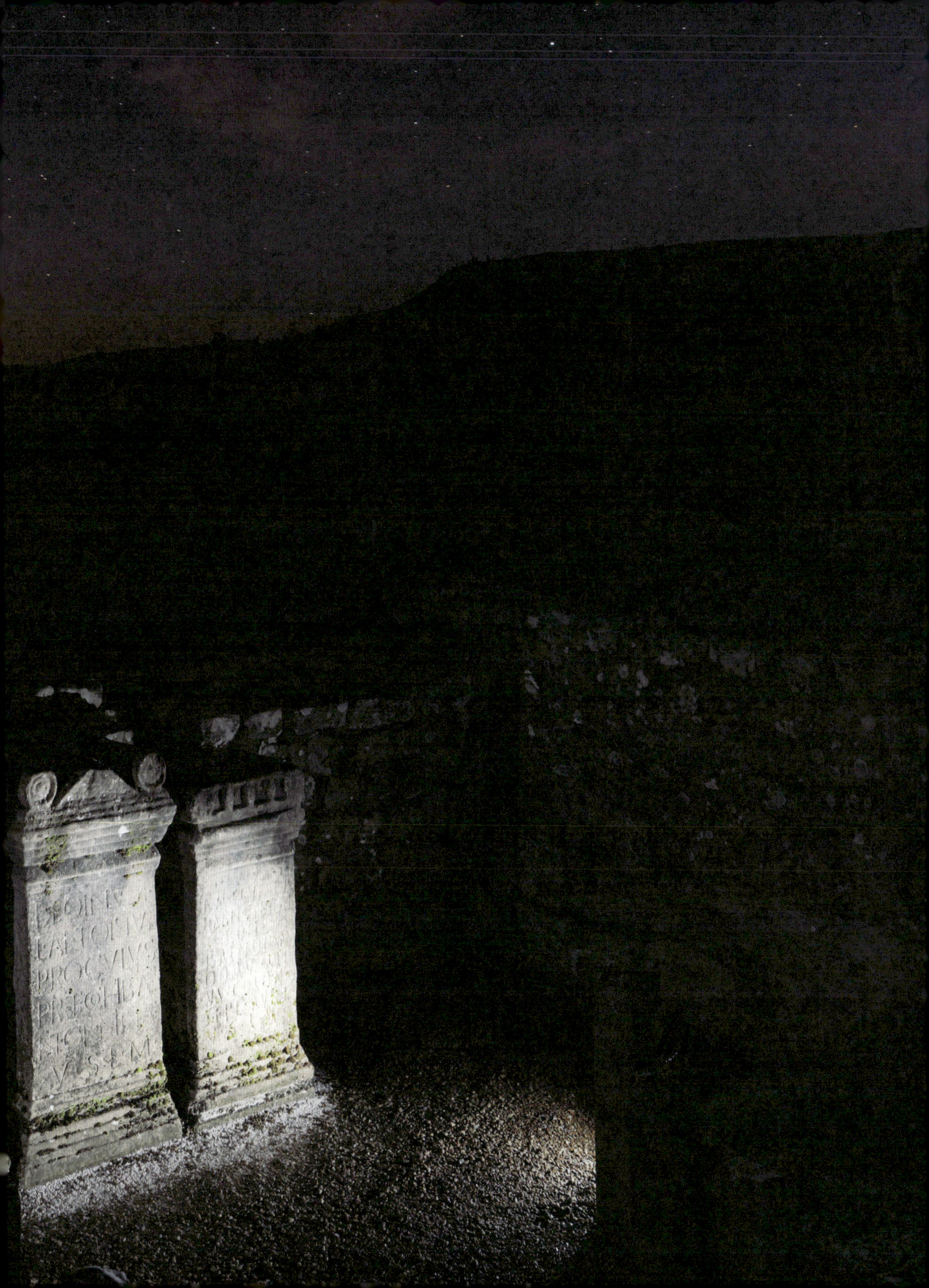

Flash Curtain Sync

A flash can fire either at the start of an exposure (*first curtain sync*) or at the end (*second curtain sync*). Generally, there's little visual difference between the two settings unless you're shooting something that's moving across the image. In that situation, the curtain sync is very important, particularly when it is combined with a slow shutter speed.

Of the two modes, second curtain sync produces the more natural effect. However, when shooting in automatic exposure modes the camera typically defaults to first curtain sync and cannot be altered.

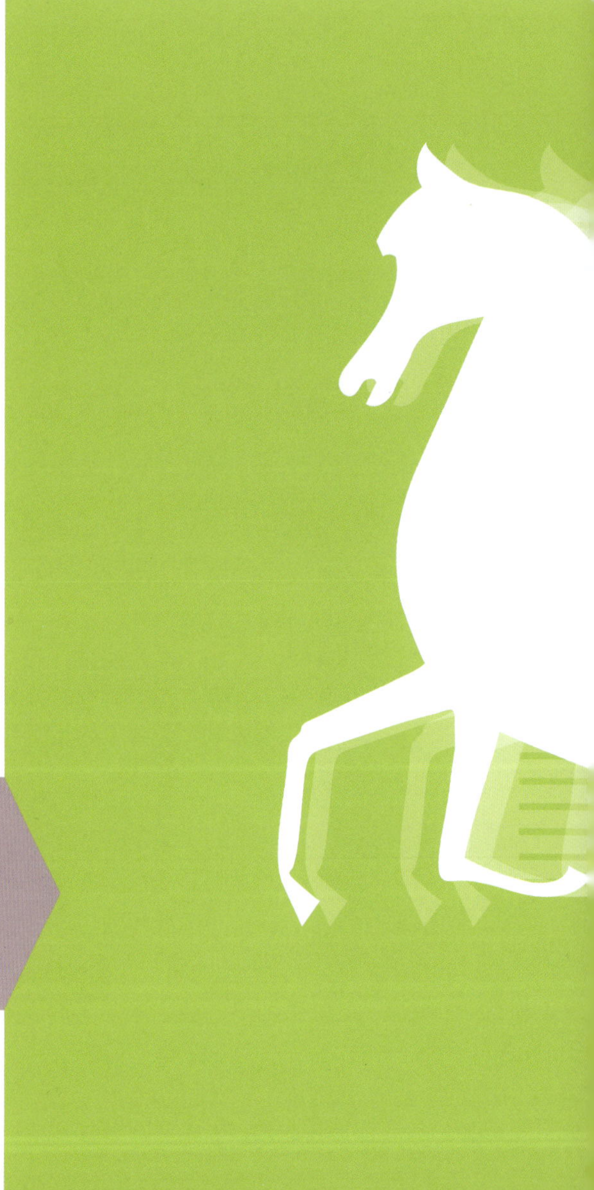

First curtain synchronization
Flash fires at start of exposure
Motion blur in front of subject

The light from the flash has frozen the movement of the horse in these two images. The blurred trail in front of and behind the horse shows how it would be captured during a long exposure when using first curtain and second curtain sync respectively.

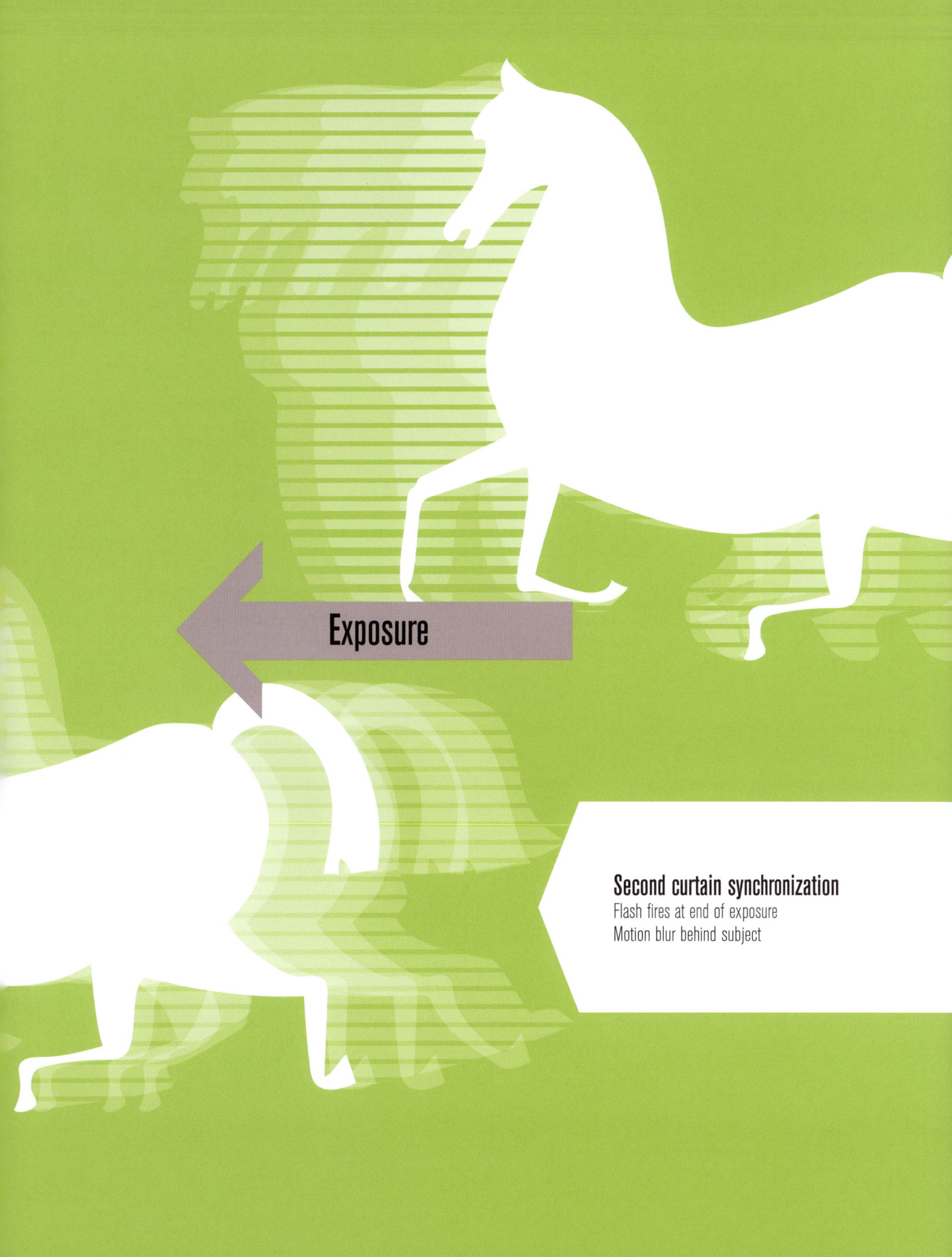

Exposure
Second curtain synchronization
Flash fires at end of exposure
Motion blur behind subject

High-Speed Sync

Usually, the camera's sync speed determines the fastest shutter speed that can be used with flash. This can make it difficult to use flash as a fill-light when you're shooting in bright conditions, but some flash units overcome this by offering a "high-speed synchronization" (or "HSS") mode. HSS works by "pulsing" the light from the flash during the exposure, so it effectively becomes a continuous light source. This allows the flash to be used with any shutter speed, no matter how fast, although the effective range of the flash is reduced.

This diagram shows how an HSS flashgun constantly pulses light during an exposure faster than a camera's sync speed. This allows the flashgun to evenly illuminate the image across the sensor during the exposure.

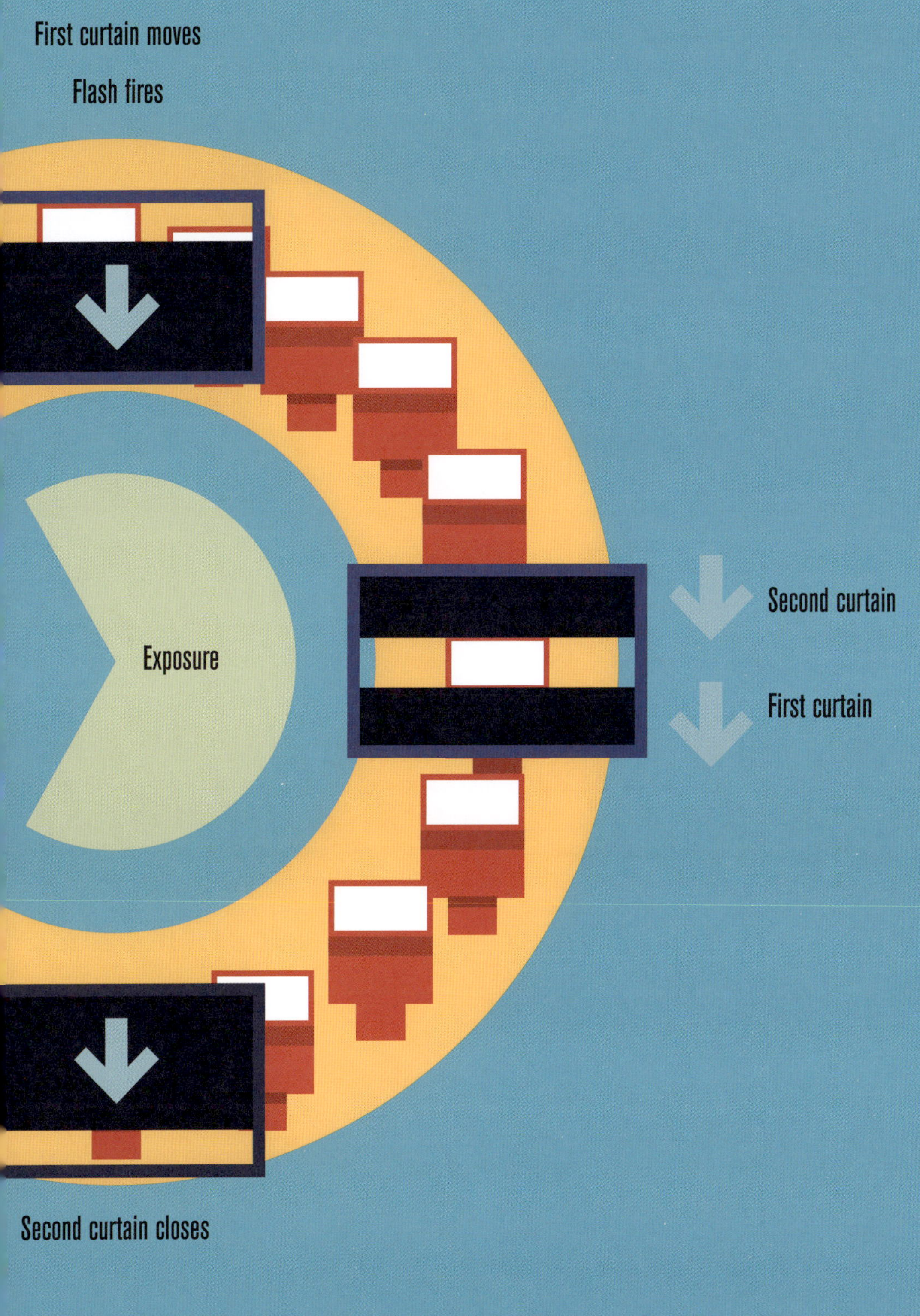

First curtain moves
Flash fires
Exposure
Second curtain
First curtain
Second curtain closes

Bounce Flash

Some flashes have an adjustable head that lets you use a "bounce flash" technique. Bounce flash helps to soften the light from the flash and also alters the direction of the light hitting your subject.

Direct flash fired from the camera position is a frontal light. This isn't particularly flattering and can produce hard, dark shadows behind your subject.

If you angle the flash head and bounce the light off a surface such as a ceiling or reflector, this will reduce contrast and produce a more pleasing effect. The surface you use should be neutral in color to avoid adding a color tint. The flash exposure should also be increased, as the light has to travel further.

Flash heads can often be swiveled from side to side as well as up and down. This gives you greater control over how your subject is lit. By bouncing the light from a wall (or reflector) to the side of your subject you can create a more side-lit effect.

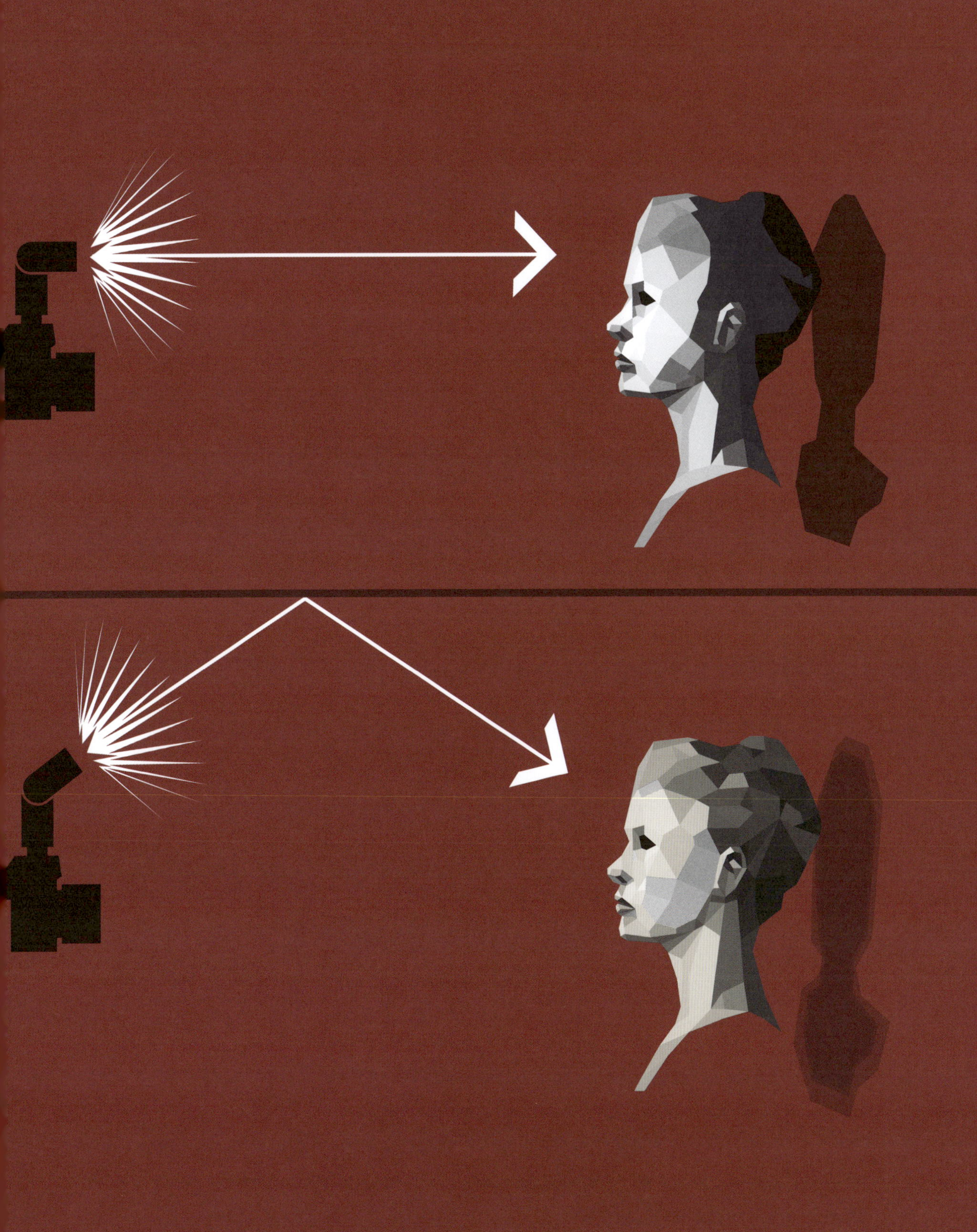

Lighting Ratios

A lighting ratio describes the difference in brightness between two sources of illumination, such as two flashes. The brighter of the two lights is known as the "key" light, while the secondary light is known as the "fill." The lighting ratio is easily adjusted by altering the relative brightness of the two lights, which is usually achieved by adjusting the power of the light or by altering the light-to-subject distance.

This diagram shows how altering the relative brightness of a key and fill light changes the balance of illumination on either side of a subject.

Fill light power 

Lighting ratio 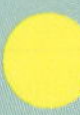

Difference in stops 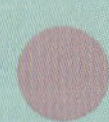

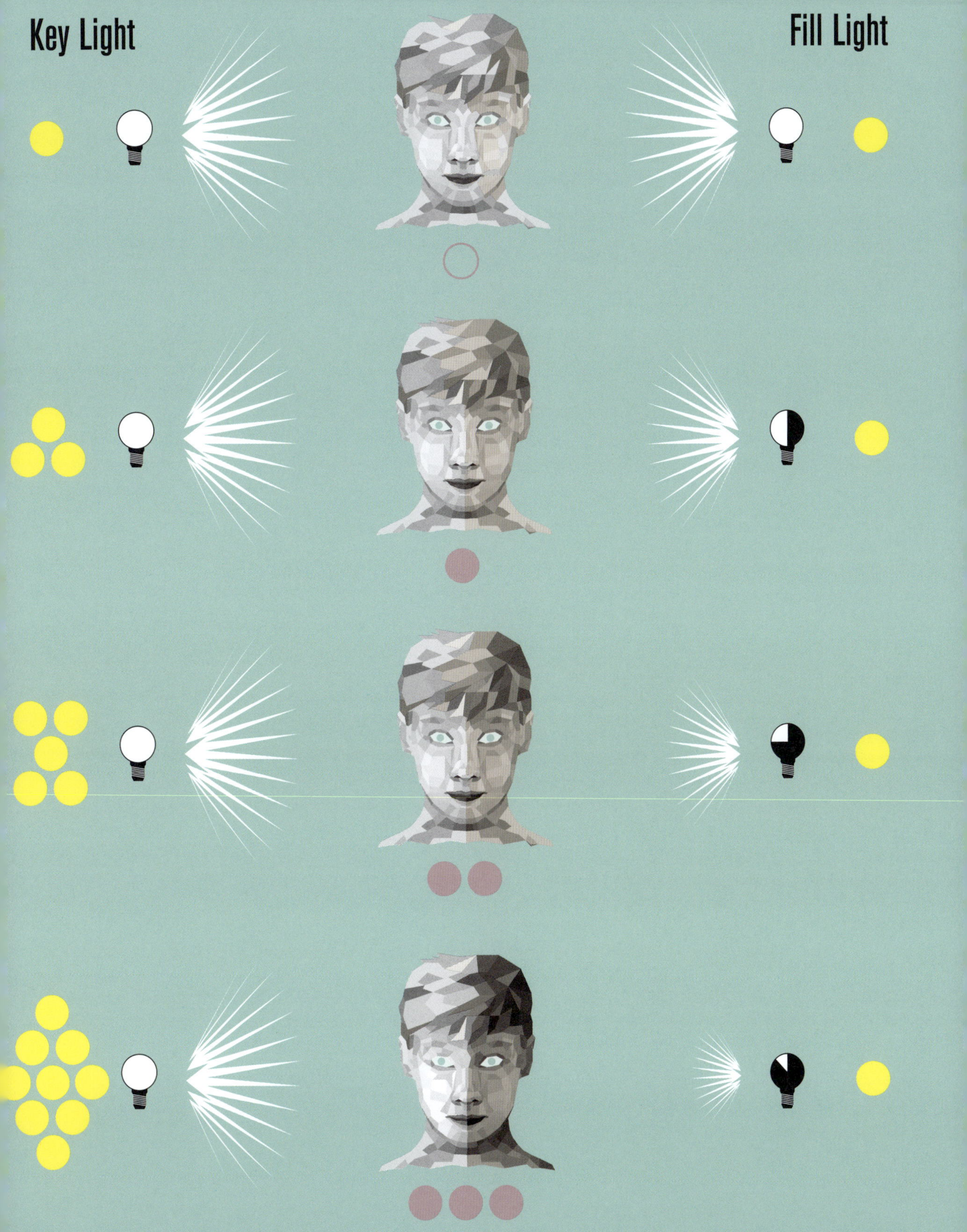

Key Light
Fill Light

Glossary

Aberration General name for a flaw visible in an image caused by the optics of a lens.

AF (Autofocus) A reliable through-the-lens focusing system allowing accurate focus without the user manually turning the lens.

Angle of view The angular extent of an image projected by a lens.

Aperture Variable iris inside a lens used to control exposure and depth of field.

Aperture priority Exposure mode in which the photographer sets the aperture and the camera sets the shutter speed.

Bracketing The act of shooting two or more images with a range of different settings (usually exposure or white balance).

Buffer A temporary memory store built into a camera where images are processed before being written to the memory card.

Bulb Exposure mode that allows the camera shutter to be held open for an indefinite period of time.

Camera shake Image flaw caused by movement of the camera during an exposure.

Center-weighted metering Metering mode that heavily biases the exposure measurement toward the center of an image.

Chromatic aberration Color fringing seen in areas of high contrast in an image. Caused by a lens' inability to focus all the wavelengths of visible light to the same point.

Clipping Term used to describe the loss of detail in underexposed shadows or overexposed highlights.

Color temperature A description of the warmth or coolness of an image; measured in degrees Kelvin.

Compact camera Fixed-lens camera designed to fit into a pocket or small bag.

CSC (Compact System Camera) A camera with a removable lens, but lacking the reflex mirror of a DSLR. For this reason, CSCs are typically far smaller and lighter than DSLRs.

Compression A reduction in the file size of an image so it requires less space on a memory card or hard drive.

Contrast The range between the highlight and shadow areas of an image, or a marked difference in illumination between colors or adjacent areas.

Crop factor Value necessary to calculate the effective angle of view when a lens is used on a non-full frame camera.

Depth of field The amount of an image that appears acceptably sharp. Depth of field is controlled by the aperture; the smaller the aperture, the greater the depth of field.

Digital sensor A microchip consisting of a grid of millions of light sensitive cells— the more cells, the greater the number of pixels, and the higher the resolution of the final image.

Distortion A lens aberration that causes what should be straight lines in an image to bow outward from the center (barrel distortion) or inward (pincushion distortion).

Drive mode Settings that determines when and how often an exposure is made after the shutter-release button is pressed down.

DSLR (Digital Single Lens Reflex) A digital camera with an optical viewfinder. The image arrives at the viewfinder from the lens via a reflex mirror and pentaprism.

Dynamic range The ability of the camera's sensor to capture shadows and highlights.

Evaluative metering A metering system whereby the exposure is based on light reflected from several subject areas, with a possible bias toward the point of focus.

Exposure The amount of light allowed to reach the sensor, as controlled by the aperture, shutter speed, and ISO. Also, the act of taking a photograph, as in "making an exposure."

Exposure compensation A control that allows intentional over- or underexposure.

Exposure lock A camera function that holds the exposure settings temporarily.

Filter A piece of colored, or coated, glass or plastic placed in front of the lens to modify the light passing through it.

Focal length The distance from the optical center of a lens to its focal point.

Focus To sharpen an image using AF or MF.

Flash External flash unit attached to a camera's hotshoe or via a cable. Some flashes can also be fired wirelessly by the camera.

FPS (Frames Per Second) A measure of the time needed for a camera to process one image and be ready to shoot the next.

f/stop Lens aperture value, expressed as a fraction. Large apertures range from f/1.0–f/5.6; small apertures cover a range from f/16 upward.

HDR (High Dynamic Range) An in-camera or post-processing effect that increases the tonal range of an image. Typically achieved by bracketing a series of images using different exposure settings and then blending the images together.

Highlights The brightest part of an image.

Histogram A graph used to represent the distribution of tones in an image.

Incident-light metering Meter reading based on the intensity of the light falling onto the subject.

ISO A measure of the sensitivity of the sensor or film; the higher the ISO, the greater the sensitivity.

JPEG An image file format found on digital cameras. JPEG files compress image data, losing some detail in the process.

LCD (Liquid Crystal Display) The flat screen on a digital camera that allows the user to compose and review digital images.

Lens A group of shaped glass elements that focus light onto the digital sensor (or film) inside a camera. The prime characteristic of a lens is its focal length, which (depending on the size of the sensor/film) determines the angle of view.

Manual exposure Exposure mode with no automation that requires the photographer to set all aspects of exposure.

Macro A term used to describe close focusing and the close-focusing ability of a lens.

Megapixel One million pixels equal one megapixel.

Metering The act of measuring the amount of light falling on a scene to determine the required exposure.

MF (Manual Focus) To adjust the focus distance of a lens by turning the focus ring by hand.

Midtone Equivalent to mid-gray; a tone exactly half way in brightness between black and white.

Mirrorless Common name given to a camera that does not have a reflex mirror (see also, CSC). The photographer views a live image streamed from the digital sensor to an LCD screen on the back of the camera, or an electronic viewfinder.

Noise Colored image interference caused by stray electrical signals.

Overexposure The result of allowing too much light to reach the digital sensor during exposure. Often, the highlights in an overexposed image will be burnt out to pure white and the shadows unnaturally bright.

Pentaprism A reflective prism with five sides, that gives a constant deviation of light through 90º. Used in the viewfinder of SLR cameras to display the image the correct way up.

Predictive AF An autofocus system that can continuously track a moving subject.

Raw A file format in which the raw data from the sensor is stored without permanent alteration being made.

Remote switch A device used to trigger the shutter of a tripod-mounted camera at a distance to avoid camera shake. Also known as a "cable release."

Resolution The number of pixels used to capture or display an image.

RGB (Red, Green, Blue) Computers and other digital devices understand color information as combinations of red, green, and blue.

Shadows The darkest part of an image.

Shutter A mechanism that opens and closes to control the amount of light reaching the sensor.

Shutter priority Exposure mode in which the photographer sets the shutter speed and the camera sets the aperture.

Spot metering A metering system that measures the intensity of light reflected by a very small portion of a scene.

Telephoto A lens with a large focal length and narrow angle of view.

TTL (Through The Lens) metering A metering system built into a camera that measures light passing through the lens at the time of shooting.

Underexposure The result of allowing too little light to reach the digital sensor during exposure. Often, the highlights in an underexposed image will be muddy and the shadows dense and lacking in detail.

Viewfinder An optical or LCD-based system used for framing the subject.

White balance A function that allows the correct color balance to be recorded for any given lighting situation.

Wide-angle lens A lens with a short focal length and a wide angle of view.

Zoom A lens with a variable focal length.

Useful Web Sites

General
Digital Photography Review www.dpreview.com
On Landscape www.onlandscape.co.uk

Photographers
David Taylor www.davidtaylorphotography.co.uk

Photographic Equipment
Canon www.canon.com
FujiFilm www.fujifilm.com
Leica www.leica-camera.com
Nikon www.nikon.com
Olympus www.olympus-global.com
Panasonic www.panasonic.net
Ricoh/Pentax www.ricoh-imaging.com
Sigma www.sigma-photo.com
Sony www.sony.com
Tamron www.tamron.com
Tokina www.tokinalens.com
Zeiss www.zeiss.com

Photography Publications
Ammonite Press www.ammonitepress.com
Black & White/ Outdoor Photography magazine
www.thegmcgroup.com

Printing
Epson www.epson.com
Hahnemühle www.hahnemuehle.de
Harman www.harman-inkjet.com
HP www.hp.com
Ilford www.ilford.com
Lexmark www.lexmark.com
Lyson www.lyson.com
Marrut www.marrutt.com

Software
Adobe www.adobe.com
AlienSkin www.alienskin.com
Apple www.apple.com
Corel www.corel.com
DxO www.dxo.com
Phase One www.phaseone.com
Photomatix Pro www.hdrsoft.com
PhotoPills www.photopills.com

Index

A
absorption 17
angle of view 46, 50–51, 52
aperture 42, 56, 57, 66, 68, 69, 70, 71, 72, 74,
    80–81, 82, 84, 86, 87, 88, 94, 96, 118,
        134, 142, 150, 151, 154
Aperture Priority mode 118, 120
APS-C sensor 51, 52
APS-H sensor 52
autofocus 45
Automatic Exposure Bracketing (AEB) 123
Automatic White Balance (AWB) 24

B
battery grip 42
black & white 146–147
blur 127
bokeh 56
bounce flash 166–167
bracketing 122–123, 124, 128, 129
brightness 88, 94, 98, 122, 124, 128, 168
Bulb (B) mode 118

C
cameras 44–45
    cellphone 42, 45
    compact 42, 45, 54, 136, 158
    Digital Single Lens Reflex (DSLR) 43, 44,
        45, 54, 136, 137
    mirrorless 43, 44, 45, 54, 136, 137
    non-system 42
    system 42
camera
    position 26
    shake 58, 88, 94, 119
Close-up mode 119
CMYK 18
color 17, 88, 116, 117, 139
    additive 19
    bias 24
    perception 20–21

primary 18
secondary 18
spectrum 18
temperature 22–23, 32, 138
wheel 18–19, 139
compact cameras 42, 45, 54, 136, 158
compression 100, 101
contrast 13, 26, 28–29, 36, 37, 43, 90, 98,
    116, 117, 124, 128
controlling exposure 102–129
crop factor 52–53

D
"dark frame subtraction" 92
depth of field 46, 70, 71, 72, 74, 82–83, 84,
    88, 119
differential focusing 84
diffusing light 13, 37
Digital Single Lens Reflex (DSLR) 43, 44, 45,
    54, 136, 137
Drive mode 123
dynamic range 90–91

E
electromagnetic spectrum 14
electronic viewfinder 43, 44, 45
equipment 40–59
exposure 28, 43, 45, 54, 58, 62, 71, 92, 94,
    96, 105, 110, 112, 118, 119, 120, 121,
    122, 123, 124, 138, 140, 143, 151
    compensation 120–121
    control 42, 70, 102–129
    Manual 96, 140
    modes 118–119
    triangle 70–71
    values 96–97
exposure basics 60–101
exposure meters 94, 105, 108–109, 118
    incident 108, 109
    reflective 108, 109

F
file formats 100–101
film 62
filters 130–147
    adapter rings 132, 133, 136, 137, 139
    color correction 138
    colored 64, 146
    effect 138
    factors 140–141
    holder sizes 136–137
    neutral density (ND) 138, 142–143
    polarizing 66, 138, 144–145
    round 132
    square 132, 133
    thread sizes 134–135, 136
    types 138–139
    uv/skylight 138
first principles 66–67
fisheye lens 51
flash 22, 25, 36, 42, 90, 119, 148–169
    bounce 166–167
    built-in 150
    curtain sync 162–163
    diffusers 13
    exposure 150, 156
        automatic 151
        manual 150, 151
        TTL 150, 151, 156
    external 42, 150
    guide numbers (GN) 154–157
    high speed sync 164–165
    sync speed 158–159
Flash Off mode 119
focal
    length 45, 46, 47, 50, 56, 74, 82
    plane shutter 54, 55, 158
focus distance 82
    point 82
frame rate 126
freezing movement 74–75
frequency 14

f-stops 68–69, 80, 81, 94
Fully Automatic (Auto) mode 119, 126, 140

G
guide numbers (GN) 154–157

H
HDR (high dynamic range) 122, 124, 128–129
high key 63
high speed sync 164–165
highlights 107, 128
histograms 98–99, 128, 129
hot pixels 92

I
image stablization 58
incident metering 108, 109
interchangeable lens 42
inverse square law 152–153
ISO 42, 45, 66, 68, 69, 70, 71, 72, 74, 86–87,
    88, 89, 94, 95, 96, 126, 150, 151, 154

J
JPEG 100, 101, 116, 128

K
Kelvin value 22–23, 24

L
Landscape mode 119
LCD screen 43, 44
lens aperture 56–57
lenses 42, 43, 44, 46–47, 50, 56, 94, 134
    fisheye 51
    interchangeable 42
    normal 46, 47, 51
    prime 56
    super-telephoto 51
    telephoto 46, 47, 50, 51, 84
    wide-angle 46, 47, 48–49, 50, 51, 84, 137
    zoom 56

light & color 10–39
light 12, 24, 80, 86, 87, 96, 108, 110, 140,
    142, 150, 152
    artificial 13, 36
    cool 22
    diffusing 13, 37
    direction 26–27, 166
    hardness 12, 13, 36, 37, 38–39, 98, 166
    intensity 12, 90,
    low 58,66
    natural 13, 23, 24, 30, 31, 36, 95, 119
    position 12, 26, 30, 31, 34, 35
    quality 36–37
    reflecting 13
    source 13, 17, 22, 28, 36, 37
    splitting 16
    visible 14
    warm 22, 32
    white 14, 16, 17
lighting
    back 26, 27, 28–29
    frontal 26, 167
    low key 62
    ratios 168–169
    side 26, 27, 166
    three-quarter 26, 27
lightmeter see exposure meter

M
Manual exposure 96, 140
Manual mode 118, 126
memory card 100, 101
metering
    exposure 94, 105, 108–109, 118
    incident 108, 109
    reflective 108, 109
metering modes 110–111, 112–113
microlenses 64
midday 32, 33, 36
midtone 105, 106, 107
midtones, shadows & highlights 106–107

mirrorless cameras 43, 44, 45, 54, 136, 137
mode
    Aperture Priority 118, 120
    Bulb (B) 118
    Close-up 119
    Drive 123
    Flash Off 119
    Fully Automatic (Auto) 119, 126, 140
    Landscape 119
    Manual 118, 126
    Portrait 119
    Program (P) 118, 120
    Shutter Priority 118, 120
    Sports/Action 119
movement 76–77, 78–79
    blurring 70, 71, 76–77
    freezing 74–75, 76–77, 78–79

N
neutral density (ND) filters 138, 142–143
noise 70, 71, 72, 88–89, 92
    reduction 92
    thermal 92
non-system cameras 42

O
optical viewfinder 43
outdoors 12, 30
overexposure 62, 66, 98, 99, 105, 114, 122
OVF 43

P
panning 78–79
photodiodes 64
picture parameters 116–117, 146
polarizer 66
polarizing filters 144–145
Portrait mode 119
postproduction 28, 92, 101, 104, 105, 116,
    124, 128, 132, 146
prime lens 56

prism 16, 44
Program (P) mode 118, 120

R
rainbow 16
Raw 100, 101, 105, 116, 128, 129
reflective metering 108, 109
reflectivity 105, 106, 107, 108, 166, 168
reflectors 13
refraction 16
remote release 59, 96
RGB 19

S
self-timer 59
sensor 43, 44, 46, 50, 51, 52, 54, 56, 62,
    64–65, 66, 68, 80, 90, 140, 142
    APS-C 51, 52
    APS-H 52
    compact 51
    filter 64
    four-thirds 51, 52
    full-frame 51, 52, 90
    microlenses 64
    photodiodes 64
sequences 124–125
shade 25
shadows 26, 36, 37, 38, 90, 95, 98, 99, 106,
    128, 167
sharpness 82, 116, 117
shutter 43, 54–55, 92, 96
    electronic 54, 62
    focal plane 54, 55, 158
    leaf 54, 55, 56, 158
    mechanical 54
    speed 42, 54, 58, 66, 68, 69, 70, 71,
        72–73, 74, 75, 76, 78, 86, 87, 88, 92,
        94, 95, 96, 118, 119, 126, 127, 142,
        151, 158, 160, 162,164
Shutter Priority mode 118, 120
silhouette 26

slow sync speed 160–161
softbox 13
solstices & equinoxes 34–35
Sports/Action mode 119
spot metering 114–115
stops 68–69, 120, 141, 142
Sunny 16 rule 94–95, 96
sunrise 23, 30–31, 32–33, 34
sunset 23, 30–31, 32–33, 34
sun's path 34–35
super-telephoto lens 51
system cameras 42, 43

T
telephoto lens 46, 47, 50, 51, 84
tonal range 90, 91, 98, 106
tripod 58–59, 128, 129, 168

U
underexposure 28, 62, 66, 98, 99, 105,
    122, 140

V
video 126–127
viewfinder
    electronic 43, 44, 45
    optical 43, 44
visible light 14, 17

W
wavelength 14–15, 16, 17, 22, 32
weather 12, 25, 38, 95
white balance 24–25, 43, 100, 101,
    105, 138
wide-angle lens 46, 47, 48–49, 50, 51,
    84, 137

Z
zoom lens 56

Acknowledgments

A big thank you to everyone who supported and encouraged me during the writing of this book. Specifically that means Jason Hook, Robin Shields, and Jonathan Bailey at Ammonite Press and my very patient editor, Chris Gatcum. Closer to home I'd like to thank my parents Bill and Carol, and my parents-in-law, Brian and Sue. Even closer to home I'd like to thank my wife Tania, to whom this book is dedicated.

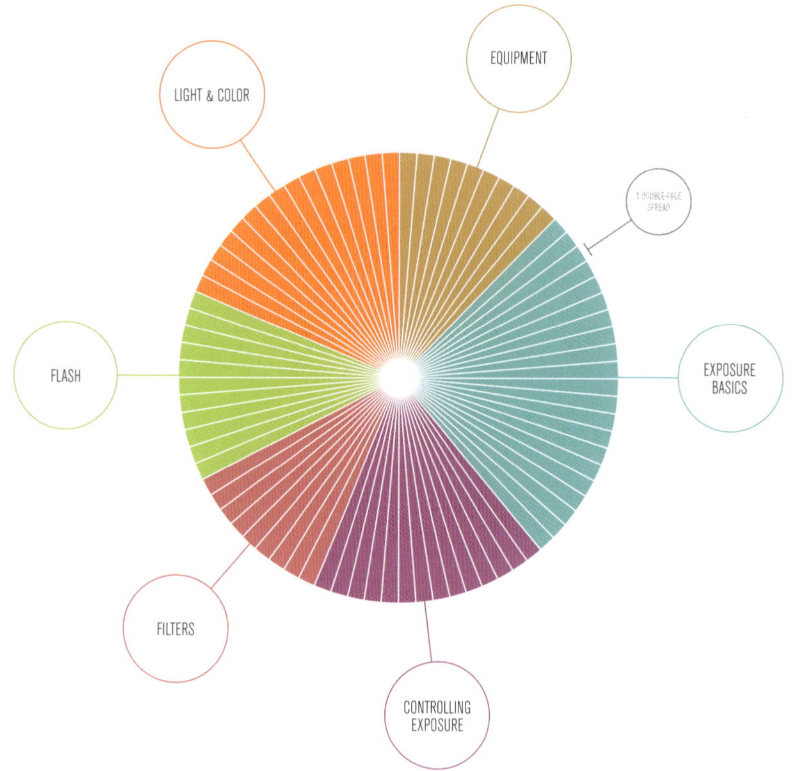

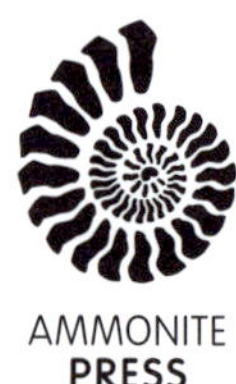

To place an order, or request a catalog, contact:
Ammonite Press
GMC Publications Ltd, Castle Place, 166 High Street, Lewes, East Sussex, BN7 1XU, United Kingdom
Tel: +44 (0)1273 488006
www.ammonitepress.com